For Dummies
COMPUTER
BOOK SERIES
FROM IDG

QuickBooks® 4 For Dummies®, 2nd Edition

Cheat Sheet

W9-CRW-917

Speedy Shortcuts That Can Save You Scads of Time

PC Shortcut	Mac Shortcut	QuickBooks Does This
Ctrl+A	⌘+A	Displays the Chart of Accounts window
Ctrl+J	⌘+J	Displays the Customer:Job List window
Ctrl+I	⌘+I	Displays the Create Invoice window
Ctrl+W	⌘+K	Displays the Write Checks window
Ctrl+P	⌘+P	Prints the list of customers, jobs, vendors, employees, or whatever, that's showing in the active window
Ctrl+Z	⌘+Z	Almost always undoes whatever you just did
Ctrl+X	⌘+X	Cuts out the current selection and places it on the Windows Clipboard
Ctrl+C	⌘+C	Copies the current selection and places it on the Windows Clipboard
Ctrl+V	⌘+V	Pastes whatever is on the Windows Clipboard into the text where the cursor is located
Ctrl+Ins	⌘+Y	Inserts a line into a list of items or expenses
Ctrl+Del	⌘+B	Deletes the selected line from a list of items or expenses
Ctrl+M	⌘+M	Memorizes a transaction
Crtl+T	⌘+T	Displays the memorized transaction
Alt+F4	⌘+Q	Exits QuickBook

Some Windows 95 Tricks

- To move quickly to list box entries that begin with a specific letter, press the letter.

- To select a list box entry and choose a dialog box's suggested command button, double-click the entry.

- To move the insertion point to the beginning of a field, press Home.

- To move the insertion point to the end of a field, press End.

- To close a window or dialog box, double-click its Control menu box (the little icon in a box in the upper-left corner) or click the box in the upper right-hand corner with an *x* in it.

- To minimize a window so that only a teensy part of the title bar is showing, click the first box with the little line in it in the window's upper-right corner. (This works both for the application window — the window for the program — and the individual windows shown within each program.)

- To show a window without covering the entire monitor screen, click the middle button in the upper right-hand corner of the window — if the button shows one box in it. When the button shows two boxes in it, clicking the button maximizes the QuickBooks desktop so that it fills the monitor screen.

- To yelp for help from just about anywhere, press F1.

Some Cool Date-Editing Tricks

If the selection cursor is on a date field, you can use these tricks to edit the date:

Press	What Happens
+	Adds one day to the date shown
t	Replaces the date shown with today's date
−	Subtracts one day from the date shown
y	Changes the date to the first day in the year
r	Changes the date to the last day in the year
m	Changes the date to the first day in the month
h	Changes the date to the last day in the month

... For Dummies: #1 Computer Book Series for Beginners

Iconbar Shortcuts for Busy People

The QuickBooks iconbar is just a row of buttons you click to do things really fast. (If your iconbar doesn't show some of these icons, you can change it by choosing Preferences➪Iconbar.)

Use This Icon	QuickBooks Does This
Invoice	Displays the Create Invoices window so that you can record a sale and, optionally, prepare a customer invoice. Equivalent to choosing Activities➪Create Invoices.
PO	Displays the Create Purchase Orders window so that you can prepare a purchase order. Equivalent to choosing Activities➪Create Purchase Orders.
Check	Displays the Write Checks windows so that you can record a bill and write a check to pay the bill. Equivalent to choosing Activities➪Write Checks.
Bill	Displays the Enter Bills window so that you can record bills that you want to pay later. Equivalent to choosing Activities➪Enter Bills.
Reg	If the Chart of Accounts window is displayed and an account is selected, clicking this icon displays the account's register. Otherwise, clicking this icon displays the Chart of Accounts window so that you can select an account.
Accnt	Displays the Chart of Accounts window. Equizvalent to choosing Lists➪Chart of Accounts.
Cust	Displays the Customer:Job List window. If you want to add a customer or job, click the New or Add Job buttons that appear in the window. Equivalent to choosing Lists➪Customers:Jobs.
Vend	Displays the Vendor List window. If you want to add a vendor, you can click the New button that appears in the window. Equivalent to choosing Lists➪Vendors.
Item	Displays the Item List window. If you want to add an item, you can click the New button that appears in the window. Equivalent to choosing Lists➪Items.
Calc	Starts the Windows Calculator accessory.
Backup	Tells QuickBooks that you want to back up the company file. Equivalent to choosing File➪Backup.

Keeping Your Debits and Credits Straight

Account Type	Debits	Credits
Assets	Increase asset accounts	Decrease asset accounts
Liabilities	Decrease liability accounts	Increase liability accounts
Owner's equity	Decrease owner's equity accounts	Increase owner's equity accounts
Income	Decrease income accounts	Increase income accounts
Expenses	Increase expense accounts	Decrease accounts

QUICKBOOKS® 4

FOR

DUMMIES®

2ND EDITION

QUICKBOOKS® 4
FOR
DUMMIES®
2ND EDITION

by Stephen L. Nelson

IDG
BOOKS
WORLDWIDE

IDG Books Worldwide, Inc.
An International Data Group Company

Foster City, CA ♦ Chicago, IL ♦ Indianapolis, IN ♦ Braintree, MA ♦ Dallas, TX

QuickBooks® 4 For Dummies®, 2nd Edition

Published by
IDG Books Worldwide, Inc.
An International Data Group Company
919 E. Hillsdale Blvd.
Suite 400
Foster City, CA 94404

Library of Congress Catalog Card No.: 95-81550

ISBN: 1-56884-947-8

Printed in the United States of America

10 9 8 7 6 5 4 3 2 1

2A/SS/QR/ZW

Distributed in the United States by IDG Books Worldwide, Inc.

Distributed by Macmillan Canada for Canada; by Computer and Technical Books for the Caribbean Basin; by Contemporanea de Ediciones for Venezuela; by Distribuidora Cuspide for Argentina; by CITEC for Brazil; by Ediciones ZETA S.C.R. Ltda. for Peru; by Editorial Limusa SA for Mexico; by Transworld Publishers Limited in the United Kingdom and Europe; by Al-Maiman Publishers & Distributors for Saudi Arabia; by Simron Pty. Ltd. for South Africa; by IDG Communications (HK) Ltd. for Hong Kong; by Toppan Company Ltd. for Japan; by Addison Wesley Publishing Company for Korea; by Longman Singapore Publishers Ltd. for Singapore, Malaysia, Thailand, and Indonesia; by Unalis Corporation for Taiwan; by WS Computer Publishing Company, Inc. for the Philippines; by WoodsLane Pty. Ltd. for Australia; by WoodsLane Enterprises Ltd. for New Zealand.

For general information on IDG Books Worldwide's books in the U.S., please call our Consumer Customer Service department at 800-762-2974. For reseller information, including discounts and premium sales, please call our Reseller Customer Service department at 800-434-3422.

For information on where to purchase IDG Books Worldwide's books outside the U.S., contact IDG Books Worldwide at 415-655-3021 or fax 415-655-3295.

For information on translations, contact Marc Jeffrey Mikulich, Director, Foreign & Subsidiary Rights, at IDG Books Worldwide, 415-655-3018 or fax 415-655-3295.

For sales inquiries and special prices for bulk quantities, write to the address above or call IDG Books Worldwide at 415-655-3200.

For information on using IDG Books Worldwide's books in the classroom, or ordering examination copies, contact Jim Kelly, Director of Corporate, Education, and Government sales, at IDG Books Worldwide, 800-434-2086.

For authorization to photocopy items for corporate, personal, or educational use, please contact Copyright Clearance Center, 222 Rosewood Drive, Danvers, MA 01923, or fax 508-750-4470.

 ™ is a trademark under exclusive license to IDG Books Worldwide, Inc., from International Data Group, Inc.

About the Author

Stephen L. Nelson

Steve Nelson has a simple purpose in life. He wants to help you (and people like you) manage your business finances by using computers. Oh, sure. This personal mandate won't win him a Nobel prize or anything, but it's his own little contribution to the world.

Steve's education and experiences mesh nicely with his special purpose. He has a B.S. in accounting and an M.B.A. in finance. He's a CPA. He used to work as a senior consultant with Arthur Andersen & Co, the world's largest public accounting firm. He also has been the controller and treasurer of a 50-person manufacturing firm. Nelson, whose books have sold more than 1,000,000 copies in English and been translated into eleven other languages, is also the bestselling author of IDG's *Quicken 5 For Windows For Dummies, 3rd Edition*.

ABOUT IDG BOOKS WORLDWIDE

Welcome to the world of IDG Books Worldwide.

IDG Books Worldwide, Inc., is a subsidiary of International Data Group, the world's largest publisher of computer-related information and the leading global provider of information services on information technology. IDG was founded more than 25 years ago and now employs more than 7,700 people worldwide. IDG publishes more than 250 computer publications in 67 countries (see listing below). More than 70 million people read one or more IDG publications each month.

Launched in 1990, IDG Books Worldwide is today the #1 publisher of best-selling computer books in the United States. We are proud to have received 8 awards from the Computer Press Association in recognition of editorial excellence and three from Computer Currents' First Annual Readers' Choice Awards, and our best-selling ...*For Dummies*® series has more than 19 million copies in print with translations in 28 languages. IDG Books Worldwide, through a joint venture with IDG's Hi-Tech Beijing, became the first U.S. publisher to publish a computer book in the People's Republic of China. In record time, IDG Books Worldwide has become the first choice for millions of readers around the world who want to learn how to better manage their businesses.

Our mission is simple: Every one of our books is designed to bring extra value and skill-building instructions to the reader. Our books are written by experts who understand and care about our readers. The knowledge base of our editorial staff comes from years of experience in publishing, education, and journalism — experience which we use to produce books for the '90s. In short, we care about books, so we attract the best people. We devote special attention to details such as audience, interior design, use of icons, and illustrations. And because we use an efficient process of authoring, editing, and desktop publishing our books electronically, we can spend more time ensuring superior content and spend less time on the technicalities of making books.

You can count on our commitment to deliver high-quality books at competitive prices on topics you want to read about. At IDG Books Worldwide, we continue in the IDG tradition of delivering quality for more than 25 years. You'll find no better book on a subject than one from IDG Books Worldwide.

John J. Kilcullen

John Kilcullen
President and CEO
IDG Books Worldwide, Inc.

WINNER
Eighth Annual Computer Press Awards ≥ 1992

WINNER
Ninth Annual Computer Press Awards ≥ 1993

IDG BOOKS WORLDWIDE

IDG Books Worldwide, Inc., is a subsidiary of International Data Group, the world's largest publisher of computer-related information and the leading global provider of information services on information technology. International Data Group publishes over 250 computer publications in 67 countries. Seventy million people read one or more International Data Group publications each month. International Data Group's publications include: **ARGENTINA:** Computerworld Argentina, GamePro, Infoworld, PC World Argentina; **AUSTRALIA:** Australian Macworld, Client/Server Journal, Computer Living, Computerworld, Digital News, Network World, PC World, Publishing Essentials, Reseller; **AUSTRIA:** Computerwelt, PC TEST; **BELARUS:** PC World Belarus; **BELGIUM:** Data News; **BRAZIL:** Annuário de Informática, Computerworld Brazil, Connections, Super Game Power, Macworld, PC World Brazil, Publish Brazil, SUPERGAME; **BULGARIA:** Computerworld Bulgaria, Networkworld/Bulgaria, PC & MacWorld Bulgaria; **CANADA:** CIO Canada, ComputerWorld Canada, InfoCanada, Network World Canada, Reseller World; **CHILE:** Computerworld Chile, GamePro, PC World Chile; **COLUMBIA:** Computerworld Colombia, GamePro, PC World Colombia; **COSTA RICA:** PC World Costa Rica/Nicaragua; **THE CZECH AND SLOVAK REPUBLICS:** Computerworld Czechoslovakia, Elektronika Czechoslovakia, PC World Czechoslovakia; **DENMARK:** Communications World, Computerworld Danmark, Macworld Danmark, PC World Danmark, PC World Danmark Supplements, TECH World; **DOMINICAN REPUBLIC:** PC World Republica Dominicana; **ECUADOR:** PC World Ecuador, GamePro; **EGYPT:** Computerworld Middle East, PC World Middle East; **EL SALVADOR:** PC World Centro America; **FINLAND:** MikroPC, Tietoverkko, Tietoviikko; **FRANCE:** Distributique, Golden, Info PC, Le Guide du Monde Informatique, Le Monde Informatique, Reseaux & Telecoms; **GERMANY:** Computer Business, Computerwoche, Computerwoche Extra, Computerwoche Focus, Electronic Entertainment, GamePro, I/M Information Management, Macwelt, PC Welt; **GREECE:** GamePro, Macworld & Publish; **GUATEMALA:** PC World Centro America; **HONDURAS:** PC World Centro America; **HONG KONG:** Computerworld Hong Kong, PCWorld Hong Kong, Publish in Asia; **HUNGARY:** ABCD CD-ROM, Computerworld Szamitastechnika, PC & Mac World Hungary, PC-X Magazine; **INDIA:** Computerworld India, PC World India, Publish in Asia; **INDONESIA:** InfoKomputer PC World, Komputek Computerworld, Publish in Asia; **IRELAND:** ComputerScope, PC Live!; **ISRAEL:** PC World 32 BIT, People & Computers; **ITALY:** Computerworld Italia, Computerworld Italia Special Editions, Lotus Italia, Macworld Italia, Networking Italia, PC Shopping, PC World Italia, PC World/Walt Disney; **JAPAN:** Macworld Japan, Nikkei Personal Computing, SunWorld Japan, Windows World Japan; **KENYA:** East African Computer News; **KOREA:** Hi-Tech Information/Computerworld, Macworld Korea, PC World Korea; **MACEDONIA:** PC World Macedonia; **MALAYSIA:** Computerworld Malaysia, PC World Malaysia, Publish in Asia; **MEXICO:** Computerworld Mexico, GamePro, Macworld, PC World Mexico; **MYANMAR:** PC World Myanmar; **NETHERLANDS:** Computable, Computer! Totaal, LAN Magazine, Macworld, Net Magazine; **NEW ZEALAND:** Computer Buyer, Computerworld New Zealand, MTB, Network World, PC World New Zealand; **NICARAGUA:** PC World Costa Rica/Nicaragua; **NIGERIA:** PC World Africa; **NORWAY:** Computerworld Norge, Computerworld Privat, CW Rapport Klient/Tjener, CW Rapport Nettverk & Telecom, CW Rapport Offentlig Sektor, IDG's KURSGUIDE, Macworld Norge, Multimedia World, PC World Ekspress, PC World Nettverk, PC World Norge, PC World's Produktguide, Windows Spesial; **PAKISTAN:** Computerworld Pakistan, PC World Pakistan; **PANAMA:** GamePro, PC World Panama; **PARAGUAY:** PC World Paraguay; **P. R. OF CHINA:** China Computerworld, China Infoworld, Computer & Communication, Electronic Product World, Electronics Today, Game Camp, PC World China, Popular Computer Week, Software World, Telecom Product World; **PERU:** Computerworld Peru, GamePro, PC World Profesional Peru, PC World Peru; **POLAND:** Computerworld Poland, Computerworld Special Report, Macworld, Networld, Networld, PC World Komputer; **PHILIPPINES:** Computerworld Philippines, PC Digest, Publish in Asia; **PORTUGAL:** Cerebro/PC World, Correio Informático/Computerworld, Mac•In/PC•In Portugal; **PUERTO RICO:** PC World Puerto Rico; **ROMANIA:** Computerworld Romania, PC World Romania, Telecom Romania; **RUSSIA:** Computerworld Rossiya, Network World Russia, PC World Russia; **SINGAPORE:** Computerworld Singapore, PC World Singapore, Publish in Asia; **SLOVENIA:** MONITOR; **SOUTH AFRICA:** Computing S.A., Network World S.A., Software World; **SPAIN:** Computerworld España, COMUNICACIONES WORLD, Dealer World, Macworld España, PC World España; **SWEDEN:** CAP&Design, Computer Sweden, Corporate Computing, MacWorld, Maxi Data, MikroDatorn, Nätverk & Kommunikation, PC/Aktiv, PC World, Windows World; **SWITZERLAND:** Computerworld Schweiz, Macworld Schweiz, PCtip; **TAIWAN:** Computerworld Taiwan, Macworld Taiwan, PC World Taiwan, Publish Taiwan, Windows World; **THAILAND:** Thai Computerworld, Publish in Asia; **TURKEY:** Computerworld Monitör, MACWORLD Turkiye, PC WORLD Turkiye; **UKRAINE:** Computerworld Kiev, Computers & Software Magazine, PC World Ukraine; **UNITED KINGDOM:** Acorn User, Amiga Action, Amiga Computing, Amiga, Appletalk, CD Powerplay, CD-ROM Now, Computing, Connexion, GamePro, Lotus Magazine, Macaction, Macworld, Open Computing, Parents and Computers, PC Home, PC Works, The WEB; **UNITED STATES:** Cable in the Classroom, CD Review, CIO Magazine, Computerworld, Computerworld Client/Server Journal, Digital Video Magazine, DOS World, Electronic, InfoWorld, I-Way, Macworld, Maximize, MULTIMEDIA WORLD, Network World, PC World, PUBLISH, SWATPro Magazine, Video Event, WebMaster; **URUGUAY:** PC World Uruguay; **VENEZUELA:** Computerworld Venezuela, GamePro, PC World Venezuela; and **VIETNAM:** PC World Vietnam   10/17/95

Dedication

To the entrepreneurs and small business people of the world. You folks create most of the new jobs.

Credits

Senior Vice President and Publisher
Milissa L. Koloski

Associate Publisher
Diane Graves Steele

Brand Manager
Judith A. Taylor

Editorial Managers
Kristin A. Cocks
Mary C. Corder

Product Development Manager
Mary Bednarek

Editorial Executive Assistant
Richard Graves

Editorial Assistants
Constance Carlisle
Chris H. Collins
Kevin Spencer

Acquisitions Assistant
Gareth Hancock

Production Director
Beth Jenkins

Production Assistant
Jacalyn L. Pennywell

Supervisor of Project Coordination
Cindy L. Phipps

Supervisor of Page Layout
Kathie S. Schnorr

Production Systems Specialist
Steve Peake

Reprint/Blueline Coordination
Tony Augsburger
Patricia R. Reynolds
Theresa Sánchez-Baker
Elizabeth Cárdenas-Nelson

Media/Archive Coordination
Leslie Popplewell
Melissa Stauffer
Michael Wilkey

Project Editor
Barb Terry

Editors
Bill Helling
Suzanne Packer
Pat Seiler
Tamara S. Castleman

Technical Reviewers
Dan Bieger
Kevin Spencer

Graphic Coordination
Shelley Lea
Gina Scott
Carla Radzikinas

Project Coordinator
Sherry Gomoll

Production Page Layout
Brett Black
Kerri Cornell
Dominique DeFelice
Angela F. Hunckler
Todd Klemme
Jane Martin
Jill Lyttle
Mark C. Owens
Anna Rohrer
Kate Snell
Michael Sullivan

Proofreaders
Melissa Buddendeck
Christine Meloy Beck
Gwenette Gaddis
Dwight Ramsey
Carl Saff
Robert Springer

Indexer
Steve Rath

Cover Design
Kavish + Kavish

Acknowledgments

Hey, reader, lots of folks spent lots of time working on this book to make QuickBooks easier for you. You should know who these people are. You may just possibly meet them some day at a produce shop, squeezing cantaloupe, eating grapes, and looking for the perfect peach.

Those folks are Diane Steele, Mary Corder, Barb Terry, Pat Seiler, Suzanne Packer, and Vincent Abella.

(The publisher and the author give special thanks to Patrick J. McGovern, without whom this book would not have been possible.)

Contents at a Glance

Cartoons at a Glance

By Rich Tennant

"OH BROTHER! I NEVER THOUGHT OF THIS AS A WAY TO DECIDE WHICH BUDGETS GET CUT."

Page 183

"WELL'P — THERE GOES THE AMBIANCE."

Page 9

I DON'T KNOW - MY SPREADSHEET TELLS ME WE SHOULD BASE OUR OVERHEAD BUDGET ON SALES FIGURES RATHER THAN FIXED, MY PLOT CHART INDICATES WE SHOULD ESCALATE OUR MARKETING THRUST, AND MY PSYCHOANALYSIS PROGRAM TELLS ME I DEPEND TOO MUCH ON OUTSIDE INPUT AND SHOULD TRUST MY INSTINCTS MORE.

Page 265

IN A BIZARRE MIX-UP, KEN BALANCES A BUS SCHEDULE INSTEAD OF HIS CHECKBOOK, AND THEN CONTINUES BY BOOKING A SEAT FOR HIM AND LAVERNE IN THE LOCAL BANK'S SAFE DEPOSIT BOX.

"From that time forward, Laverne handled their financial affairs.

Page 69

NETWORK JONES AND THE LOST FILE OF WENDY

Oh Netty - be careful!

Page 54

TESTING THE '686 CHIP

"IT'S FAST ENOUGH FOR ME."

Page 305

ORIGINAL VAN-GOGH OF THE MONTH CLUB

"I JUST DON'T KNOW WHERE THE MONEY'S GOING."

Page 254

"I TOLD HIM WE WERE LOOKING FOR SOFTWARE THAT WOULD GIVE US GREATER PRODUCTIVITY, SO HE SOLD ME A DATABASE THAT CAME WITH THESE SIGNS."

Page 312

"WE HARDLY GET ANY COMPLAINTS FROM TAXPAYERS ANYMORE. THINK IT'S BECAUSE WE HIRED A TROGLODYTE TO RUN THE DEPARTMENT?"

Page 270

Table of Contents

Introduction

I think that running or working in a small business is one of the coolest things a person can do. Really. I mean it. Sure. Sometimes it's a dangerous environment. Kind of like the Old West. But it's also an environment where you have the opportunity to make tons of money. And it's an environment where you can build a company or a job that fits you. In comparison, many of our brothers and sisters who are working in big-company corporate America are furiously trying to fit their round pegs into painfully square holes. Yuck.

You're wondering, of course, what any of this has to do with this book or with QuickBooks. Quite a lot, actually. The whole purpose of this book is to make it easier for you to run or work in a small business by using QuickBooks.

About this Book

This book isn't meant to be read from cover to cover like some John Grisham page-turner. Instead, it's organized into tiny, no-sweat descriptions of how you do the things you need to do. If you're the sort of person who just doesn't feel right not reading a book from cover to cover, you can, of course, go ahead and read this thing from front to back.

I should, however, mention one thing. Accounting software programs require you to do a certain amount of up-front preparation before you can use them to get real work done. If you haven't started to use QuickBooks yet, I recommend that you read through the first three chapters of this book to find out what you need to do first.

About the Author

If you're going to spend your time reading what I have to say, you deserve to know what my qualifications are. So let me tell you briefly.

I have an undergraduate degree in accounting and a master's degree in finance and accounting. I also am a certified public accountant (CPA).

I have spent most of the last 12 years helping businesses set up computerized financial management systems. I started with Arthur Andersen & Co., which is one of the world's largest public accounting and systems consulting firms. More recently, I have been working as a sole proprietor. When I wasn't doing financial systems work, I served as the controller of a 50-person computer software company.

One other thing: I use QuickBooks in my own business.

I don't mean to sound goofy by telling you this stuff. But knowing a little something about me should give you a bit more confidence in applying what's covered in the pages that follow. All joking aside, this topic is something that's extremely important: your business.

How to Use this Book

You can use this book in one of two ways. One way is to start reading Chapter 1 and continue all the way to the end (which means through Chapter 20 and the appendixes). I actually don't think this from-start-to-finish approach is bad. You'll learn a bunch of stuff.

But you also can use this book like an encyclopedia. If you want to know about a subject, you can look it up in the table of contents or in the index. Then you can flip to the correct chapter or page and read as much as you need or enjoy. No muss. No fuss.

If you want to learn about anything else, of course, you just repeat the process.

What You Can Safely Ignore

Sometimes I provide step-by-step descriptions of tasks. I feel very bad about having to do this. So to make things easier for you, I describe the tasks by using bold text. That way, you know exactly what you're supposed to do. I also provide a more detailed explanation in regular text. You can skip the regular text that accompanies the step-by-step descriptions if you already understand the process.

Here's an example that shows what I mean:

1. Press Enter.

Find the key that's labeled *Enter* or *Return*. Extend your index finger so that it rests ever so gently on the Enter key. In one sure, fluid motion, press the Enter key by using your index finger. Then release your finger.

Okay, that example is kind of extreme. I never actually go into that much detail. But you get the idea. If you know how to press Enter, you can just do that and not read further. If you need help — maybe with the finger part or something — just read the nitty-gritty details.

Is there anything else you can skip? Let me see now. . . . You can skip the Technical Stuff sidebars, too. The information in these sidebars is really there only for those of you who like that kind of stuff.

For that matter, I guess that you can safely ignore the stuff in the Tip sidebars, too. Even if the accumulated wisdom, gleaned from long hours slaving over a hot keyboard, could save you much weeping and gnashing of teeth. If you're someone who enjoys trying to do something another way, go ahead and read the Tips.

What You Should Not Ignore (Unless You're a Masochist)

Don't skip the Warning sidebars. They're the ones flagged with the picture of the nineteenth-century bomb. They describe some things that you really shouldn't do.

Out of respect for you, I'm not going to put stuff such as "don't smoke" in these sidebars. I figure that you're an adult. You can make your own lifestyle decisions.

So I'm reserving the Warning sidebars for more urgent and immediate dangers — things akin to "Don't smoke while you're filling your car with gasoline."

Three Foolish Assumptions

I am making three assumptions:

- ✔ You have a PC with Microsoft Windows or a Mac.
- ✔ You know how to turn on the computer.
- ✔ You want to use QuickBooks.

By the way, if you haven't already installed QuickBooks and need some help, refer to Appendix A. It describes how to install QuickBooks if you're really lazy or really busy. And if you're just starting out with Microsoft Windows, peruse Chapter 1 of *Windows User's Guide* and *Windows For Dummies* by Andy Rathbone (IDG Books Worldwide).

By the way, for the new edition of this book, although this is primarily a QuickBooks for Windows book, I've added some tips and procedures specifically for those of you who are using the Mac version of QuickBooks. I flag those notes with this icon for easy reference. The book will help you with the practical side of using QuickBooks for your business, and, hopefully, throw in a few extras for you.

How this Book Is Organized

This book is organized into five mostly coherent parts.

Part I: You Gotta Start Someplace

Part I, "You Gotta Start Someplace," covers some up-front stuff that you need to take care of before you can start using QuickBooks. I promise I won't waste your time here. I just want to make sure that you get off on the right foot.

Part II: Daily Chores

This second part of *QuickBooks 4 For Dummies* explains how you use QuickBooks for your daily financial record-keeping: preparing customer invoices, collecting cash, paying bills. That kind of stuff.

I guess that you could say that these chores are just data-entry stuff. And you'd be correct. But I think that you'll be amazed at how much easier QuickBooks will make your life. QuickBooks is a really cool program.

Part III: Stuff You Do Every So Often

Part III talks about the kinds of things you should do at the end of the week, the end of the month, or the end of the year. This part explains, for example, how you print checks, balance your bank account, do payroll, and take care of some other housekeeping tasks as well.

While I'm on the subject, I also want to categorically deny that Part III contains any secret messages that you can decipher by reading it backward. *Yllaer.*

Part IV: The Part of Tens

Gravity isn't just a good idea; it's also a law.

By tradition, the same is true for this part of a . . . *For Dummies* book. The Part of Tens provides a collection of lists: ten things you should do if you get audited, ten things you should do if you own a business, ten things to do when you next visit Acapulco — oops, sorry about that last one. Wrong book.

By the way, also by tradition, these ten-item lists don't need to have exactly ten items on them. You know the concept of a baker's dozen, right? You order a dozen doughnuts but get 13 for the same price. Well, . . . *For Dummies* ten-item lists have roughly ten items. (If Mr. Dummies were running the bakery, a ten-doughnut order might mean that you get anywhere from 8 to 13 doughnuts.)

Part V: Appendixes

It's an unwritten rule that computer books have appendixes, so I have included three. Appendix A tells you how to install QuickBooks in ten easy steps. Appendix B explains small business accounting, provides a short biography of an Italian monk, and explains double-entry bookkeeping. Appendix C describes project estimating.

Conventions Used in this Book

To make the best use of your time and energy, you should know about the following conventions used in this book:

When I want you to type something such as **Hydraulics screamed as the pilot lowered his landing gear**, it's in bold letters. When I want you to type something that's short and uncomplicated, such as **Jennifer**, it still appears in boldface type.

By the way, with QuickBooks you don't have to worry about the case of the stuff you type. If I tell you to type Jennifer, you can type **JENNIFER**. Or you can follow e. e. cummings' lead and type **jennifer**.

Whenever I describe a message or information that you'll see on the screen, I present it as follows:

```
            Surprise! This is a message on-screen.
```

Whenever I tell you to choose a command, I say something such as, "Choose Lists⇨Items," which simply means to first choose the Lists menu and then choose Items. The ⇨ separates one part of the command from the next part.

You can choose menus and commands and select dialog box elements with the mouse or with the keyboard. To select them with the mouse, you just click them. To select them with the keyboard, you press Alt and the underlined letter in the menu, command, or dialog box. For example, the letter *F* in *File* and the letter *O* in *Open* are underlined, so you can choose the File Open command by pressing Alt and F at the same time and then pressing O. (I also identify the keyboard selection keys by underlining them in the steps.) You can select many commands by clicking icons on the iconbar as well.

One thing I don't do, I should confess, is give the Alt+key combinations for selecting window and dialog box elements: text boxes, option buttons, list boxes, and so on. I have an excuse. Sort of. QuickBooks isn't very consistent about its use of this interface convention. So because you can't use it much of the time, I figured, "Why bother?"

Special Icons

Like many computer books, this book uses *icons,* or little pictures, to flag things that don't quite fit into the flow of things. The *. . . For Dummies* books use a standard set of icons that flag little digressions, such as the following:

This icon says, "Look here, you Mac users. You've got something special going on here. Better pay attention."

This icon points out nerdy technical material that you may want to skip (or read, if you're feeling particularly bright).

Whee, here's a shortcut to make your life easier!

This icon is just a friendly reminder to do something.

And this icon is a friendly reminder *not* to do something . . . or else.

Part I
You Gotta
Start Someplace

The 5th Wave   By Rich Tennant

"WELL'P — THERE GOES THE AMBIANCE."

In this part . . .

All accounting programs — including QuickBooks — make you do a bunch of preliminary stuff. Sure, this is sort of a bummer. But getting depressed about it won't make things go any faster. So if you want to get up and going with QuickBooks, peruse the chapters in this first part. I promise that I'll get you through this stuff as quickly as possible.

Chapter 1

Setting Up Shop

● ●

In This Chapter

▶ Starting QuickBooks

▶ Setting up a company

▶ Choosing an invoice style

▶ Setting up the chart of accounts

● ●

1 know that you're anxious to get started. You've got a business to run. But before you can start using QuickBooks, you need to complete the preliminaries described in this chapter and the next two chapters. I won't waste your time. I want to get through with this stuff as quickly as you do.

This chapter explains how to start QuickBooks and how to describe (or set up) the company for which you want to keep financial records.

Note: I assume that you know how Windows works. If you don't, take the time to read Chapter 1 of *Windows User's Guide* or one of the *Windows For Dummies* books by Andy Rathbone from IDG Books Worldwide.

Starting QuickBooks

To start QuickBooks, choose Start⇨Programs and then click the menu choices that lead to QuickBooks. (For example, on my computer, I choose Start⇨Programs⇨QuickBooks⇨QuickBooks CD-ROM because I have the CD-ROM version. If you are starting QuickBooks for the first time, QuickBooks displays a window that gives you several options, depending on your version. After QuickBooks starts, you see a message box that asks whether you want to register QuickBooks.

To start QuickBooks, open the folder where you installed QuickBooks, and then double-click the QuickBooks icon.

As a default, QuickBooks also has this habit (which is annoying to me) of showing an Inside Tip every time you start up the program. It's an extra window that is supposed to heighten your consciousness about things inside the program that you normally wouldn't be looking for. I suspect it's an insidious Intuit plot to recruit people into the organization while seeming to help them with things they didn't know QuickBooks had. If you relish the thought of remaining an outsider, beating ceaselessly against the current, you can make QuickBooks skip the Inside Tips by removing the check mark in the Show Tips When QuickBooks Starts Up check box in the Inside Tips screen. (You do this by clicking in the check box.)

Registering QuickBooks

The folks at Intuit make you register QuickBooks. You can use the product roughly a couple of dozen times and then — whammo — either you register it or you can't use it. I don't like being forced to do something, but getting worked up about having to register QuickBooks is a waste of time. The simplest thing to do is just register.

Here's how: When QuickBooks displays the message box that asks whether you want to register, click Register. Then QuickBooks displays another dialog box that gives you a telephone number to call and provides a space for you to enter your customer number.

You can get a customer number in two ways. One way is to call Intuit and register. If you ordered QuickBooks directly from Intuit, you can also get your customer number directly from your invoice. Enter the customer number in the Registration dialog box, and then click OK. If you bought the CD-ROM multimedia version of QuickBooks, the program gives you the option of playing the SoundAdvice introduction. For the time being, just skip it and click Done.

A dialog box appears that welcomes you to QuickBooks and gives you some option buttons. You're going to jump right into this, so click the Set Up a New Data File For a Company option button and then click OK.

The first screen that you see is a new feature in QuickBooks — the EasyStep Interview (see Figure 1-1). When you see this screen, click Next. The next screen asks whether you're upgrading from a previous version of Quicken, QuickBooks, or QuickBooks Pro. You're probably not (or you wouldn't be reading this book), so click the option that says, "No, I'm not upgrading," and then click Next.

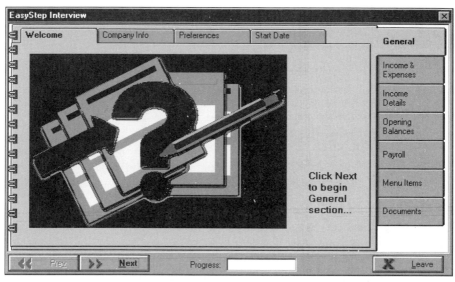

Figure 1-1:
The
EasyStep
Interview
window.

The next screen gives you some options in setting up a new company. The EasyStep Interview process is rather drawn out, but it has several advantages. One is that it gives you context-sensitive help as you go through the process. For example, let's say that you state that you're a musician, operating as an independent contractor to clubs. During the interview process, QuickBooks adds hints and tips that are specific to your situation. Pretty cool.

There is one thing, though. It's not that the interview is all that evil or anything, but it asks for more information than you really need to give QuickBooks at this point. You could spend a long time collecting all the information and making decisions that you don't really need to make yet.

By clicking the tabs in the EasyStep Interview window, you can see the kinds of information the process requires. Feel free to leaf through the tabs and, if it doesn't seem too daunting, go ahead and use them — Intuit's instructions are pretty self-explanatory. If you get partway through the interview process and decide it's not worth it, just click the Leave button in the lower-right corner, and QuickBooks will close the EasyStep Interview window.

Just in case you're like me and decide that the interview process is too much work, I'm giving you a short, easier way to set up your company — with some additional information along the way. Since you're still at the screen shown in Figure 1-1, click Next, and Quicken will ask whether you're upgrading from another product. Click the appropriate choice, and then click Next. The Skip Interview button will be right smack-dab in the middle of your screen. Click it, and we're on our way!

Here are a few extra notes that might come in handy:

- ✓ The EasyStep Interview window appears every time you start a new company (which you do by choosing File↔New Company).

- ✓ Note that, when you click the tabs on the right of the EasyStep Interview window, the tabs at the top change accordingly. This change comes in handy while you're leafing through the tabs.

- ✓ QuickBooks purposely makes deleting a company you create in QuickBooks hard, so don't make up an imaginary company to play with unless you're familiar enough with your operating system to delete files.

Keeping Good Company

The first thing you need to do after you start QuickBooks is describe your business. Or, in the parlance of accounting programs, you need to *set up the company files.* Follow these steps:

1. Click Skip Interview.

QuickBooks displays a message box telling you that it's about to ask you a number of different questions.

2. Click Yes to display the Creating New Company dialog box, shown in Figure 1-2.

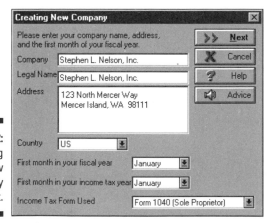

Figure 1-2: The Creating New Company dialog box.

3. Give your company name and address.

You can probably figure out how to fill in this dialog box yourself, right? You enter the doing-business-as name in the Company text box, click in the Legal Name text box and, oddly enough, then enter your business's legal name — the name that must appear on your legal documents. Enter the business address and, optionally, the telephone and fax numbers in the Address text box. This information will appear at the top of financial reports, and it can appear at the top of invoices. Figure 1-2 shows how I filled out the dialog box for my little company. (Yes, as weird as it may sound, a company named Stephen L. Nelson, Inc. really exists.) The address and telephone information isn't real, however. (I know that *you* would never do it, but if I provided my real address and telephone number, some people would start writing letters and phoning, wanting me to become their "works-for-free" accountant.)

4. Specify the first month in your fiscal (or accounting) year, the first month in your income tax year, and the income tax form that you use to report your taxes.

QuickBooks wants you to specify the first month in the accounting year for which you'll use QuickBooks for accounting. To specify the first month, use the drop-down list for First month in your fiscal year. The first month is probably January. Because you may not use the standard calendar year for taxes, you can choose a different month in the next drop-down list box. Then make sure that the name of the form in the list box for Income Tax Form Used is accurate.

TIP

Qcards

The Windows version of QuickBooks has a really cool feature called *Qcards*. Qcards are basically pop-up message boxes that tell you what you're supposed to plop into the active text box. (The *active text box* is the one where you have placed the cursor.) I have not included the Qcards in the figures in this book because, as cool as Qcards are, they can obscure parts of the dialog box or window that I want you to be able to see. You can turn Qcards on and off by clicking the Qcard icon. (You can change the iconbar by choosing Preferences⇨Iconbar from the menu and following the instructions.)

5. Click Next.

After you complete the first Creating New Company dialog box, click Next. QuickBooks displays another Creating New Company dialog box that asks what you want the invoices to look like (see Figure 1-3).

6. Choose the type of invoice you want.

When the dialog box shown in Figure 1-3 appears, choose the type of invoice that you want. To make this choice, you select the Service, Professional, or Product button. Notice, if you will, that beneath the Service, Professional, and Product buttons are samples showing how the different invoice types look.

7. Click Next.

After you complete the second Creating New Company dialog box, click Next.

8. Tell QuickBooks what type of business you're in.

After you click Next, QuickBooks displays a third Creating New Company dialog box, shown in Figure 1-4. You use this dialog box to tell QuickBooks what kind of business you're in. This step is very important because QuickBooks sets up many of its components — its *chart of accounts* (the list of the assets, liabilities, owners equity, and income and expense categories that you'll use), its *item lists*, and even the iconbar — based on your type of business. The choices you make will affect everything you do with QuickBooks from here on out.

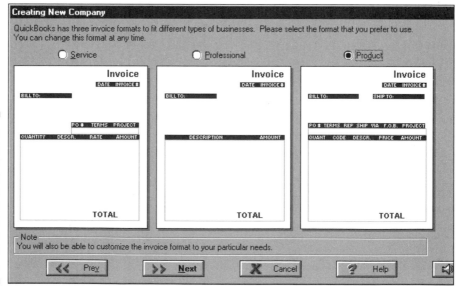

Figure 1-3: The Creating New Company dialog box that asks what the invoices should look like.

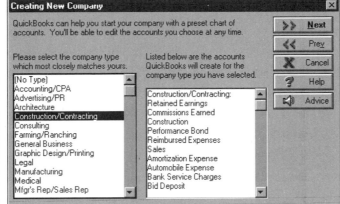

Figure 1-4:
The dialog
box that
asks, "And
what type of
business
are you in?"

To choose a type of business, click an entry in the list box on the left. After you select a type of business, QuickBooks displays the chart of accounts that is tailored for that type of business in the list box on the right. (If this chart of accounts doesn't look right to you, you can select another type of business in the box on the left.)

9. Click Next.

QuickBooks displays a dialog box that asks whether you need to set up any sales tax accounts.

10. Indicate whether you're supposed to collect sales tax.

If you're supposed to charge your customers or clients sales tax, click Yes. If you're not supposed to charge your customers or clients sales tax, click No. If you click Yes, QuickBooks displays the Setting up Sales Tax dialog box shown in Figure 1-5. QuickBooks asks whether you'll pay one tax rate to a single tax agency or multiple tax rates to multiple tax agencies.

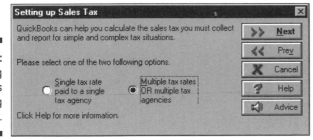

Figure 1-5:
The Setting
Up Sales
Tax dialog
box.

11. (Optional) Tell QuickBooks whether you're supposed to set up one sales tax rate or several sales tax rates.

If you indicate that you don't charge sales tax, QuickBooks skips the next two questions. If you'll pay one tax rate to a single tax agency, click the left option button. If you'll pay more than one tax rate or pay tax to more than one tax agency, click the right option button. Click Next when you're done.

12. (Optional) Describe any sales tax that you're supposed to collect.

If you indicate that you'll pay a single tax rate to a single agency, QuickBooks displays the dialog box shown in Figure 1-6, asking you to name the tax, describe it, give the sales tax percentage, and identify the tax agency. I filled in the text boxes in Figure 1-6 to give you some idea of what goes where. After you describe the sales tax, click Next.

Figure 1-6:
If you collect sales tax, you use this dialog box to describe the sales tax.

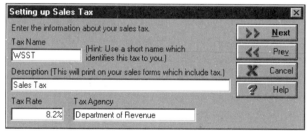

If you indicate that you'll pay more than one tax rate or pay tax to more than one agency, QuickBooks displays a cute little dialog box saying that you need to set up the sales taxes manually. Don't worry about those taxes for now; the next chapter tells you how to set up taxes manually. Click Next to continue.

13. Indicate whether you stock inventory or write purchase orders.

After you complete Step 12, QuickBooks displays a dialog box that asks whether you stock inventory (for resale) or write purchase orders. Just so you know, *purchase orders* are just written orders for the stuff you buy. Click Yes or No to answer the question. When you answer Yes to Step 13, the program asks you a few extra questions about whether your company uses require verbal or written estimates and whether you will be using the program for time tracking. These features are included with QuickBooks Pro, not the standard QuickBooks package. So, as you can guess, if you are using the regular QuickBooks and answer Yes, the program drops a not-so-subtle hint about upgrading to QuickBooks Pro. Either way, just follow the instructions and answer the questions appropriately.

14. **Indicate whether you want to use QuickBooks for payroll.**

    If you are not planning to use QuickBooks for payroll, click No and go to
    the next step. If you click Yes, a dialog box that asks for your federal and
    state employer identification numbers appears. If you don't have them
    handy, you can provide that information in the Company Identification
    screen later. When you are ready to leave this dialog box, click Next.

15. **Give QuickBooks the thumbs-up signal.**

    After you answer the inventory or purchase orders questions at length,
    QuickBooks displays, lo and behold, another message box. It tells you that
    QuickBooks is about to take all the information that you have entered and
    create a new company. All you need to do, per QuickBooks, is click Next.
    Go ahead. Do it. QuickBooks next displays the Filename For New Company
    dialog box (see Figure 1-7).

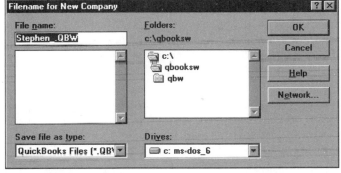

Figure 1-7:
The
Filename
for New
Company
dialog box.

16. **(Optional) Name the file and specify a file location.**

    If you don't want to accept the name and file location that QuickBooks
    suggests, use the File Name, Folders, and Drives boxes to specify a differ-
    ent name and location for the file. Even if you're using Windows 95,
    whatever you specify as a filename has to be a valid DOS filename. In other
    words, it needs to be up to eight characters in length, and it can't include
    any kooky characters that DOS uses in special ways on its command line.
    (As long as you stick with letter and number characters, you'll be fine.)

    Of course, Mac users have never been tied to the DOS filename con-
    straints. Any characters can be used, but the filename can be no more
    than 31 characters in System 7.

17. Click OK.

QuickBooks sets up the company that you have described. (This process may take a few seconds.) After QuickBooks finishes, you may see some additional windows. (One is a window that tells you the version numbers of the payroll tax table and payroll forms QuickBooks will use — you may want to have a pencil and paper around for that. If your versions aren't current, the window also includes instructions on how to order them.) Eventually, you see the full QuickBooks window (see Figure 1-8). The window now shows an iconbar. (The iconbar is the row of buttons at the top of the screen.) In the middle of the window, you also see the Reminders window. (Later chapters discuss the Reminders window and the iconbar.)

Fiddling with the Chart of Accounts

I feel a bit awkward about what I'm going to suggest next. But I really have thought about you and what you want to accomplish with QuickBooks. So I think that it probably makes sense for you to take a peek at the suggested chart of accounts that QuickBooks has created. And I think that it also makes sense for you to make any obvious changes.

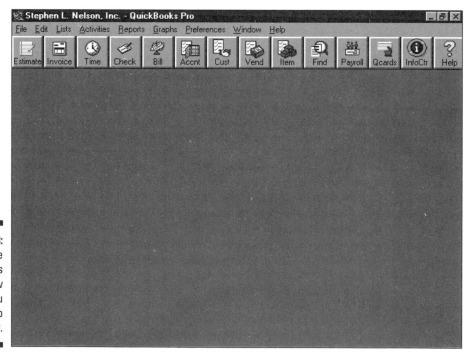

Figure 1-8:
The QuickBooks window after you have set up a company.

"Jeepers," you're saying to yourself. "A few paragraphs ago, I'd never even heard the term *chart of accounts,* and now you're asking me to muck about with it?"

Okay. I know it sounds risky. But with a little bit of friendly help from me, I don't think that you'll have too much trouble.

If you're still pretty new to accounting, consider reading Appendix B, a primer on accounting and bookkeeping.

A bit of background

What I want you to do is take a peek at the chart of accounts as it now exists. You can see it by choosing Lists➪Chart of Accounts. QuickBooks then displays the Chart of Accounts dialog box shown in Figure 1-9.

Figure 1-9:
The Chart of
Accounts
dialog box.

Name	Type	Balance
◆ Undeposited Funds	Other Current Asset	0.00
◆ Payroll Liabilities	Other Current Liability	0.00
◆ Sales Tax Payable	Other Current Liability	0.00
◆ Opening Balance Equity	Equity	0.00
◆ Owner's Capital	Equity	0.00
◆ Draws	Equity	0.00
◆ Investments	Equity	0.00
◆ Retained Earnings	Equity	
◆ Sales	Income	
◆ Sales Discounts	Income	

Chart of Accounts

| Use | Use Register | New | Edit | SoundAdvice |

If you want to review a printed copy of the chart of accounts rather than an on-screen copy, choose File➪Print List and click OK.

What you want to do now is to make sure that you don't have any other asset (such as a corporate jet), liability (a loan from your mother-in-law — heaven forbid), or other type of owners equity (such as preferred stock) that need its own account. To track or monitor the dollar value of some asset, liability, or type of owners equity, you need to give each item that you want to track its own account on the chart of accounts.

As you're doing this checking, you also should peruse the income and expense accounts. What you want to look for here is pretty much the same thing. If you want to track some other income or expense category, you need to add an account to the chart of accounts for it.

Adding accounts

Adding accounts to the chart of accounts isn't difficult. Follow these steps:

1. **Display the Chart of Accounts dialog box.**

   If the Chart of Accounts dialog box isn't already displayed, choose Lists⇨Chart of Accounts. *Voilà!* The dialog box appears. (*Voilà* is one of the words I have learned in my self-study course on French. Every morning on the way to work, I listen to CDs of people who are speaking French. As a result, my pronunciation is pretty good. Unfortunately, because I can't drive my car and read the book at the same time, I have no idea what I'm saying, but I can pronounce it correctly.)

2. **Click New.**

   QuickBooks displays the New Account dialog box. You use this dialog box to describe any new accounts you want to add to the chart of accounts (see Figure 1-10).

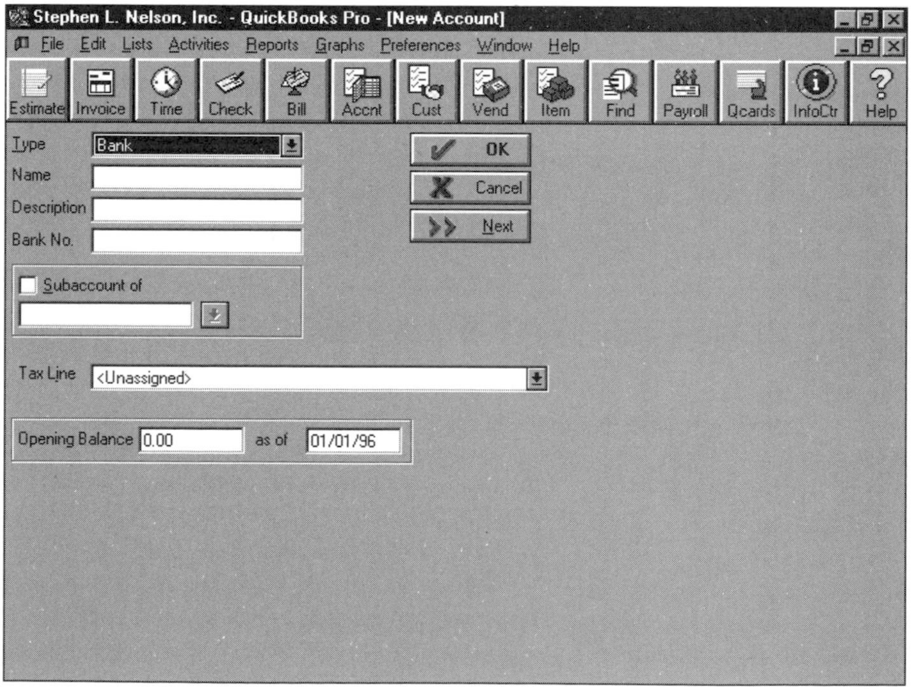

Figure 1-10:
The New
Account
dialog box.

3. Select the account type.

Activate the Type drop-down list box. Then select the entry that best describes the new account: Bank, Accounts Receivable, Other Current Asset, Fixed Asset, Other Asset, Accounts Payable, Credit Card, Other Current Liability, Long Term Liability, Equity, Income, Cost Of Goods Sold, Expense, Other Income, or Other Expense.

4. Name the account.

You can guess how this works, right? Move the cursor to the Name text box. Then type the account name you want to use to identify the account. You need to enter this name each and every time you reference the account in QuickBooks, so don't go entering some monstrously long name. Short and sweet works much, much better.

5. Describe the account.

Because the account name will be short and very possibly cryptic, you should use the Description text box to describe the account. What you enter as the description appears on the reports.

6. (Optional) Supply the bank account number.

If you're setting up an additional bank account, give QuickBooks the bank account number. Just move the cursor to the Bank No. text box and then bang away on the keyboard. (If you're setting up some other type of account, QuickBooks relabels this text box *Note*. I guess that you can enter some note into it.)

7. (Optional) Indicate whether the account is a subaccount.

In QuickBooks, you can create *subaccounts,* which are accounts within accounts. To specify that an account should be rolled into, or combined with, another account, click the Subacccount Of check box. Then activate the drop-down list box below the Subaccount Of check box and select the account.

8. (Optional) Indicate the tax line that applies to account entries.

If you activate the drop-down list box in the Tax Line entry, QuickBooks lists different tax schedules. Whenever you enter a transaction to this account, it will affect your tax reports for the line or schedule that you list here. If you have any doubts, ask your accountant how this account might affect your taxes.

Don't enter anything into the Opening Balance text box yet. Refer to Chapter 3 for more information on entering this balance (also referred to as the *trial balance*).

9. Click OK.

After you finish describing the account, click OK. QuickBooks closes the New Account dialog box. To add more accounts, repeat Steps 1 through 7.

Deleting accounts

Get rid of any accounts you know you won't need. They just mess up your chart of accounts. To remove an account, choose Lists⇨Chart of Accounts to display the Chart of Accounts dialog box. Then select the account you want to delete and choose Edit⇨Delete Account. QuickBooks, ever the careful one, displays a message box asking you to rethink your big decision. If you're sure that you want to delete the account, click OK.

Note: Delete any accounts now, before you go any further. You won't be able to delete accounts after somebody uses the account. So, if somebody uses the account erroneously (because it shouldn't have been there), you'll have a mess that you can never clean up. Ugh.

But don't delete any of the QuickBooks payroll accounts unless you really, really know what you're doing. QuickBooks automatically sets up the payroll accounts that you need for preparing employee payroll checks.

A Quick Word About Conversion Dates

Hey, I need to tell you one other thing before I go any further. You're going to have to decide on the date that you want to start using QuickBooks — your *conversion date*. The conversion date is important because it's the date that you stop doing your accounting the old way and start doing your accounting the new way — with QuickBooks.

But you can benefit from knowing a couple of things before you choose a conversion date.

First, to convert to QuickBooks on the conversion date, you need a list that shows the dollar values of your assets, liabilities, owner's equity, and, if it's any time other than the very beginning of the year, your year-to-date income and expense figures. If you don't have this list, you need to create it. You can probably pay your accountant to create it for you. Or you can read Appendix B and do the work yourself.

Note: Accountants call this list a *trial balance.* I mention this term not because you care. I know that you don't. I mention it because your old accounting system may produce a trial balance, and your accountant may be able to help get at it.

The easiest conversion date to use is the start of the fiscal year, or accounting year, which is probably January 1. This date is the easiest one to use because, at the very start of the year, the year-to-date income and expense figures are all zero because you haven't yet done any business for the year. So you don't have to worry about calculating year-to-date income and expense amounts.

One other thing I want to mention is this: You need to have detailed information on the dollar amounts that you hold in inventory, the amounts that you owe your vendors, and the amounts that your customers owe you.

Note: In your business, you may not call the people or businesses you sell to or provide services to *customers.* You may have other names for them. And I don't mean those names you use behind their backs. No way. Doctors call their customers *patients,* for example. Lawyers call their customers *clients.* In this book, however, I call the people you sell to or provide services to *customers* just to keep things easy.

Chapter 2

Lists, Lists, and More Lists

● ●

In This Chapter

▶ Setting up the Item List

▶ Describing employees

▶ Describing customers

▶ Describing vendors

▶ Using the Other Names List

▶ Describing payment methods and terms

▶ Describing shipping methods

▶ Understanding and using the other lists

● ●

*H*ere's a wacky little accounting system concept: All accounting programs, including QuickBooks, make your life easier by storing information you use over and over again. They store this information in lists.

This concept may sound kooky, but take the example of one of your vendors. Every time you want to pay a bill from this vendor, you need to know several pieces of information. You need to know the vendor's name and address. You need to know how and when the vendor expects to be paid. And you may need to know other stuff as well — such as your account number.

Whenever you want to pay a bill from this vendor, you can hunt down all this information by digging through a stack of paper. Or, if you have the information stored in a list somewhere on your computer, you can get at it with a mouse click or two.

Does that explanation make sense? Good. This chapter describes how you collect information and enter it into lists that QuickBooks can use. By the way, before you create these lists, you need to set up the chart of accounts described in Chapter 1.

Note: You need to create the lists in a certain order — the same order in which I describe them in the pages that follow.

The Magic and Mystery of Items

The first list that you need to create is a list of the items you sell. Cleverly, this list's name is the *Item List*.

Before you start creating this list, I need to tell you that QuickBooks isn't very smart about its view of what you sell. It thinks that anything you stick on an invoice is something you're selling.

If you sell blue, yellow, and red thingamajigs, for example, you probably figure (and correctly so) that you need to add descriptions of each of these items to the Item List: blue thingamajig, yellow thingamajig, and red thingamajig. But if you add freight charges to an invoice, QuickBooks thinks that you are adding another thingamajig. And if you add sales tax to an invoice, well, guess what? QuickBooks again thinks that you are adding another thingamajig.

This wacky definition of items is confusing at first. But just remember one thing and you'll be okay. It's not you who's stupid. It's QuickBooks. No, I'm not saying that QuickBooks is a bad program. It's a wonderful accounting program and a great tool. I am saying that QuickBooks is only a dumb computer program. It's not an artificial intelligence program. It doesn't pick up on the little subtleties of business — such as the fact that, even though you charge customers for freight, you're not really in the shipping business.

Each item on the invoice — the thingamajigs you sell, the subtotal, the discount, the freight charges, and the sales tax — is an item. Yes, I know. This is weird. But you may as well get used to the wackiness. The discussions that follow will be much easier to understand. (If you want to see a sample invoice, take a peek at Figure 2-1.)

Adding items you may include on invoices

To add invoice items to the Item List, follow these steps:

1. **Choose Lists⇨Items or click the Item icon on the iconbar.**

   QuickBooks, with restrained but obvious enthusiasm, displays the Item List window (see Figure 2-2).

Stephen L. Nelson, Inc.
123 North Mercer Way
Mercer Island, WA 98111
Tel: (206) 555-1234
FAX: (206) 555-4321

Invoice

DATE	INVOICE #
1/1/96	10

BILL TO:

SNG, Ltd.
345 Parkway
Tukwila, WA 98435

SHIP TO:

SNG, Ltd.
345 Parkway
Tukwila, WA 98435

P.O. NUMBER	TERMS	REP	SHIP	VIA	F.O.B.	PROJECT
	Net 30		1/1/96			

QUANTITY	ITEM CODE	DESCRIPTION	PRICE EACH	AMOUNT
20	Doohickey	20 oz. doohickey	12.25	245.00T
40	Thingamajig	12 oz. Thingamajig	11.00	440.00T
25	Gizmo	16 oz. Gizmo with Key Chain	8.00	200.00T
				885.00
		Sales Tax	8.20%	72.57

	TOTAL	$957.57

Figure 2-1:
A sample
invoice
form.

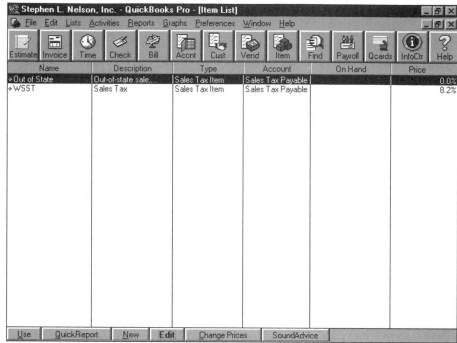

Figure 2-2:
The Item List window.

2. Click New.

QuickBooks displays the New Item dialog box (see Figure 2-3).

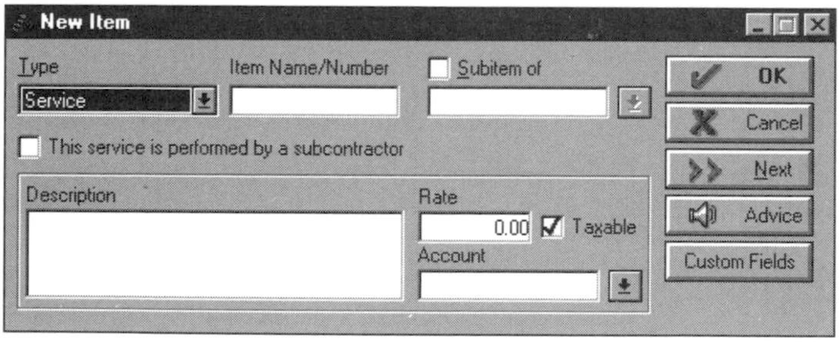

Figure 2-3:
The New Item dialog box that QuickBooks displays.

3. Categorize the item.

Activate the Type drop-down list box. The item list you see here is dependent on the type of business you're in, so use the following as a sample — your mileage may vary. Select one of the following item types:

- **Service:** Select this type if you charge for a service — such as an hour of labor or a repair job.

- **Inventory Part:** Select this type if what you're selling is something that you buy from someone else. If you sell thingamajigs that you purchase from the manufacturer Thingamajigs Amalgamated, for example, you specify the item type as Inventory Part.

- **Non-inventory Part:** Select this type if what you're selling is something that you don't want to track as inventory. (You usually don't use this item for things that you sell, by the way. Instead, you use it for items that you buy and want to include on purchase orders.)

- **Other Charge:** Select this item type for things such as freight and handling charges that you include on invoices.

- **Subtotal:** This item type adds everything up before you subtract any discount, add the sales tax, and so on.

- **Group:** Use this item type to enter a bunch of items (which are already on the list) at one time. For example, Subtotal and Sales Tax Items will always appear on every invoice if you charge sales tax. By using Group, you won't have to specify those items individually every time you write an invoice.

- **Discount:** This item type calculates an amount to be subtracted from a subtotal.

- **Payment:** This is wacky, but if your invoice sometimes includes an entry that reduces the invoice total — customer deposits, for example — select this item type. If you're confused by this item type, just ignore it.

- **Sales Tax Item:** Select this item type for the sales tax that you include on the invoice.

- **Sales Tax Group:** This item type is similar to the Group item type, but you use it only for *sales taxes* that always appear on the same invoice. A very nice time-saver.

4. Enter an item number or name.

Move the cursor to the text box to the right of the Type drop-down list box. (The name of the text box changes, depending on the item type.) Then enter a short description of the item.

5. (Optional) Make the item a subitem.

If you want to work with *subitems* — items that appear within other items — check the Subitem Of box and use the corresponding drop-down list box to specify the parent item to which a subitem belongs. If you set up a parent item for thingamajigs and subitems for blue, yellow, and red thingamajigs, for example, you can produce reports that show parent items (such as thingamajigs) or subitems (such as the different-colored thingamajigs). Subitems are just an extra complexity, so if you're new to this, I suggest that you keep things simple by avoiding them.

6. Describe the item in more detail.

Move the cursor to the Description text box and enter a description. This description then appears on the invoice. Note that, if you specify the item type as Inventory Part, you see two description text boxes: Purchase Description and Sales Description. The purchase description appears on purchase orders, and the sales description appears on sales invoices.

7. If the item type is Service, Non-inventory Part, or Other Charge, tell QuickBooks how much to charge for the item, whether the item is taxable for sales tax purposes, and which income account to use for tracking the income you receive from selling the item.

- For a **Service** type, use the Rate text box to specify the price you charge for one unit of the service. If you're charging by the hour, for example, the rate is the charge for an hour of service. If you're charging for a job — such as a repair job or the completion of a specific task — the rate is the charge for the job or task.

- For a **Non-inventory Part** type, use the Sales Price text box, which replaces the Rate text box, to specify the amount you charge for the item.

- For an **Other Charge** type, use the Amount or % text box, which replaces the Rate text box, to specify the amount you charge for the item. You can enter an amount, such as 20 for $20.00, or you can enter a percentage. If you enter a percentage, QuickBooks calculates the Other Charge Amount as the percentage multiplied by the preceding item shown on the invoice. (You usually do this after using a Subtotal Item — something I talk about later in this chapter.)

- For all three types, use the Taxable check box to indicate whether the item is taxed.

- For all three types, use the Account drop-down list to specify which income account you want to use to track income you receive from the sale of this item.

8. **If the item type is Inventory Part, tell QuickBooks how much to charge for the inventory part, how much the inventory part costs, and which income account to use for tracking the product sales income.**

For an Inventory Part item type, QuickBooks displays the New Item dialog box, shown in Figure 2-4.

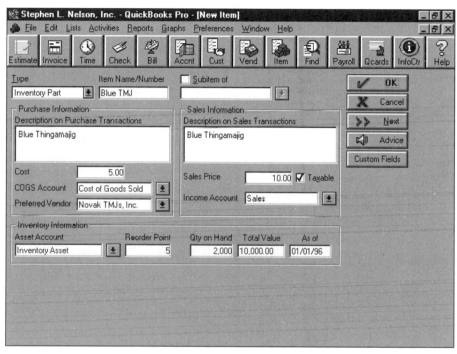

Figure 2-4:
The New Item dialog box that QuickBooks displays when the item type is Inventory Part.

You use the extra fields this special version of the dialog box displays to record the following information:

- **Description On Purchase Transactions:** Describe the part. This description then appears on the documents (such as purchase orders) used when you buy items for your inventory.

- **Cost:** Specify the average cost per unit of the items you currently have.

- **COGS (Cost of Goods Sold) Account:** Specify the account you want QuickBooks to use for tracking this item's cost when you sell it. (QuickBooks may suggest an account if you have a single cost of goods sold account on the chart of accounts.)

- **Preferred Vendor:** Specify your first choice when ordering the item for your business. (If the vendor is not on your Vendor List, QuickBooks asks you to add it, either through the QuickAdd option or the more detailed Set Up option. Your choice of options should depend on either the detail to which you plan to use QuickBooks or whether you're trying to make that appointment that was scheduled for 10 minutes ago.)

- **Description On Sales Transactions:** Describe the item as you would like it to appear on documents such as invoices, and so on, that are seen by your customers. (QuickBooks may suggest the same description you used in the Description On Purchase Transactions text box as a default.)

- **Sales Price:** Enter the amount that you charge for the item.

- **Taxable**: Indicate whether the item is taxed. Use the Income Account drop-down list to specify the income account you want to use to track income you receive from the sale of this item.

- **Asset Account:** Specify the other current asset account that you want QuickBooks to use for tracking this inventory item's value.

- **Reorder Point:** Specify the lowest inventory quantity of this item before you order more. When the inventory level drops to this quantity, QuickBooks displays the Reminders window to remind you that you need to reorder the item.

- **Qty On Hand:** Specify how many units of this inventory item you're currently holding.

- **Total Value:** Verify that this text box shows the correct and current total dollar value of this item. If it doesn't — perhaps there's a minor rounding error or something — fix the problem by replacing whatever the Total Value text box shows with the correct amount.

- **As Of:** Enter the conversion date in this text box.

9. **If the item type is Sales Tax Item, tell QuickBooks what sales tax rate to charge and what government agency to pay.**

   If the item type is Sales Tax Item, QuickBooks displays the New Item dialog box shown in Figure 2-5. You use this version of the New Item dialog box to record the following information:

   Note: You already set up one Sales Tax item as part of setting up QuickBooks if you told QuickBooks that you sell items that are subject to sales tax. If you're required to calculate and collect only one tax or if you don't have to calculate and collect sales tax (because you sell something that isn't subject to the tax), you don't need to set up additional Sales Tax items.

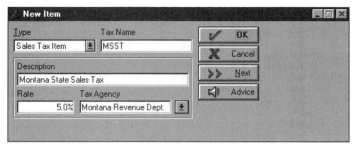

Figure 2-5:
The New
Item dialog
box for the
Sales Tax
Item.

- **Tax Name** and **Description:** Specify further details for later identification.

- **Rate:** Specify the sales tax rate.

- **Tax Agency:** Name the state tax agency that's getting all the loot you collect.

10. **If the item type is Payment, describe the payment method and how you want QuickBooks to handle the payment.**

    If you're setting up a Payment item, you see a Payment Method drop-down list box. After you specify the item type, name the item, and describe it, you use the Payment Method drop-down list to specify the method of payment. QuickBooks provides a starting list of several of the usual payment methods. (Activate the Payment Method drop-down list box to see the list.) You can easily add more payment types. Choose Lists⇨Other Lists⇨Payment Methods so that QuickBooks displays the Payment Methods Types window. Click New to see the New Payment Method dialog box. Then, in the dialog box's only text box, identify the payment method: chickens, beads, shells, or some other what-have-you.

    After you're finished, use the area in the lower-left corner of the dialog box to either group the payment with other undeposited funds or, if you use the drop-down list box, deposit the payment to a specific account.

11. **Click OK or Next when you're finished.**

    When you finish describing one item, click OK to add the item to the list and return to the Item List window. Or click Next to add the item to the list and keep the New Item dialog box displayed on your screen so that you can add more items.

Creating other wacky items for invoices

The preceding discussion does not describe all the items that you can add. Some lines on invoices are actually calculations. For example, an invoice usually shows a subtotal of the items already listed. (You usually need this subtotal when you want to calculate a sales tax on the invoice's items.) The invoice also may contain other wacky items, such as discounts. The next few paragraphs describe these special types of items.

Creating subtotal items to stick subtotals on invoices

To add a subtotal item to the list, choose Lists⇨Items to display the New Item dialog box — the same one you have seen several times already in this chapter. Specify the Item Type as Subtotal, and then provide an item name or number and a description.

When you want to subtotal, items on an invoice, all you do is stick this subtotal item on the invoice after the items you want to subtotal.

Creating group items to batch stuff you sell together

You can create an item that puts one line on an invoice that's actually a combination of several other items. If you purchase three inventory parts — a thingamajig, a gizmo, and a doohickey — but sell the items in a "gadgets" set, for example, you can create a gadgets item that groups the other three items.

To add a group item, choose the Lists⇨Items command to display the New Item dialog box. Specify the Item Type as Group. QuickBooks shows the New Item dialog box shown in Figure 2-6. Use the Item/Description/Qty list box to list each item included in the group. When you click an item line in the Item/Description/Qty list box, QuickBooks places a downward-pointing arrow at the right end of the Item column. You click this arrow to open a drop-down list of items. (If the list is longer than can be shown, you can use the scroll bar on the right to move up and down the list.) If you select the Print Items In Group check box, QuickBooks lists all the items in the group on invoices.

Creating discount items to add discounts to invoices

You can create an item that calculates a discount and sticks the discount on an invoice as another line item. To add a discount item to the list, choose the Lists⇨Items command to display the New Item dialog box. Specify the Item Type as Discount and provide an item name or number and a description.

Use the Amount or % text box to specify how the discount is calculated. If the discount is a set amount (such as $50.00), enter an amount. If the discount is calculated as a percentage, enter the percentage, including the percent symbol.

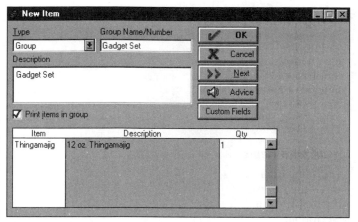

Figure 2-6:
The New
Item dialog
box for the
Group item.

When you enter a percentage, QuickBooks calculates the Discount amount as the percentage multiplied by the preceding item shown on the invoice. (If you want to apply the discount to a group of items, you need to use a subtotal item and follow it with the discount.)

Use the Account drop-down list to specify the expense account that you want to use to track the cost of the discounts you offer.

Select Apply Discount Before Taxes if you want to use this option. (This option appears only if you created it in the EasyStep Interview and you indicate that you need to charge sales tax.)

Creating Sales Tax Group items to batch sales taxes together

Sales Tax Groups enable you to batch several sales taxes that you're supposed to charge as one sales tax so that they appear as a single sales tax on the invoice. Combining the taxes is necessary — or at least possible — when you're supposed to charge, say, a 6 percent state sales tax, a 1.5 percent county sales tax, and a 0.5 percent city sales tax, but you want to show one, all-encompassing 8 percent sales tax on the invoice.

To add a Sales Tax Group item, choose the Lists⇔Items command to display the New Item dialog box. Specify the Item Type as Sales Tax Group. QuickBooks shows the New Item dialog box shown in Figure 2-7. Use the Tax Item/Rate/Tax Agency/Description list box to list the other sales tax items that you want to include in the group. When you click an item line in the list box, QuickBooks places a down arrow at the right end of the Tax Item column. You can click this arrow to open a drop-down list of Sales Tax items.

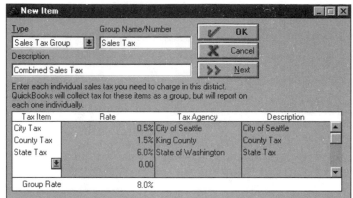

Figure 2-7:
The New
Item dialog
box for the
Sales Tax
Group item.

Editing items

If you make a mistake, you can change any piece of item information by displaying the Item List window, selecting the item by clicking it, and then clicking the Edit button so that QuickBooks displays the Edit Item dialog box. You then can use the Edit Item dialog box to make changes.

Describing Your Employees

If you're going to do payroll in QuickBooks or if you want to track sales by employees, you need to describe each employee. Describing employees is pretty dang easy. Choose Lists➪Employees so that QuickBooks displays the empty Employee List window shown in Figure 2-8. Then click New to have QuickBooks display the New Employee dialog box shown in Figure 2-9.

Figure 2-8:
The empty
Employee
List window.

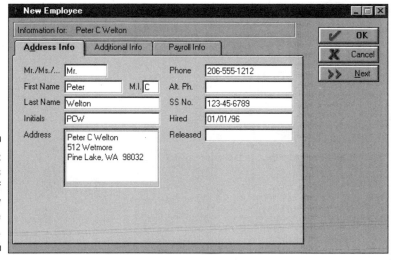

Figure 2-9:
The Address
Info tab of
the New
Employee
dialog box.

See Figure 2-9? It's pretty straightforward, right? You just fill in the fields to describe the employee.

Lesser computer book writers would probably provide step-by-step descriptions of how you move the cursor to the First Name text box and enter the person's first name, how you move the cursor to the next text box, enter something there, and so on. Not me, boy. No way. I know that you can tell just by looking at this dialog box that all you do is click a text box and type the obvious bit of information. Right?

Note that QuickBooks automatically types the employee's initials in the Initials text box. When you later describe your customers, you can use employee initials to identify the sales representative who is assigned to them.

Note, too, that you can include the information shown in Figure 2-10 by clicking the Payroll Info tab. Again, I think that what you need to do in this tab is fairly straightforward. The Additional Info tab enables you to create customizable fields, in case you want to keep information that isn't covered by the QuickBooks default fields. Favorite color and that type of thing.

After you finish describing an employee, click OK to add the employee to the list and return to the Employee List window. Or click Next to add the employee to the list but leave the New Employee dialog box displayed on the screen so that you can add more employees.

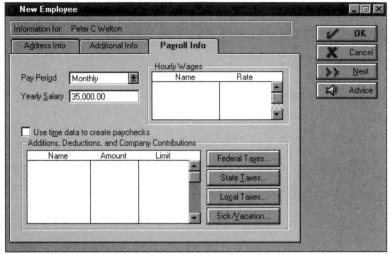

Figure 2-10:
The New
Employee
Payroll Info
tab for Peter
C. Welton.

Customers Are Your Business

This is sort of off the subject, but I read about a survey that some business school had done. In the survey, people who wanted to start a business were asked what the most important thing is that a person needs to start a business. Almost all of them answered, "Cash." The same survey also asked a large number of people who had already started businesses — many of whom had been running their businesses successfully for years — what the most important thing is that a person needs to start a business. They all answered, "Customers."

Weird, huh? I do think that it's true, though. You need customers to get into business. Everything else — including cash — is secondary. But I've sort of gotten off the track. I'm supposed to be describing how you create your Customer List. Here's the blow-by-blow:

1. **Choose Lists⇨Customers:Jobs, or click the Cust icon on the iconbar.**

   QuickBooks displays the Customer:Job List window (see Figure 2-11).

2. **Click the New button.**

   QuickBooks displays the Address Info tab of the New Customer dialog box (see Figure 2-12). You use this dialog box to describe the customer in as much detail as possible.

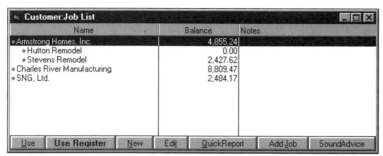

Figure 2-11:
The
Customer:
Job List
window.

3. Give the customer's name.

This step is pretty obvious, right? The cursor is already in the Customer text box. All you have to do is type the customer's name. Hunt, peck, hunt, peck, hunt, peck. If you make a mistake, use Backspace to backspace over, or erase, your mistake.

4. Give the company name.

That's right, the customer's company name.

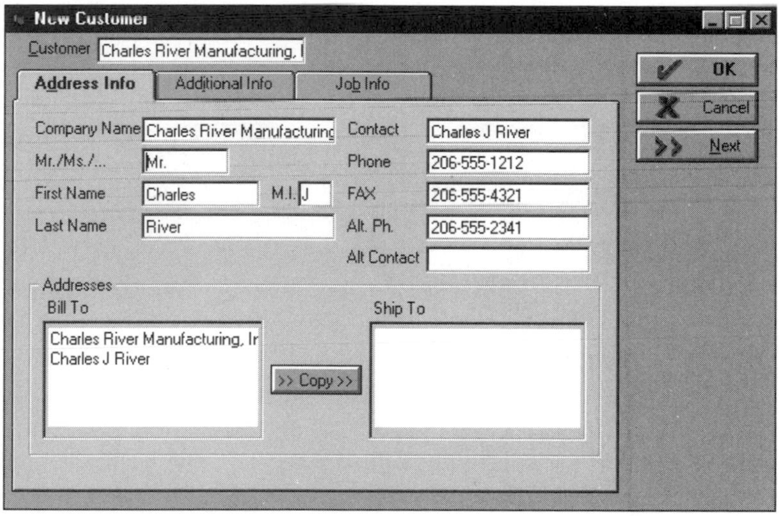

Figure 2-12:
The Address
Info tab of
the New
Customer
dialog box.

5. (Optional) Give the name of your contact, along with other pertinent information.

Press Tab to move the cursor to the Mr./Ms. text box and type the appropriate title. Same with the First Name, M.I., and Last Name text boxes.

(QuickBooks automatically types the name in the Contact text box as you type it. Nice touch, eh?)

Go ahead and fill in the Phone, FAX, and Alt. Ph. (alternative phone) text boxes while you're at it.

6. **(Really optional) Give the name of your alternative contact.**

Move the cursor to the Alt Contact text box and type the name of the alternative contact.

7. **Give the billing address.**

You can use the Bill To block of fields to provide the customer's billing address. QuickBooks copies the Customer name to the first line of the billing address, so you probably need to enter only the address. To move from the end of one line to the start of the next, press Enter.

8. **Give the shipping address.**

You can use the Ship To block of fields to provide the customer's shipping address if this address differs from the Bill To address. (If it's the same, just click Copy.) You enter this information in the same way that you enter the Bill To address. A few deft mouse clicks. Some typing. You're done.

9. **Click the Additional Info tab.**

If you don't, you'll be wondering where in the world the rest of the stuff I'm talking about is. (By the way, your screen will look like Figure 2-13.)

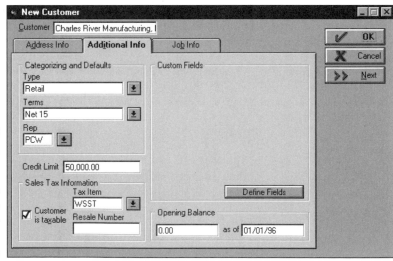

Figure 2-13:
The Additional Info tab of the New Customer dialog box.

10. (Massively optional) Categorize the customer.

See that Type drop-down list box? You can use it to assign the customer a particular type. You can create a huge list of customer types by choosing Lists⇨Other Lists⇨Customer Types (to display the Customer Type List window), clicking New (so QuickBooks displays the New Customer Type dialog box), and then filling in the dialog box blanks. If you have some clever scheme you want to use for categorizing customers, hey, be my guest. If not, don't worry about the customer type.

11. Specify the payment terms that you want the customer to observe.

Did I say "Observe"? I guess that's probably not really accurate, is it? You want the customer to do more than just *observe,* by golly. You want the customer to *honor* the terms. To specify the payment terms, activate the Terms drop-down list and select one of its terms. QuickBooks has already set up all the usual terms. (If you want to, you can use the Lists⇨Other Lists⇨Terms command to set up additional payment terms.)

12. (Optional) Name the sales representative.

QuickBooks lets you assign each customer to a sales representative by selecting the sales representative's initials from the Rep drop-down list. (To activate the Rep drop-down list box, click the down arrow at the right end of the Rep box.)

TIP

The little things do too matter

If you're not familiar with how payment terms work, you can get a bird's-eye view here. For the most part, payment terms just tell the customer how quickly you expect to be paid. At the bottom of the invoice is a phrase that states the payment terms. For example, *Net Due Upon Receipt* means that you expect to be paid as soon as possible. If *Net* is followed by some number, as in *Net 15* or *Net 30,* the number indicates the number of days after the invoice date within which the customer is supposed to pay.

So *Net 15* means that the customer is supposed to pay within 15 days of the invoice date.

Some payment terms, such as *2% 10 Net 30,* include early payment discounts. The percentage and first number indicate that the customer can deduct the percentage from the payment if the payment is made within the first number of days. The payment term *2% 10 Net 30* means that the customer can deduct 2 percent from the bill if it's paid within 10 days and the customer must pay the bill within 30 days.

13. **(Optional) Specify the customer's credit limit if you have set one.**

    Move the cursor to the Credit Limit field. Hmmm. I know. How about clicking it? Then type the credit limit. (The *credit limit,* as you probably know, is just a record of the amount of credit that you have decided to extend to the customer.) QuickBooks helps you track this amount by monitoring the customer's remaining credit limit and alerting you when the customer's reached the credit limit. If you leave this field blank, QuickBooks figures that you don't care about this customer's limit and so ignores the credit limit.

14. **Identify the Sales Tax item you use to track the sales taxes that you collect and later pay.**

    Activate the Tax Item drop-down list, and select the sales tax item you use to calculate sales tax on sales to this customer.

15. **Store the resale number if you're supposed to do so.**

    If you're supposed to collect resale certificate numbers for customers who don't pay sales tax, move the cursor to the Resale Number text box and enter the number there.

16. **Indicate whether the customer is taxable.**

    Select the Customer Is Taxable check box if the customer is, well, taxable.

17. **If you're not going to set up jobs, enter the amount that this customer currently owes you.**

    If you will track what customers owe in total rather than what customers owe by job, move the cursor to the Opening Balance text box and enter the amount that the customer owes on the conversion date. (If you track what customers owe by job, don't worry about this step. But do read the next section, "It's Just a Job.")

18. **Enter the conversion date.**

    Move the cursor to the As Of field and enter the conversion date.

19. **(Optional) Add specific job information.**

    Because you're creating a new customer account here, I'll wait and explain this step in the next section. If you're the "can't-wait" type, feel free to take a look. You can add a specific job to the new customer's information.

20. **Save the customer information.**

    When you finish describing a customer, click OK to add the customer to the list and return to the Customer:Job List window. Or click Next to add the customer to the list and keep the New Customer dialog box displayed on the screen so that you can add more customers.

If you want to change some bit of customer information, display the Customer:Job List window, click the customer to select it, click the Edit button, and then make changes by using the Edit Customer dialog box.

It's Just a Job

In QuickBooks, you can track invoices by customer or by customer and job. I know. This sounds kooky. But it makes sense in businesses that invoice customers, often several times, for specific jobs.

Take the case of a construction subcontractor who does foundation work for a handful of builders of single-family homes. This construction subcontractor invoices his customers by job, and he invoices each customer several times for the same job. For example, he invoices Poverty Rock Realty for the foundation job at 512 Wetmore when he pours the footing, and then again when he lays the block. At 1028 Fairview, the same foundation job takes more than one invoice, too.

To set up jobs for customers, you need to first describe the customers (as explained in the preceding section). Then follow these steps:

1. **Choose Lists⇨Customers:Jobs, or click the Cust icon on the iconbar.**

   QuickBooks displays the Customer:Job List window.

2. **Select the customer for which you want to set up a job.**

   This step is simple. Just click the customer name.

3. **Click the Add Job button from the bottom of the window.**

   QuickBooks displays the New Job dialog box (see Figure 2-14). You use this dialog box to describe the job. A great deal of the information in this dialog box appears on the invoice.

4. **Give the job name.**

   The cursor is in the Job Name text box. Just type the name of the job or project.

5. **Identify the customer.**

   Just on the off chance that you selected the wrong customer in Step 2, take a peek at the Customer drop-down list box. Does it name the right customer? If not, activate the drop-down list and select the right customer.

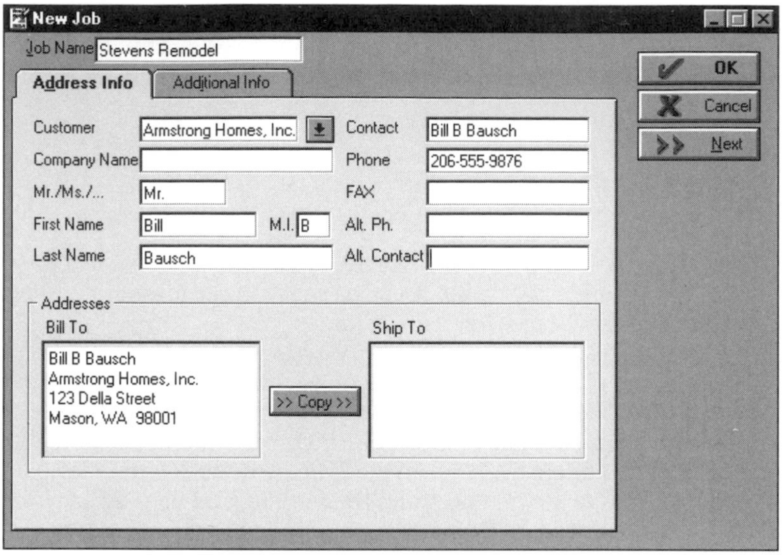

Figure 2-14:
The Address
Info tab of
the New
Job dialog
box.

6. (Optional) Name your contact, and fill in other relevant information.

You can enter the name of your contact and alternate contact in the Mr./Ms., First Name, M.I., and Last Name text boxes. QuickBooks fills in the Contact text box for you. You probably don't need to be told this, but fill in the Phone and FAX text boxes just so that you have that information on hand. If you want to get *really* optional, fill in the Alt. Ph. and Alt. Contact text boxes. Go ahead, take a walk on the wild side.

7. Give the job's billing address.

You can use the Bill To text box to provide the customer's job billing address. Because chances are good that the job billing address is the same as the customer billing address, QuickBooks copies the billing address from the Customer List. But, if need be, make changes.

8. Give the Ship To address.

You can use the Ship To block of fields to provide the job's shipping address. Click the Copy button if the shipping address is the same as the Bill To address.

To get to the second dialog box, click the Additional Info tab. Figure 2-15 illustrates the resulting screen quite admirably.

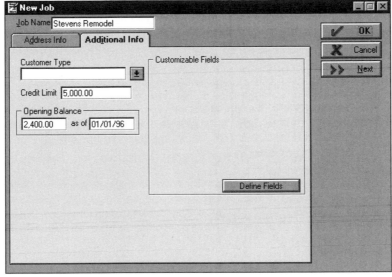

Figure 2-15:
The
Additional
Info tab of
the New Job
dialog box.

9. **(Massively optional) Categorize the job.**

   You can use the Customer Type drop-down list box to give the job type. As noted earlier in the chapter, the only initial type in the default list is From Advertisement. You can create other types by choosing Lists⇨Other Lists⇨Customer Types (which displays the Customer Types window), clicking New (so that QuickBooks displays the New Customer Type dialog box), and then filling in the dialog box blanks.

10. **Set the customer's credit limit.**

    That is, if you have set one. Which I strongly recommend.

11. **Enter the amount that this customer currently owes you on this job.**

    Move the cursor to the Opening Balance text box and enter the amount that the customer owes on this job as of the conversion date.

12. **Enter the conversion date.**

    Move the cursor to the As Of text box and enter the conversion date.

13. **(Optional) Add specific job information.**

    Click the Job Info tab, and fill in the information on the job. You can use the Job Status drop-down list box to choose None, Pending, Awarded, In Progress, Closed, or Not Awarded, whichever is most appropriate. The Start Date is (I know this is hard to believe) the day you start the job. As anyone knows, the Projected End and the End Date are not necessarily the same. Don't fill in the End Date until the job is actually finished. The Job Description field can contain any information you can fit in one line that will help you, and the Job Type is an extra field you can use. (If you do use this field, you can get to a list of Job Types by choosing Lists⇨Other Lists⇨Job Types.)

14. **Save the job information.**

After you finish describing the job, click OK to add the job to the list and return to the Customer:Job List window. Or click Next to add the job to the list and keep the New Job dialog box displayed on the screen so that you can add more jobs.

You can edit job information the same way that you edit customer information. Display the Customer:Job List window by choosing Lists⇨Customers:Jobs. When QuickBooks displays the list, select the job, click the Edit button, and use the dialog box that QuickBooks displays to make the changes.

Setting Up Your Vendors

You also need to set up your vendors on a list. Setting up a Vendor List works the same basic way as setting up a Customer List does. If you set up your Customer List in the preceding section, you will have no problem setting up one for vendors. Here's how to get the job done:

1. **Choose Lists⇨Vendors, or click the Vend icon on the iconbar.**

QuickBooks displays the Vendor List window (see Figure 2-16). It lists any sales tax agencies that you identified as part of setting up Sales Tax items.

Name	Balance
City of Seattle	0.00
Department of Revenue	0.00
King County	0.00
Montana Revenue Dept.	0.00
Novak TMJs, Inc.	0.00
State of Washington	0.00

Figure 2-16:
The Vendor List window.

Vendor List

Use   QuickReport   New   Edit

2. Click New.

QuickBooks displays the Address Info tab of the New Vendor dialog box (see Figure 2-17). You use this dialog box to describe the vendors and all their little idiosyncrasies.

3. Give the vendor's name.

The cursor is already in the Vendor text box. All you have to do is type the vendor's name.

4. (Optional) Give the name of your contact.

Fill in the Mr./Ms., First Name, M.I., and Last Name text boxes. You remember this, right?

5. Give the address to which you're supposed to mail checks.

You can use the Address text box to provide the vendor's Payment To address. QuickBooks copies the vendor's name to the first line of the address, so you probably need to enter only the street address and city. To move from the end of one line to the start of the next, press Enter.

6. (Optional) Give the vendor's telephone and fax numbers.

If you want, provide the vendor's telephone and fax numbers. The dialog box also has an Alt. Ph. text box for a second telephone number. Hey. They thought of everything, didn't they?

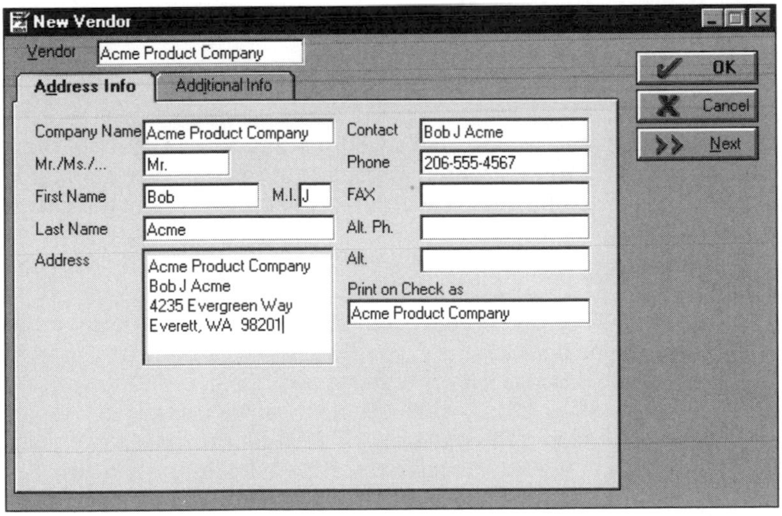

Figure 2-17:
The Address
Info tab of
the New
Vendor
dialog box.

7. Check the Print On Check As text box.

QuickBooks assumes that you want the company name to appear on any checks you write for this vendor. If not, change the text box to whatever you feel is more appropriate.

At this point, click the Additional Info tab to get the second set of dialog boxes. Their resemblance to Figure 2-18 is uncanny.

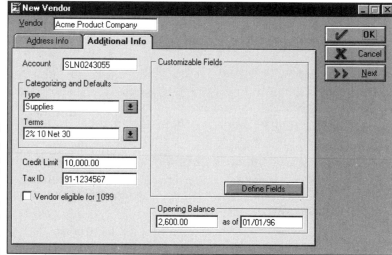

Figure 2-18: The Additional Info tab of the New Vendor dialog box.

8. (Optional) Give your account number.

If the vendor has assigned account numbers or customer numbers to keep track of customers, enter your account or customer number in the Account text box. You can probably get this piece of information from the vendor's last invoice.

9. Categorize the vendor.

See that Type drop-down list box? You can use it to assign the vendor a Type. If you activate the drop-down list by clicking its arrow, you see the initial QuickBooks list of vendor types. You can pick any of these types, but my suggestion is that you diligently identify vendors to whom you need to send a 1099 as *1099 contractor*. (A *1099 contractor* is any unincorporated business to whom you pay more than $600 during the year.)

Note: You can create a new vendor type by choosing Lists⇨Other Lists⇨Vendor Types (to display the Vendor Type List), clicking New (so

QuickBooks displays the New Vendor Type dialog box), and then filling in the dialog box blanks.

10. **Specify the payment terms that you're supposed to observe.**

    Activate the Terms drop-down list and select one of its terms. QuickBooks has already set up all the usual ones. (If you want to, you can choose Lists⇨Terms and set up additional payment terms.)

    If a vendor offers an early payment discount, it will usually be too good of a deal to pass up. Interested in more information about this? Is yours an inquiring mind that needs to know? Refer to Chapter 17 to learn about the advantages of early payment discounts.

11. **(Optional) Specify your credit limit if the vendor has set one.**

    This procedure is obvious, right? You click the Credit Limit text box and enter the number.

12. **(If applicable) Store the vendor's federal tax identification number and check the Vendor Eligible For 1099 check box.**

    This number may be the vendor's social security number if the vendor is a one-man or one-woman business. If the vendor has employees, the federal tax identification number is the vendor's employer identification number. You need this information only if you are required to prepare a 1099 for the vendor.

13. **Enter the amount that you currently owe this vendor.**

    Move the cursor to the Opening Balance text box and enter the amount you owe the vendor. If you don't know this figure, you can easily get it by adding up all the unpaid invoices you have received.

14. **Enter the conversion date.**

    Move the cursor to the As Of field and enter the conversion date.

15. **Save the customer information.**

    After you finish describing the vendor, click OK to add the vendor to the list and return to the Vendor List window. Or click Next to add the vendor to the list and leave the New Vendor dialog box displayed on the screen so that you can add more vendors.

The Little Things Never Bother Me

I have covered almost all the most important List menu commands. The menu contains a few other commands that I haven't talked about yet: Classes, Other Names, Ship Via, Customer Messages, Purchase Orders, Memorized Transactions, Reminders, and Re-sort List. I'm not going to give blow-by-blow descriptions of how you use these commands because you don't need to use these commands to build other lists. QuickBooks provides lists that are generally more than adequate. You can usually use them as is without building other lists.

Just so I don't leave you stranded, however, I want to give you quick-and-dirty descriptions of these other lists and what they do.

The Classes List

Classes are another way to organize your income and expenses. Classes are cool, really cool. But they add another dimension to the accounting model that you use in QuickBooks. So I'm not going to describe them here. I urge you — nay, I implore you — to get comfortable with how the rest of QuickBooks works before you begin mucking about with classes. If, after learning how the rest of QuickBooks works, you want to wrestle with classes, you can get whatever help you need from the user's guide.

Let me also point out that whatever you want to do with classes, you can probably do it easier and better with a clever chart of accounts or a Customers:Jobs List.

The Other Names List

QuickBooks provides an Other Names List that works as a watered-down, wimpy, Vendor and Employee List combination. You can write checks to people named on this Other Names List. But you can't do anything else. You can't create invoices or purchase orders for them, for example. And you don't get any of the other information that you want to collect for vendors or employees.

I think that you're really better off working with good, accurate, rich Vendor and Employee Lists. If you don't like this suggestion, however, just choose Lists⇨Other Names to display the Other Names List window, click its New button, and fill in the blanks in the New Name dialog box.

The Ship Via List

QuickBooks provides descriptions for the usual shipping methods. These descriptions are probably entirely adequate. If you need to add more, however, you can do so by using the Lists⇨Other Lists⇨Ship Via command. When you choose the command, QuickBooks displays the Ship Via window, which lists all the shipping methods that you or QuickBooks has said are available. To add more methods, click New and fill in the dialog box that QuickBooks displays. Friends, it doesn't get much easier than this.

The Customer Messages List

This list is another minor player in the QuickBooks drama. You can stick messages at the bottom of invoices if you first type the message in the Customer Messages List. QuickBooks provides a handful of boilerplate messages. You can add more messages by choosing the Lists⇔Other Lists⇔ Customer Messages command. When QuickBooks displays the Customer Messages List window, click its New button. Then use the New Message dialog box, which QuickBooks displays, to create a new message. You can create a message of up to three lines. Use Enter or Return to move from one line to the next.

The Purchase Orders List

The Lists⇔Purchase Orders command displays the Purchase Orders List window. You can add purchase orders to the list by clicking the window's New command button. If you're interested in using purchase orders or want to set up any existing purchase orders, refer to Chapter 7 for the straight scoop.

The Memorized Transactions List

The Memorized Transactions List isn't really a list. At least, it's not like the other lists I've described thus far. The Memorized Transactions List is a list of accounting transactions — invoices, bills, checks, purchase orders, and so forth — that you've asked QuickBooks to memorize.

You can have QuickBooks memorize transactions so that you can reuse them. QuickBooks uses this list for QuickFill operations.

The Reminders List

QuickBooks keeps track of a bunch of different stuff that it knows you need to monitor. If you choose Lists⇔Reminders, QuickBooks displays this Reminders List. On it you see things such as invoices and checks that need to be printed, inventory items you should probably reorder, and so on.

And what about the Re-sort List command?

Ah, yes. I almost forgot. The Re-sort List command alphabetizes whatever list is shown in the active document window. How the command itself is worded on the menu changes, according to the active window — for example, if the Item List window is open, the command will read Re-sort Item List. (The active document window is the one that is on top of any other windows in the QuickBooks application window.)

To use the Re-sort List command, first display the list that you want to alphabetize by choosing one of the other Lists menu commands. If you want to alphabetize the customer and job names shown in the Customer:Job List window, choose Lists⇨Customers:Jobs. Then choose Lists⇨Re-sort List. QuickBooks, sensing that you definitely mean business and don't want it fooling around, displays a message box that says that it's about to alphabetize the list. Click OK to alphabetize.

Chapter 3

The Rest of the Story

In This Chapter

▶ Adjusting for accrual-basis accounting

▶ Describing your current financial condition

▶ Describing your year-to-date income and expenses

▶ Some other nits and gnats

*T*he preceding two chapters describe *most* of the things you do to set up QuickBooks, but you do need to take care of two other things. You need to make an adjustment if you want to use accrual-basis accounting. And you need to describe your current business finances. These tasks aren't time consuming. But they are the two most complicated things that you need to do to set up QuickBooks. (If you're not sure what the big deal is about accrual-basis accounting, I respectfully suggest that you take a break here and read Appendix B.)

Should You Get Your Accountant's Help?

Oh, shoot. I don't know. If you follow my directions carefully and your business's financial affairs are *not* wildly complex, I think that you can probably figure out all this stuff on your own. You don't have to be a rocket scientist.

That said, however, I suggest that you at least think about getting your accountant's help at this juncture. Your accountant can do a much better job of giving you some advice that may be specific to your situation. The accountant probably knows your business and can keep you from making a terrible mess of things just in case you don't follow my directions carefully.

By the way, if you do call upon your accountant to help you with the tasks in this chapter, stick a bookmark in the page with the technical stuff sidebar and ask your financial wizard to read it. It summarizes what you've accomplished thus far. (If you're going to do all this stuff yourself, reading the technical stuff sidebar is not a bad idea.)

For accountants only

If you're reading this, I assume that you're an accountant who has been asked to help your client with the last piece of the QuickBooks conversion. I also assume that you understand double-entry bookkeeping and that you are at least passingly familiar with the general mechanics involved in converting to new accounting systems. With those two caveats, you're ready to start.

First, your client should already have installed QuickBooks and set up a chart of accounts (tasks I described in Chapter 1), and three master files should be loaded. The Item List master file describes the inventory account balances. (QuickBooks uses an average costing assumption.) The Customer List master file describes the accounts receivable balances. And the Vendor List master file describes the accounts payable balances. Because your client has set up these master files, QuickBooks has made three journal entries, as described in the following paragraphs. (I'm using *Xs* to represent numbers, in case you're not familiar with this convention. But, of course, you are. You're an accountant.)

To set up the conversion date inventory balance (if inventory exists), QuickBooks has created the following entry:

	Debit	Credit
Inventory Asset	$X,XXX	
Opening Bal Equity		$X,XXX

To set up the conversion date accounts receivable (A/R) balance (if A/R exists), QuickBooks has created the following entry:

	Debit	Credit
Accounts Receivable	$X,XXX	
Uncategorized Income		$X,XXX

To set up the conversion date accounts payable (A/P) balance (if A/P exists), QuickBooks has created the following entry:

	Debit	Credit
Accounts Payable		$X,XXX
Uncategorized Expenses	$X,XXX	

To complete the picture, you need to do two things. If your client will use accrual-basis accounting, you need to get rid of the credit to the Uncategorized Income account and the debit to the Uncategorized Expenses account. (These two accounts are really just suspense accounts.) And you need to load the rest of the trial balance. The steps for accomplishing these tasks are described in the next two sections.

Adjusting for Accrual-Basis Accounting

If you want to use accrual-basis accounting — and I recommend that you do — you need to camouflage a couple of goofy accounts, called *suspense accounts,* that QuickBooks creates when you set up the Item, Customer, and Vendor Lists.

Figure 3-1 shows the example trial balance after I've entered the inventory, accounts receivable, and accounts payable balances. (These account balances get set up indirectly, as noted in the information for accountants. When you set up your Item, Customers, and Vendors Lists, you also create account balances for inventory, accounts receivable, and accounts payable.)

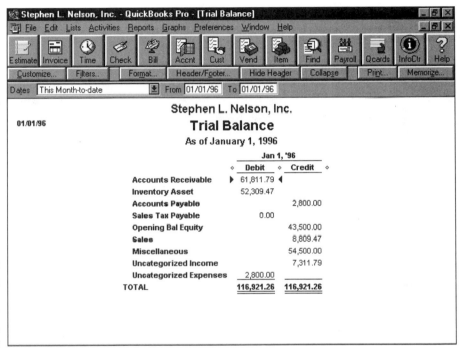

Figure 3-1:
A sample trial balance.

You can produce your own half-complete trial balance from inside QuickBooks by choosing Reports⇨Other Reports⇨Trial Balance. QuickBooks displays the trial balance report in a document window.

If you need to do so, enter the conversion date in the From and To date boxes by clicking these date boxes and typing the conversion date in MM/DD/YY fashion. Figure 3-1, for example, shows the conversion date 01/01/96 in both boxes. Make a note of the credit and debit balances shown for the Uncategorized Income and Uncategorized Expenses accounts.

If you want, you can print the report by clicking the Print button and then, when QuickBooks displays the Print Report dialog box, clicking its Print button. Yes, you click two Print buttons.

After you have the conversion date balances for the Uncategorized Income and Uncategorized Expenses accounts, you're ready to make the accrual accounting adjustment. To do so, follow these steps:

1. **Display the Chart of Accounts window.**

   Choose Lists⇨Chart of Accounts. QuickBooks displays the Chart of Accounts window, as shown in Figure 3-2. Hubba, hubba.

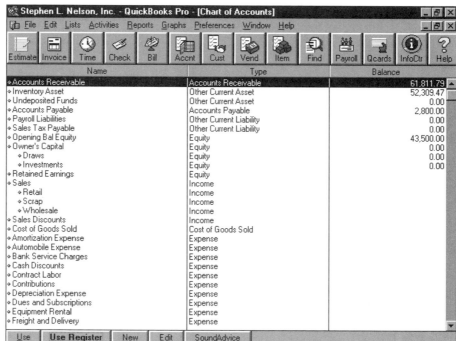

Figure 3-2:
The Chart of Accounts window.

2. **Select the Opening Bal Equity account.**

   Scroll through the chart of accounts list until you see the account Opening Bal Equity. (It's after the liability accounts.) Click it.

3. **Click the Use Register button.**

   QuickBooks displays the *register* — just a list of transactions — for the account named Opening Bal Equity. Figure 3-3, coincidentally, shows this register.

4. **If it is not already selected — and it probably is — select the next empty row of the register.**

   You can select it by clicking it, or you can use the up- or down-arrow key to move to the next empty row.

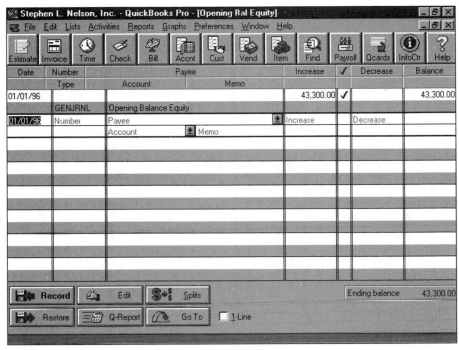

Date	Number	Payee			Increase	✓	Decrease	Balance
	Type	Account		Memo				
01/01/96					43,300.00	✓		43,300.00
	GENJRNL	Opening Balance Equity						
01/01/96	Number	Payee		⬇	Increase		Decrease	
		Account	⬇	Memo				

Ending balance   43,300.00

Record   **Edit**   **$→$ Splits**

Restore   **Q-Report**   **Go To**   ☐ 1-Line

Figure 3-3:
The Opening
Bal Equity
register.

5. Enter the conversion date in the Date field.

Move the cursor to the Date field (if it isn't already there) and type the date. Use the MM/DD/YY format. For example, you can type either **010196** or **1/1/96** to enter January 1, 1996.

6. Enter the Uncategorized Income account balance in the Increase field.

In Figure 3-1, for example, the Uncategorized Income account balance is $7,311.79. In this case, you select the Increase field by clicking it, and then you type **7311.79** in the field. (You don't need to include the dollar signs. QuickBooks adds the punctuation for you.)

7. Type the account name, Uncategorized Income, **in the Account field.**

Select the Account field, which is on the row under the word *Payee,* and begin typing **Uncategorized Income,** the account name. As soon as you type enough of the name for QuickBooks to figure out what you're typing, it fills in the rest of the name for you. When this happens, you can stop typing. Figure 3-4 shows the Opening Bal Equity register with this Uncategorized Income transaction entered.

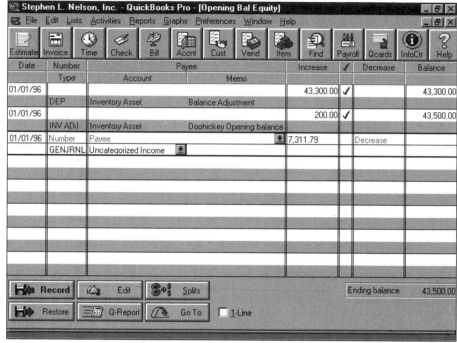

Figure 3-4:
The transaction that fixes the Uncategorized Income account balance.

8. **Click the Record button to record the Uncategorized Income adjustment transaction.**

9. **Again, select the next empty row of the register.**

   Click it or use the up- or down-arrow key.

10. **Enter the conversion date in the Date field.**

   Move the cursor to the Date field (if it isn't already there) and type the date. As noted earlier, you use the MM/DD/YY format. You type **1/1/96**, for example, to enter January 1, 1996.

11. **Enter the Uncategorized Expenses account balance in the Decrease field.**

   In Figure 3-1, for example, the Uncategorized Expenses account balance is $2,800. In this case, you select the Decrease field by clicking it, and then you type **2800** in the field. I have said this before, but I'll say it again because you're just starting out: You don't need to include any punctuation, such as dollar signs.

12. **Type the account name,** Uncategorized Expenses, **in the Account field.**

Select the Account field, which is on the second line of the register transaction, and begin typing **Uncategorized Expenses**, the account name. As soon as you type enough of the name for QuickBooks to figure out what you're typing, it fills in the rest of the name for you. When this happens, you can stop typing. Figure 3-5 shows the Opening Bal Equity register with this Uncategorized Expenses transaction entered.

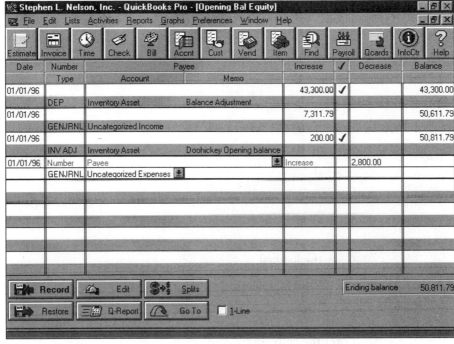

Figure 3-5:
The transaction that fixes the Uncategorized Expenses account balance.

13. **Click the Record button to record the Uncategorized Expenses adjustment transaction.**

You can close the Opening Bal Equity register, too, at this point. You're finished with it. (One way to close it is to double-click the Control menu button at the left end of the menu bar.)

You can check your work thus far — and checking it is a good idea — by producing another copy of the trial balance report. What you want to check are the Uncategorized Income and Uncategorized Expenses account balances. They should both be zero, as shown in Figure 3-6.

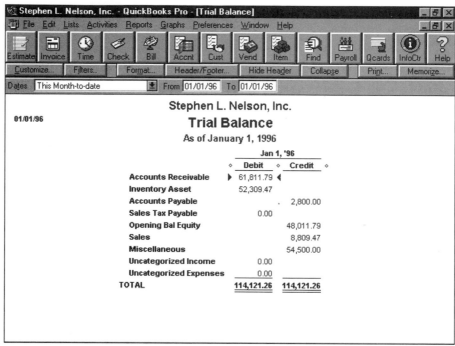

Figure 3-6:
Another
sample trial
balance.

As you may remember, you can produce a trial balance by choosing Reports⇨Other Reports⇨Trial Balance. QuickBooks displays the trial balance report in a document window. If you need to enter the conversion date in the From and To date boxes, click the boxes, and type the conversion date in MM/DD/YY fashion in both boxes. Figure 3-6, for example, shows the conversion date 01/01/96 in both boxes.

If the Uncategorized Income and the Uncategorized Expenses account balances don't show as zero, it means that you (with my help, of course) botched the accrual adjustment. To fix your mistake, redisplay the Opening Bal Equity register, select the adjustment transactions, and then check the account, amount, and field (increase versus decrease). If one of the fields is wrong, select the field and then replace its contents by typing over them.

Supplying the Missing Numbers

You're almost done. Really. Your only other task is to enter the rest of the trial balance into QuickBooks. To perform this task, of course, you need to already have a trial balance as of the conversion date. But you should have one. A *trial balance* is simply a list of your asset, liability, owners equity, and year-to-date income and expense account balances. (I'll stop plugging Appendix B, but if you have questions about what trial balances are and how they work, you really should read that appendix.)

Oh where, oh where, has my trial balance gone?

If you have been using another small business accounting system, such as Microsoft Profit, you may be able to have your old system produce a trial balance on the conversion date. In that case, you can get the balances from your old system. (You can consider yourself lucky if this is the case.)

If your old system is rather informal (perhaps it's a shoe box full of receipts) or if it tracks only cash (perhaps you have been using Quicken), you need to do a bit more work.

To get your asset account balances, you need to tell QuickBooks what each asset costs. For depreciable fixed assets, you also need to provide any accumulated depreciation that you've charged. (*Accumulated depreciation* is just the total depreciation that you have charged on an asset.)

To get your liability account balances, you need to tell QuickBooks how much you owe on each liability. If you trust your creditors — the people you owe the money to — you may also be able to get this information from their statements.

You don't need to worry about the owners equity accounts. QuickBooks calculates a single owners equity account for you, based on the difference between your total assets and your total liabilities. Okay? This method is a bit sloppy. Accountants may not like it. But I think that it's a pretty good compromise.

If you do have detailed account balances for your owners equity accounts, you should use these figures. (If you have these figures, you also should know that you're very unique. Yes, indeed.)

To get your income, cost of goods sold, expense, other income, and other expense account balances, you need to calculate the year-to-date amount of each account. If you can get this information from your old system, that's super. If not, you need to get it manually. (If you suddenly have images of yourself sitting at your desk, late at night, tapping away on a ten-key, you're right.)

Because the year-to-date income and expense account balances equal zero at the very start of a fiscal year, the easiest time to convert to a new accounting system such as QuickBooks is at the very beginning of the new year. In fact, if you are reading this book late in the year, keep reading, but postpone the actual conversion until the start of the new year. And you know what else? If it's early in the year, I would honestly consider starting the year over again — only this time by just using QuickBooks. (In other words, if it's early February, go ahead and use January 1 as the conversion date, and record all the information for the year so far.)

Entering the trial balance information

After you collect the trial balance information, entering it is a snap. Let's say, for purposes of illustration, that your trial balance looks like the one shown in Table 3-1.

Table 3-1	A Sample Trial Balance	
Trial Balance Information	**Debit**	**Credit**
Assets		
Checking	$5,000	
Fixed Assets	10,000	
Accumulated Depreciation (Fixed Assets)		$ 2,000
Liabilities Information		
Loan Payable		10,000
Owners Equity and Income Statement Information		
Opening Bal Equity	30,000	
Sales		60,000
Cost of Goods Sold	20,000	
Supplies Expense	2,100	
Rent Expense	4,900	
Totals	**$72,000**	**$72,000**

After you have the trial balance information organized in a fashion similar to that shown in Table 3-1, you're ready to enter it in the QuickBooks system. Follow these steps:

1. **Display the Special Transactions dialog box.**

    Choose Activities⇨Enter Special Transactions. QuickBooks displays the General Journal Entry dialog box shown in Figure 3-7.

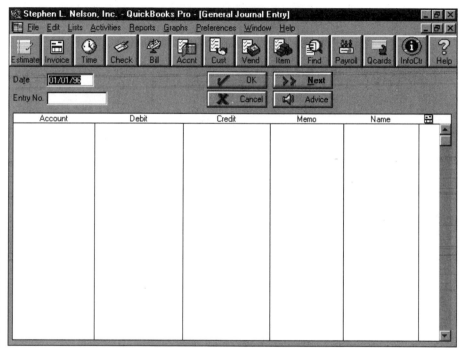

Figure 3-7:
The empty
General
Journal
Entry dialog
box.

2. **Enter the conversion date.**

    Move the cursor to the Date field (if it isn't already there) and type the date. As you may know by now, you use the MM/DD/YY format. For example, you type **1/1/96** for January 1, 1996. (Or **010196**, if you don't want to put the slashes in.)

3. **Enter each trial balance account and balance that isn't already in the half-completed trial balance.**

    Okay. This step sounds confusing. But remember that you already entered your accounts receivable, inventory, and accounts payable account balances and a portion of the Opening Bal Equity account balance as part of setting up the Item, Customers, and Vendors Lists. So what you need to

do now is enter the rest of the trial balance: cash, fixed assets, the accumulated depreciation on the fixed assets, the loan, the year-to-date income
and expense account balances, and the remaining portion of the opening
balance equity. To enter each account and balance, use a row of the
General Journal Entry dialog box's list box. Figure 3-8 shows how this
dialog box looks after you enter the rest of the trial balance into the list
box rows.

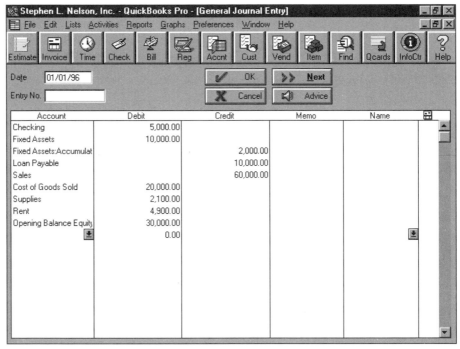

Figure 3-8:
The
completed
General
Journal
Entry dialog
box.

4. **Click OK to record the general journal entry that sets up the rest of your
trial balance.**

Checking your work one more time

Checking your work again is a good idea. Produce another copy of the trial
balance report. What you want to check is that the QuickBooks trial balance is
the same one that you want to enter. For example, I would compare the
QuickBooks trial balance (shown in Figure 3-9) with the one shown in Table 3-1.

About those debits and credits

You have to keep the debits and credits thing straight for a few minutes. Here's the straight scoop. For assets and expenses, a debit balance is the same thing as a positive balance. So a cash debit balance of $5,000 means that you have $5,000 in your account. And $20,000 of cost of goods sold means that you incurred $20,000 of costs of goods expense. For assets and expenses, a credit balance is the same thing as a negative balance. So, if you have a cash balance of –$5,000, your account is overdrawn by $5,000. In the example trial balance shown in Table 3-1, the accumulated depreciation shows a credit balance of $2,000, which is, in effect, a negative account balance.

For liabilities, owners equity accounts, and income accounts, things are flip-flopped. A credit balance is the same thing as a positive balance. So an accounts payable credit balance of $2,600 means that you owe your creditors $2,600. A bank loan credit balance of $10,000 means that you owe the bank $10,000. And a sales account credit balance of $60,000 means that you have enjoyed $60,000 of sales.

I know that I keep saying this, but do remember that those income and expense account balances are year-to-date figures. They exist only if the conversion date is after the start of the financial year.

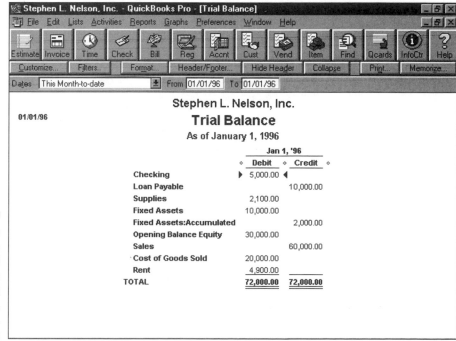

Figure 3-9: The completed conversion date trial balance. At last.

Stephen L. Nelson, Inc. - QuickBooks Pro - [Trial Balance]

File Edit Lists Activities Reports Graphs Preferences Window Help

Estimate Invoice Time Check Bill Reg Accnt Cust Vend Item Find Qcards InfoCtr Help

Customize... Filters.. Format... Header/Footer... Hide Header Collapse Print.. Memorize

Dates This Month-to-date From 01/01/96 To 01/01/96

01/01/96

Stephen L. Nelson, Inc.
Trial Balance
As of January 1, 1996

	Jan 1, '96	
	Debit	Credit
Checking	5,000.00	
Loan Payable		10,000.00
Supplies	2,100.00	
Fixed Assets	10,000.00	
Fixed Assets:Accumulated		2,000.00
Opening Balance Equity	30,000.00	
Sales		60,000.00
Cost of Goods Sold	20,000.00	
Rent	4,900.00	
TOTAL	**72,000.00**	**72,000.00**

Remember that you can produce a trial balance by choosing Reports⇨Other Reports⇨Trial Balance. Be sure to enter the conversion date in the From and To date boxes. If the QuickBooks trial balance report agrees with what your records show, you're finished.

If the QuickBooks trial balance doesn't agree with what your records show, you need to fix the problem. Fixing it is a bit awkward, but it's not complicated. Choose Reports⇨Other Reports⇨Journal. QuickBooks displays a report, or journal, listing all the transactions that you or QuickBooks has entered as part of setting up. (The Dates, From, and To text boxes need to specify the conversion date.) Scroll through the list of transactions until you get to the last one. It is the one that you entered to set up the rest of the trial balance, and it names recognizable accounts and uses familiar debit and credit amounts. Double-click this transaction. QuickBooks displays the register window. Don't worry about this register window. Just click the Edit button. QuickBooks redisplays the General Journal Entry dialog box with the botched transaction. Find the mistake. Then fix the erroneous account or amount by clicking it and typing the correct account or amount.

Part II
Daily Chores

The 5th Wave   By Rich Tennant

IN A BIZARRE MIX-UP, KEN BALANCES A BUS SCHEDULE INSTEAD OF HIS CHECKBOOK, AND THEN CONTINUES BY BOOKING A SEAT FOR HIM AND LAVERNE IN THE LOCAL BANK'S SAFE DEPOSIT BOX.*

* From that time forward, Laverne handled their financial affairs.

In this part . . .

Okay. You've got QuickBooks set up. Or maybe you were lucky enough to have someone else do all the dirty work. But all that doesn't matter now. It's in this part where the rubber really hits the road. You need to start using QuickBooks to do a bunch of stuff on a regular, and maybe daily, basis. Invoice customers. Record customer payments. Pay bills. This part describes how you do all these things.

Chapter 4

Billing Customers

. . . .

In This Chapter

▶ Preparing invoices

▶ Fixing invoice mistakes

▶ Preparing credit memos

▶ Fixing credit memo mistakes

▶ Printing invoices and credit memos one at a time

▶ Printing invoices in a batch

▶ Printing credit memos in a batch

. . . .

*T*he big difference between Quicken and QuickBooks is this: QuickBooks enables you to create and print invoices to send to your customers so that they know that they're supposed to pay you and how much and why they're supposed to pay you. This chapter, you'll be surprised to hear, describes how you create and print invoices in QuickBooks.

Making Sure That You're Ready

I know that you're probably all set to go. But first you need to check a few things, Okay? Good.

You should already have installed QuickBooks, of course. (Appendix A describes how to install it.) You should have set up a company and a chart of accounts, as described in Chapter 1. You should already have set up your lists — particularly your Item and Customer lists, as described in Chapter 2. And, to make things cleanest and most straightforward, you should already have entered your starting trial balance or have talked your accountant into entering it for you, as described in Chapter 3.

As long as you have all this prerequisite stuff done, you're ready to start. If you don't have one of the prerequisites done, you need to complete it before going any further.

Sorry. I don't make the rules. I just tell you what the rules are.

Preparing an Invoice

After you complete all the preliminary work, preparing an invoice with QuickBooks is a snap. To give you the abbreviated version of the story, you display the Create Invoices window — by clicking the Invoice icon, for example — and then you fill in this window and click the Print button. If you want more help than a single sentence provides, keep reading for step-by-step instructions.

The following steps describe how to create the most complicated and involved invoice there is: a product invoice. Some of the fields on the product invoice don't appear on the service or professional invoice, but don't worry if your business is a service or professional one. Creating a service or professional invoice works basically the same way as creating a product one — you just fill in fewer fields.

1. **Display the Create Invoices window.**

   You display it by choosing Activities⇨Create Invoices or by clicking the Invoice icon. QuickBooks then displays the Create Invoices window shown in Figure 4-1.

2. **Identify the customer and, if necessary, the job.**

   Activate the Customer:Job drop-down list by clicking the down arrow at the right end of the box. Scroll through the Customer:Job list until you see the customer or job name, and then click it.

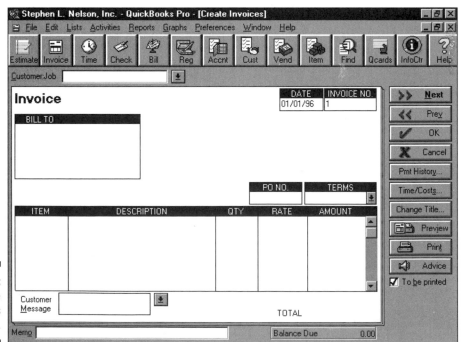

Figure 4-1:
The Create
Invoices
window.

3. Give the invoice date.

Press Tab to move the cursor to the Date text box. Then enter the correct date in MM/DD/YY format. You also can use the following secret codes to change the date:

- Press + (the plus symbol) to move the date ahead one day.

- Press – (the minus symbol) to move the date back one day.

- Press T to change the date to today's date (as specified by the system time that your computer's internal clock provides).

- Press M to change the date to the first day in the current month (because *M* is the first letter in the word *month*).

- Press H to change the date to the last day in the current month (because *H* is the last letter in the word *month*).

- Press Y to change the date to the first day in the current year (because, as you've no doubt guessed, *Y* is the first letter in the word *year*).

- Press R to change the date to the last day in the current year (because *R* is the last letter in the word *year*).

4. (Optional) Enter an invoice number.

QuickBooks suggests an invoice number by adding 1 to the last invoice number that you used. You can accept this addition, or, if you need to have it your way, you can tab to the Invoice No. text box and change it to whatever you want.

5. Fix the Bill To address if needed.

QuickBooks grabs the billing address from the Customer List. You can change the address for the invoice, however, by replacing some portion of the usual billing address. You can, for example, insert another line that says, "Attention: William Bobbins," if that is the name of the person to whom the invoice should go.

6. Fix the Ship To address if needed.

I feel like a broken record, but here's the deal: QuickBooks also grabs the shipping address from the Customer List. So, if the shipping address has something unusual about it for just this one invoice, you can change it by replacing or adding information to the Ship To address block.

7. (Optional . . . sort of) Provide the purchase order number.

If the customer issues purchase orders, enter the number of the purchase order that authorizes this purchase in the PO No. text box. Just for the record, *PO* is pronounced *pee-oh*. Not *poh* or *poo*.

8. Specify the payment terms.

To specify the payment terms, activate the Terms drop-down list box and select something from it. I have only one request to make: Don't offer a customer an early payment discount without reading the first couple of sections in Chapter 17. Please. I'm only looking out for your welfare. Really.

9. **(Optional) Name the sales representative.**

   Rep does *not* stand for *Reputation,* so don't put three-letter editorial comments in here. (Although I can't, for the life of me, imagine what you could do with three letters.) If you want to track sales by sales representative, you use the Rep drop-down list box. Just activate the list box, by clicking its arrow, for example, and then pick a name. I don't want to do the "I told you so" routine, but to specify sales representatives, you need to have set up the Employee List.

10. **Specify the shipping date if it's something other than the invoice date.**

    To specify the date, just move the cursor to the Ship Date text box, and then type the date in MM/DD/YY fashion. You can move the cursor by pressing Tab or by clicking the text box. Oh. One other quick point. Remember all those secret codes I talked about earlier in the chapter for changing the invoice date? They also work for changing the shipping date.

11. **Specify the shipping method.**

    You can probably guess how you specify the shipping method. But parallel structure and a compulsive personality force me to continue. So . . . to specify the shipping method, move the cursor to the Ship Via drop-down list, activate the list, and then select a shipping method. By the way, you can add new shipping methods to the list by choosing Lists⇨Other Lists⇨Ship Via to display the Ship Via List window, clicking its New button, and filling out the cute little dialog box that QuickBooks displays. Oh sure. It may sound difficult the first time you read the sentence, but setting up new shipping methods is really easy. Really easy.

12. **Specify the FOB point.**

    FOB stands for *free-on-board.* The FOB point is more important than it first seems — at least in a business sense — because the FOB point determines when the transfer of ownership occurs, who pays freight, and who bears the risks of damage to the goods during shipping. If a shipment is free-on-board at the shipping point, the ownership of the goods being sold transfers to the purchaser as soon as the goods leave the seller's shipping dock. (Remember that you're the seller.) This means that the purchaser pays the freight and that the purchaser bears the risk of shipping damage. The FOB shipping point can be specified either as FOB Shipping Point or by using the name of the city. If the shipping point is Seattle, for example, FOB Seattle is the same thing as FOB Shipping Point. Most goods are shipped as FOB Shipping Point, by the way.

    If a shipment is free-on-board at the destination point, the ownership of the goods that are being sold transfers to the purchaser as soon as the goods arrive on the purchaser's shipping dock. The seller pays the freight and bears the risk of shipping damage. The FOB destination point can be specified either as FOB Destination Point or by using the name of the city. If the destination point is Omaha, for example, FOB Omaha is the same thing as FOB Destination Point.

13. Describe each item that you're selling.

Move the cursor to the first row of the Item/Description/Qty/Rate/Amount/ Tax list box. Okay. I know that isn't a very good name for it, but you know what I mean, right? You need to start filling in the line items that go on the invoice. After you move the cursor to a row in the list box, QuickBooks turns the Item field into a drop-down list box. Activate the Item drop-down list box of the first empty row in the list box and then select the item.

When you do, QuickBooks fills in the Description and Rate text boxes with whatever sales description and sales price you entered in the Item List. (You can edit the information for this particular invoice if you need to.) Enter the number of items sold in the Qty text box. (After you enter this number, QuickBooks calculates the amount by multiplying the Qty by the Rate.) If you need other items on the invoice, use the remaining empty rows of the list box to enter each one. If you checked the Taxable check box when you added the item to the Item List, a small *T* appears in the Tax column to indicate that the item will be taxed.

Note: You can put as many items on an invoice as you want. If you don't have enough room on a single page, QuickBooks just adds as many pages as are needed to the invoice. The invoice total information, of course, goes only on the last page.

14. Describe any special items that should be included on the invoice.

If you didn't set up the QuickBooks item file, you have no idea what I'm talking about. But here's the scoop: QuickBooks thinks that anything you stick on an invoice is something that you're selling. If you sell blue, yellow, and red thingamajigs, you obviously need to add descriptions of each of these items to the Item List. But if you add freight charges to your invoice, QuickBooks thinks that the freight charge is just another thingamajig and so requires you to add another item to the list box. The same is true for a volume discount that you want to stick on the invoice. And if you add sales tax to your invoice, well, guess what? QuickBooks again thinks that it is just another item that you need to include in the list box.

To describe any of the special items, activate the Item drop-down list box of the next empty row in the list box and then select the special item. After QuickBooks fills in the Description and Rate text boxes, edit this information if necessary. Describe each of the other special items — subtotals, discounts, freight, and so on — that you're itemizing on the invoice by filling in the following empty rows of the list box.

If you want to include a discount item, you need to stick a subtotal item on the invoice after the inventory or other items you want to discount. Then you stick a discount item directly after the subtotal item. Then QuickBooks calculates the discount as a percentage of the subtotal.

15. (Optional) Add a customer message.

Click the Customer Message box, activate its drop-down list, and select a clever customer message. (You can add customer messages to the customer message list. Choose Lists⇨Other Lists⇨Customer Messages to have QuickBooks display the Customer Message List window. Click New and then fill in the dialog box that QuickBooks displays. (I know that I talked about the Customer Message box in Chapter 2, but I wanted to quickly describe how to add a customer message again so you don't have to flip back 30 pages or so.)

16. Specify the sales tax.

If you have only one sales tax, QuickBooks uses it as a default. If it isn't correct, move the cursor to the Tax list box, activate the drop-down list, and select the correct sales tax.

17. (Truly optional) Add a memo.

You can add a memo description to the invoice, if you want. This memo isn't for your customer. It doesn't even print. It's for your eyes only. Memo descriptions give you a way of storing information related to an invoice with that invoice. Figure 4-2 shows a completed Create Invoices window.

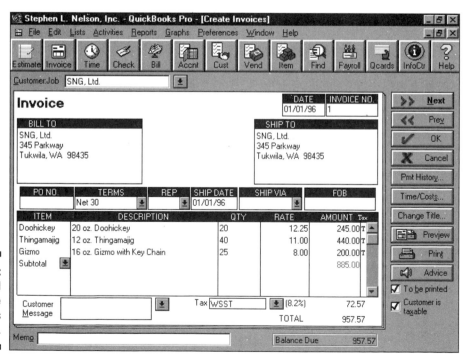

Figure 4-2:
A completed
Create
Invoices
window.

18. **If you want to delay printing this invoice, unmark the To Be Printed check box that's below the column of buttons on the right.**

   I want to postpone talking about what checking the To Be Printed check box does until I finish the discussion of invoice creation. I'll talk about printing invoices just a little bit later in the chapter. I promise.

19. **Save the invoice.**

   You can save a completed invoice in one of several ways:

   - If you want to create more invoices, click Next. QuickBooks saves the invoice that's on the screen and then redisplays an empty Create Invoices window so that you can create another invoice. (Note that you can return to invoices that you created earlier by clicking the Next button's cousin: Prev).

   - If you don't want to create additional invoices, click OK. QuickBooks saves the invoice and closes the Create Invoices window.

   - If you want to print the invoice and save it, click the Print button. I discuss printing invoices in detail a little bit later in the chapter.

Fixing Invoice Mistakes

I'm not a perfect person. You're not a perfect person. Heck, very few people are. So we make mistakes. You don't need to get worked up over mistakes that you make while entering information in invoices, however. Fixing them is easy.

If the invoice is still displayed on the screen

If the invoice is still displayed on the screen, you can just move the cursor to the box or button that's wrong and then fix the mistake. Because most of the bits of information that you enter in the Create Invoices window are short and sweet, you can easily replace the contents of some fields by typing over whatever is already there. To save your correction, click OK, Next, or Prev.

If the invoice isn't displayed on the screen

If the invoice isn't displayed on the screen but you haven't yet printed it, you can use the Next and Prev buttons to page through the invoices. When you get to the one with the error, just fix the error as described in the preceding section.

If you have printed the invoice, you also can make the sort of change described in the preceding paragraphs. For example, you can page through the invoices until you find the one (now printed) that has the error. And you can change the error and print the invoice again. I'm not so sure that you want to go this route, however, if you've already sent out the invoice. You may want to consider fixing the invoice by issuing either a credit memo (if the original invoice overcharged) or another invoice (if the original invoice undercharged). The reason that I suggest issuing a credit memo or another invoice is that life gets awfully messy if you or your customer have multiple copies of the same invoice floating around and causing confusion.

Deleting an invoice

I hesitate to mention this, but you also can delete invoices. Procedurally, deleting an invoice is easy. You just display the invoice in the Create Invoices window (choose Activities⇨Create Invoices or click the Invoice button to display the window). Use the Next and Prev buttons to page through the invoices until you see the invoice that you want to delete. Then choose Edit⇨Delete Invoice. When QuickBooks asks you to confirm your deletion, click Yes. But read the next paragraph first. You may not want to delete the invoice . . . .

Even though deleting invoices is easy, it isn't something that you should do casually or for fun. I do think that it's okay to delete an invoice if you've just created it, only you have seen it, and you haven't yet printed it. In this case, no one needs to know that you made a mistake. But the rest of the time — even if you created an invoice that you don't want later — you should keep a copy of the invoice in the QuickBooks system. By doing so, you have a record that the invoice existed, which usually makes answering questions easier later.

"But how am I to correct my books if I leave the bogus invoice?" you ask.

Good question. To correct your financial records for the invoice that you don't want to count anymore, just void the invoice. The invoice remains in the QuickBooks system, but QuickBooks doesn't count it. To void an invoice, display it in the Create Invoices window and then choose Edit⇨Void Invoice.

Preparing a Credit Memo

Credit memos can be a handy way to fix data entry mistakes that you didn't find or correct earlier. Credit memos are also handy ways to handle things such as customer returns and refunds. If you have prepared an invoice or two in your time, you'll find that preparing a QuickBooks credit memo is super-easy — and handy.

The following steps describe how to create the most complicated and involved kind of credit memo: a product credit memo. Creating a service or professional credit memo works basically the same way, however. You just fill in fewer fields.

1. **Display the Create Credit Memos/Refunds window.**

   Choose Activities⇨Create Credit Memos/Refunds. When you do, QuickBooks displays the Create Credit Memos/Refunds window as shown in Figure 4-3. Note that the Credit Memos are red and the Invoices are blue. This creates a color scheme that brings out the highlights in your hair and throws the emphasis on . . . okay, I'll stop.

2. **Identify the customer and, if necessary, the job.**

   Activate the Customer:Job drop-down list box. Then select the customer or job by clicking it.

3. **Give the credit memo date.**

   Press Tab to move the cursor to the Date text box. Then enter the correct date in MM/DD/YY format. You also can use the secret date-editing codes that I described earlier in the chapter in the section on preparing invoices. Oh, boy.

4. **(Optional) Enter a credit memo number.**

   QuickBooks suggests a credit memo number by adding 1 to the last credit memo number you used. You can accept the number or tab to the Credit No. text box and change the number to whatever you want.

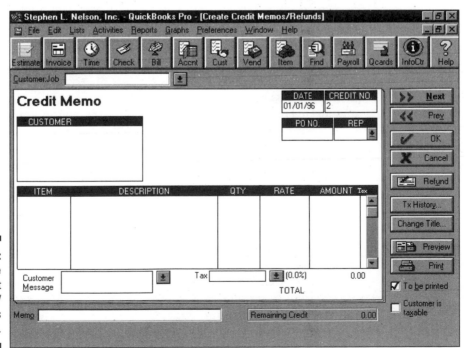

Figure 4-3:
The Create
Credit
Memos/
Refunds
window.

5. Fix the Customer address if needed.

QuickBooks grabs the billing address from the Customer List. You can change the address for the credit memo, however, by replacing some portion of the usual billing address. Typically, you should use the same address for the credit memo that you used for the original invoice or invoices.

6. (Optional . . . sort of) Provide the purchase order number.

If the credit memo adjusts the total remaining balance on a customer purchase order, you should probably enter the number of the purchase order into the PO No. text box.

Here's my logic on this suggestion for those readers who care: If you billed your customer $1,000 on PO No. 1984, which authorizes a $1,000 purchase, you have "used up" the entire purchase order — at least according to the customer's accounts payable clerk who processes your invoices. If you make sure that a credit memo for $1,000 is identified as related to PO No. 1984, however, you essentially free up the $1,000 purchase balance, which may mean that you can use, or bill on, the purchase order again.

7. (Optional) Name the sales representative.

If you want to track sales by sales representative, use the Rep drop-down list box to identify the salesperson whose sales are being reduced by the credit memo.

8. If the customer is returning items, describe each item.

Move the cursor to the first row of the Item/Description/Qty/Rate/Amount/ Tax list box. In the first empty row of the box, activate the Item drop-down list and then select the item. After you select it, QuickBooks fills in the Description and Rate text boxes with whatever sales description and sales price you entered in the Item List. (You can edit this information if you want, but it's not necessary.) Enter the number of items that the customer is returning (or not paying for) in the Qty text box. (After you enter this number, QuickBooks calculates the amount by multiplying the Qty by the Rate.) Enter each of the other items that the customer is returning by filling in the following empty rows of the list box.

Note: As with invoices, you can put as many items on a credit memo as you want. If you don't have enough room on a single page, QuickBooks just keeps adding pages to the credit memo until you're finished. The total information, of course, goes on the last page.

9. Describe any special items that should be included on the credit memo.

If you want to issue a credit memo for other items that appear on the original invoice — freight, discounts, other charges, and so on — add descriptions of each of these items to the Item List.

To add descriptions of these items, activate the Item drop-down list of the next empty row in the list box and then select the special item. (You activate the list by clicking the field once to turn it into a drop-down list box and then clicking the field's down arrow to drop down the list box.)

After QuickBooks fills in the Description and Rate text boxes, edit this information if necessary. Enter each of the other special items — subtotals, discounts, freight, and so on — that you're itemizing on the credit memo.

If you want to include a discount item, you need to stick a subtotal item on the invoice after the inventory or other items you want to discount. Then stick a discount item directly after the subtotal item. In this way, QuickBooks calculates the discount as a percentage of the subtotal.

10. (Optional) Add a customer message.

Activate the Customer Message list and select a clever customer message.

11. Specify the sales tax.

Move the cursor to the Tax list box, activate the list box, and select the correct sales tax.

12. (Optional, but a really good idea . . :) Add a memo.

You can use the Memo text box to add a memo description to the credit memo. I suggest that you use this description to explain your reasons for issuing the credit memo and to cross-reference the original invoice or invoices. Figure 4-4 shows a completed Create Credit Memos/Refunds window.

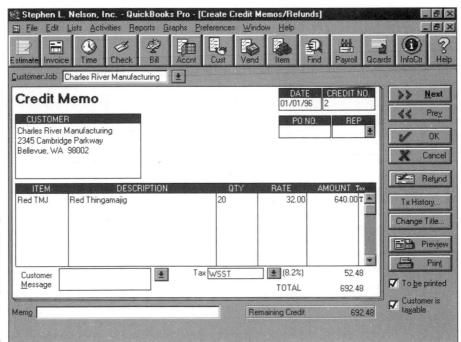

Figure 4-4:
A completed Create Credit Memos/Refunds window.

13. **If you want to delay printing this credit memo, check the To B̲e Printed check box.**

    I want to postpone talking about what checking the To B̲e Printed check box does until I finish the discussion of credit memo creation. I discuss printing invoices and credit memos a little later in this chapter.

14. **Save the invoice.**

    You can save a completed credit memo in one of three ways:

    - To create more credit memos, click N̲ext. QuickBooks saves the credit memo that's on the screen and then displays an empty Create Credit Memos/Refunds window so that you can enter another credit memo. (Note that you can return to credit memos that you created earlier by clicking the Prev button.)

    - If you don't want to create additional credit memos, click OK. QuickBooks saves the credit memo and closes the Create Credit Memos/Refunds window.

    - If you want to print the credit memo and save it, click the Prin̲t button. I discuss printing invoices and credit memos a little later in this chapter.

Fixing Credit Memo Mistakes

Sure. I could repeat the same information I gave in the "Fixing Invoice Mistakes" section and leave you with a strange feeling of déjà vu. But I won't.

Here's everything you need to know about fixing credit memo mistakes: You can fix credit memo mistakes the same way that you fix invoice mistakes. If you need more help, refer to the earlier section of this chapter, "Fixing Invoice Mistakes."

Printing Invoices and Credit Memos

As part of setting up QuickBooks, you picked an invoice type. I assume that you have the raw stock for whatever you chose. If you're going to print on blank letterhead, for example, I assume that you have some letterhead lying around. If you decided to use preprinted forms, I assume that you ordered those forms and have now received them.

I also assume that you have already set up your printer. If you have ever printed anything, your printer is already set up. Really.

Loading the forms into the printer

This part is easy. Just load the invoice forms into the printer the same way you always load paper. Because there are about a jillion different printers, I can't give you the precise steps that you need to take, but, if you have used the printer a bit, you should have no problem.

Wait a minute. What's that? Your printer is brand new, and you've never used it before? Okay, here's one of my weird ideas: Use a pencil or something else that is heat-resistant (so it won't gum up the insides of the printer) to draw an arrow on a piece of paper. (Do not, repeat, *do not*, use crayon. And don't let your children watch you do this.) Draw the arrow so that it points toward the top edge of the paper. Load the paper in the printer, with the arrow face up, and note which direction the arrow is pointing. Print something. Anything. When the paper comes out, notice whether the image faces the same direction as the arrow and whether it is on the same side of the paper as the arrow. With this information and a little logic, you should be able to figure out how to load forms correctly.

Setting up the invoice printer

You need to set up the invoice printer only once, but you need to specify a handful of general invoice printing rules. These rules also apply to credit memos and to purchase orders, by the way.

To set up your printer for invoice printing, follow these steps:

1. **Display the Invoice Printer Setup dialog box.**

   Choose File⇨Printer Setup⇨Invoice Printer. QuickBooks displays the Invoice Printer Setup dialog box shown in Figure 4-5.

2. **Select the printer that you want to use to print invoices.**

   Activate the Printer drop-down list. It shows the installed printers. Select the one that you want to use for printing invoices and purchase orders.

   The Macintosh assumes you will use the printer that is currently active. It doesn't allow for using different printers at the same time.

3. **(Optional) Select the Paper Feed setting.**

   You have three choices: Auto-detect, Continuous, and Page-oriented. You can probably stick with Auto-detect unless you know — perhaps you're some sort of printer expert — that you should go with one of the other two settings.

4. **Select the type of invoice form.**

   Activate the Print On drop-down list. Then select the type of form that you want to print on: Preprinted form, Blank paper, Blank paper (w/drawn-in boxes), Letterhead paper, or Letterhead (w/drawn-in boxes).

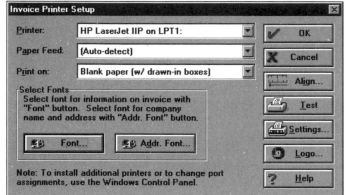

Figure 4-5:
The Invoice
Printer
Setup
dialog box.

5. (Optional) Choose the font for the invoice detail.

See the Font button? If you click it, QuickBooks displays the Invoice Printing Font dialog box shown in Figure 4-6. Use the Font list box to specify the font that you want QuickBooks to use for the body of the invoice. Use the Font style list box to choose a font style from among the choices: Regular, Italic, Bold, and Bold Italic. Use the Size list box to choose a point size. (One point equals $1/72$ of an inch.) If you want to get really wacky — and your printer is willing and able — you can use the Effects check boxes and the Color drop-down list to further customize the font. Be sure, however, to watch the Sample box. It shows what your font specification looks like. (By the way, the only choice I was able to get out of the Script text box was Western. I could try to guess what it might be for, but I get embarrassed too easily. Especially when I'm wrong.)

Of course, the Mac choices are slightly different. You have check boxes for Outline, Shadow, Condense, and Extend, for example. A caution, similar to the one above, though: Getting too crazy with font styles, using Bold, Outline, and Shadow on 10-point Monotype Corsiva, for example, is almost always associated with a computer beginner. Unless you have a good feel for typographic design, simplicity should be your guide.

6. (Optional) Choose the font for the company name and address.

You choose this font the same way that you choose the font for the invoice details. The only difference is that you click the Addr. Font button instead of the Font button.

7. (Optional) Add a logo to the invoice form.

You can add a logo to the invoice form as long as it's stored as a small bitmap image somewhere on your computer. To add it, click the Logo button. (You guessed this much, right?) QuickBooks displays the Invoice Logo dialog box. Click its File button to tell QuickBooks to display the Open Logo File dialog box and then specify the name and location of the logo file. (The file must be in bitmap format, and the filename must have a

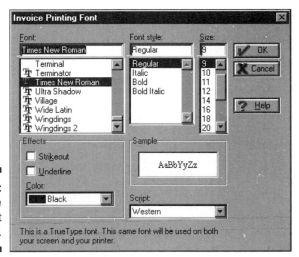

Figure 4-6:
The Invoice
Printing Font
dialog box.

.BMP extension.) Then click OK. QuickBooks redisplays the Invoice Logo dialog box — only this time it shows a picture of the invoice logo (see Figure 4-7). Click OK to return to the Invoice Printer Setup dialog box.

Rather than a Logo button, the Macintosh has a Paste Logo button. In order to use it, you must first load the logo by copying it into the Clipboard. Then press the Paste Logo button to open the appropriate window (in this case, the Invoice Logo window), and press the Paste button. To remove it, make sure that the appropriate window is open again, and press the Clear button. To close the window, press either OK or Cancel.

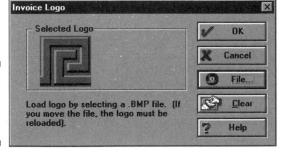

Figure 4-7:
The Invoice
Logo dialog
box.

8. (Optional, but a really good idea . . .) Print a test invoice on real invoice paper.

Click the Test button. QuickBooks prints a dummy invoice on whatever paper you have loaded on the invoice printer. This dummy invoice gives you a chance to see what your invoices will look like.

9. Fix any form alignment problems.

If you see any alignment problems after you complete Step 8, you need to fix them. (These problems will probably occur only with impact printers. With laser printers or inkjet printers, the sheets of paper feed into the printer the same way every time, so you almost never need to fiddle with the form alignment.)

To fix any big alignment problems — like stuff printing in completely the wrong place — you need to adjust the way the paper feeds into the printer. When you finally get the paper loaded as best you can, be sure to note exactly how you have it loaded. You need to have the printer and paper set up the same way every time you print.

For minor, but nonetheless still annoying, alignment problems, click the Align button. QuickBooks displays the Fine Alignment dialog box shown in Figure 4-8. Click its Print Sample button to print another dummy invoice. As the dummy invoice in Figure 4-9 shows, this invoice has a set of alignment gridlines that prints over the invoice number. Use this second dummy invoice to figure out whether the dummy invoice's vertical or horizontal alignment is off. If the alignment is off, use the Fine Alignment dialog box's Vertical and Horizontal boxes to adjust the form's alignment. Then print another sample invoice. Go ahead and experiment a bit with this. You'll only need to fine-tune the printing of the invoice form once. Click OK in the Fine Alignment dialog box when you finish to have QuickBooks redisplay the Invoice Printer Setup dialog box.

Figure 4-8:
The Fine
Alignment
dialog box.

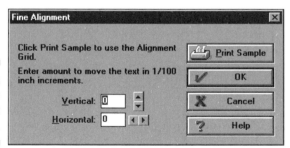

Note: Clicking the Settings button in the Invoice Printer Setup dialog box opens the selected printer's Windows printer setup information. Because this information relates to Windows and not to QuickBooks, I'm not going to explain it. You shouldn't have to worry about the Settings button. But if you're the curious type or accidentally click it and then have questions about what you see, refer either to your *Windows User's Guide* or to the printer's user guide.

10. Save your printer settings stuff.

After you're finished fiddling with all the Invoice Printer Setup dialog box boxes and buttons, click OK to save your changes.

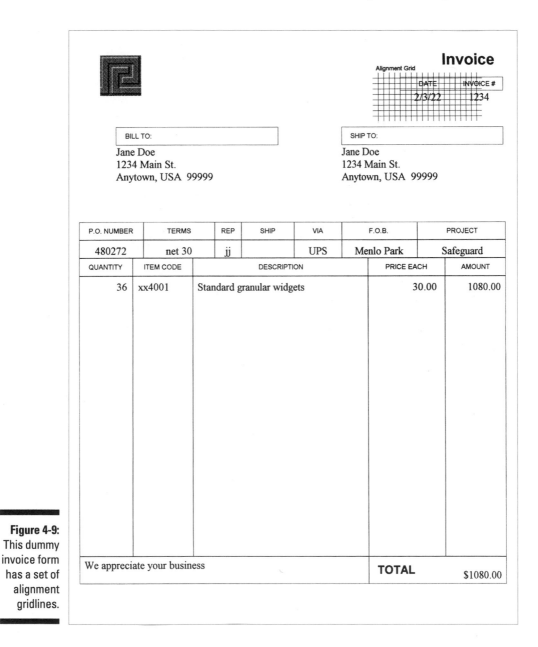

Figure 4-9:
This dummy
invoice form
has a set of
alignment
gridlines.

And now for the main event

You can print invoices and credit memos either one at a time or in a batch. It makes no difference to QuickBooks or to me, your humble author and new friend. Pick whatever way seems to fit your style the best.

Printing invoices and credit memos as you create them

If you want to print invoices and credit memos as you create them, follow these steps:

1. **Click the Print button after you create the invoice or credit memo.**

   After you fill in each of the boxes in the Create Invoices window or the Create Credit Memos/Refunds window, click the Print button or choose File⇨Print Forms⇨Print Invoice or File⇨Print Forms⇨Print Credit Memo. QuickBooks, ever the faithful servant, displays either the Print One Invoice dialog box (see Figure 4-10) or the Print One Credit Memo/Refund dialog box (which looks almost like the Print One Invoice dialog box).

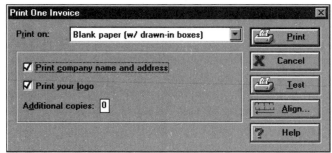

Figure 4-10:
The Print One Invoice dialog box.

2. **(Optional) Select the type of invoice or credit memo form.**

   If you're using a different invoice or credit memo form type than you described for the Invoice Printer Setup, activate the Print On drop-down list. Then select the type of form that you want to print on: Preprinted form, Blank paper, or Blank paper (w/drawn-in boxes).

3. **(Optional) Add the company name to the top of the invoice or credit memo.**

   If you're printing the invoice or credit memo on blank paper — not on a preprinted form or on letterhead — check the Print Company Name And Address check box. (You don't need to add the company name and address to the top of the invoice form if it's already printed there.)

4. **(Optional) Add the company logo to the invoice or to the credit memo.**

   If you described a logo that will sometimes go on invoice, credit memo, and purchase order forms when you set up the invoice printer, you can tell QuickBooks to place it on this invoice or credit memo form by checking the Print Your Logo check box.

What am I printing on?

Sometimes people get confused about preprinted forms versus letterhead versus plain paper. Here's the scoop. Preprinted forms have your company name, perhaps your logo, and a bunch of other boxes and lines (often in another color of ink) already printed on them. Preprinted forms are often multipart forms. (Examples of preprinted forms come in the QuickBooks box.)

Letterhead is what you usually use for letters that you write. It has your company name and address, for example, but nothing else. To save

you from having to purchase preprinted forms, QuickBooks enables you to use letterhead. (To make the letterhead look a little more bookkeeperish, QuickBooks draws lines and boxes on the letterhead so that it looks sort of like a preprinted invoice.)

Plain paper is, well, plain paper. Nothing is printed on it. So QuickBooks needs to print everything — your company name, all the invoice stuff, and optionally, lines and boxes.

5. (Optional) Specify any extra copies.

If you want additional copies of the invoice or credit memo — perhaps you want to keep a paper file of these documents — in the Additional Copies text box enter the number of additional copies that you want. You can print as many copies as you want, of course. It's your business. But I doubt that you'll need more than one additional copy.

Note: You shouldn't have to worry about printing test invoice or credit memo forms or fiddling with form alignment problems if you addressed these issues when you set up the invoice printer. So I'm not going to talk about the Test and Align buttons here. If you want to do this kind of stuff and you need help, refer to the preceding section, "Setting up the invoice printer." It describes how to print test forms and fix form alignment problems.

6. Print the form.

Click the Print button to send the form to the printer. QuickBooks prints the form (see Figures 4-11 and 4-12). Then it displays a message box that asks whether the form printed correctly (see Figure 4-13). QuickBooks displays this message box whether you're printing a single invoice or a batch of invoices.

Two tips for Macintosh users:

First, the Select Invoices to Print dialog box has a Print Mailing Labels button. Pressing this button opens a Select Mailing Labels to Print dialog box, in which you can format mailing labels for your invoices and the

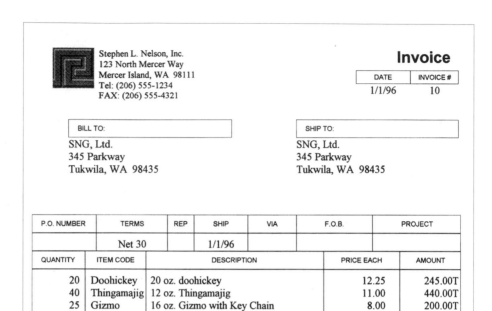

Stephen L. Nelson, Inc.
123 North Mercer Way
Mercer Island, WA 98111
Tel: (206) 555-1234
FAX: (206) 555-4321

Invoice

DATE	INVOICE #
1/1/96	10

BILL TO:

SNG, Ltd.
345 Parkway
Tukwila, WA 98435

SHIP TO:

SNG, Ltd.
345 Parkway
Tukwila, WA 98435

P.O. NUMBER	TERMS	REP	SHIP	VIA	F.O.B.	PROJECT
	Net 30		1/1/96			

QUANTITY	ITEM CODE	DESCRIPTION	PRICE EACH	AMOUNT
20	Doohickey	20 oz. doohickey	12.25	245.00T
40	Thingamajig	12 oz. Thingamajig	11.00	440.00T
25	Gizmo	16 oz. Gizmo with Key Chain	8.00	200.00T
				885.00
		Sales Tax	8.20%	72.57

	TOTAL	$957.57

Figure 4-11:
A real live
invoice
form.

names of individuals or lists to use on the labels. To use this option, your printer must be set up to handle labels, or the program won't let you continue.

Second, before actually printing the invoices or credit memos, the Macintosh displays a standard printer window, with the name of the installed printer at the top. This window usually appears every time you

Stephen L. Nelson, Inc.
123 North Mercer Way
Mercer Island, WA 98111

Credit Memo

DATE	CREDIT NO.
1/1/96	2

BILL TO:

Charles River Manufacturing
2345 Cambridge Parkway
Bellevue, WA 98002

SHIP TO:

P.O. NUMBER	TERMS	REP	SHIP	VIA	F.O.B.	PROJECT
			1/1/96			

QUANTITY	ITEM CODE	DESCRIPTION	PRICE EACH	AMOUNT
-20	Red TMJ	Red Thingamajig	32.00	-640.00T
		Sales Tax	8.20%	-52.48

TOTAL $-692.48

Figure 4-12:
A real live
credit memo
form.

try to print something and allows you to choose the number of copies,
pages to print, and so on. Most of the choices are pretty self-explanatory
by now, if you need them at all (which you probably won't), so I won't go
into it here.

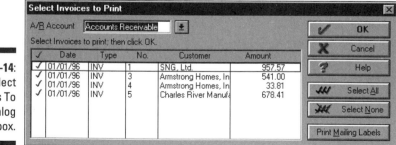

Figure 4-13:
The Did
Form(s)
Print OK?
message
box.

7. Review the invoice or credit memo and reprint the form if necessary.

Review the invoice or credit memo to see whether QuickBooks printed it correctly. If the form looks okay, just click OK in the message box. If the form doesn't look okay, enter the form's number — its invoice number or credit memo number — in the message box. Then fix whatever problem fouled up the form (perhaps you printed it on the wrong paper, for example) and reprint the form by clicking the Print button again in the Print One Invoice or Print One Credit Memo dialog box.

Printing invoices in a batch

If you want to print invoices in a batch, you need to check the To Be Printed check box that appears in the lower-right corner of the Create Invoices window. This check mark tells QuickBooks to put a copy of the invoice on a special invoices-to-be-printed list.

When you later want to print the invoices-to-be-printed list, follow these steps:

1. Choose File⇨Print Forms⇨Print Invoice.

QuickBooks displays the Select Invoices To Print dialog box that is shown in Figure 4-14. This box lists all the invoices that you marked as To Be Printed that you haven't yet printed.

Figure 4-14:
The Select
Invoices To
Print dialog
box.

2. Select the invoices that you want to print.

Initially, QuickBooks marks all the invoices with a check mark, indicating that they will be printed. You can check and uncheck individual invoices on the list by clicking them. You also can use the Select All and the Select None buttons. Click Select All to check all the invoices. Click Select None to uncheck all the invoices.

3. Click OK.

After you have correctly marked all the invoices you want to print — and none of the ones you don't want to print — click OK. QuickBooks displays the Print Invoices dialog box shown in Figure 4-15.

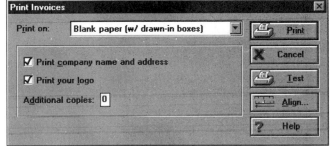

Figure 4-15:
The Print
Invoices
dialog box.

4. (Optional) Select the type of invoice form.

If you're using a different type of invoice form than you described during the Invoice and PO printer setup, activate the Print On drop-down list. Then select the type of form that you want to print on: Preprinted form, Blank paper, or Blank paper (w/drawn-in boxes).

5. (Optional) Add the company name to the top of the invoice.

If you're printing the invoice or credit memo on blank paper — not on a preprinted form or on letterhead — check the Print Company Name And Address check box. Obviously, you don't need to add the company name and address to the top of the invoice form if it's already printed there.

6. (Optional) Add the company logo to the invoice.

If, when you set up the invoice printer, you described a logo that will sometimes go on the invoice, credit memo, and purchase order forms, you can tell QuickBooks to place it on this invoice form by checking Print Your Logo.

7. (Optional) Specify any extra copies.

In the Additional copies text box, enter the number of additional copies that you want.

Note: I'm not going to talk about the Test and Align buttons here. If you need to use them and you want help, refer to the earlier chapter section, "Setting up the invoice printer." It describes how to print test forms and fix form alignment problems.

8. Print the forms.

Click the Print button to send the selected invoice forms to the printer. QuickBooks prints the forms. Then it displays a message box that asks whether the forms printed correctly (refer to Figure 4-13).

9. Review the invoice forms and reprint forms if necessary.

Review the invoices to see whether QuickBooks printed all of them correctly. If all the forms look okay, just click OK in the message box. If one or more forms don't look okay, enter the invoice number of the first bad form in the message box. Then fix whatever problem fouled up the form (perhaps you printed it on the wrong paper, for example) and reprint the bad form(s) by clicking the Print button again. (The Print button is in the Print Invoices dialog box.)

Printing credit memos in a batch

If you want to print credit memos in a batch, you need to check the To Be Printed check box that appears in the lower-right corner of the Create Credit Memos/Refunds window. Checking this box tells QuickBooks to put a copy of the credit memo on a special credit-memos-to-be-printed list.

Note: Printing credit memos in a batch works very similarly to printing invoices in a batch. Because the preceding section describes how to print invoices in a batch, I'm going to speed through the following description of printing credit memos in a batch. If you get lost or have questions, refer to the preceding section.

When you are ready to print the credit memos that are on the to-be-printed list, follow these steps:

1. Choose File⇨Print Forms⇨Print Credit Memo.

QuickBooks displays the Select Credit Memos to Print dialog box.

2. Select the credit memos that you want to print.

3. Click OK to display the Print Credit Memos dialog box.

4. Use the Print Credit Memos dialog box to describe how you want your credit memos printed.

5. Click the Print button to send the selected credit memos to the printer.

QuickBooks prints the forms.

Chapter 5
Cash on the Barrelhead

· ·

· ·

*Y*ou need to record the cash that customers pay you when they fork over cash at the time of the sale or after you invoice them. This chapter describes how to record these payments, and it explains how to make bank deposits, track the amounts that customers owe and pay, and assess finance charges.

Making Sure That You're Ready

If you have been using QuickBooks to prepare customer invoices, you're ready to begin recording payments. You'll have no problem.

If you haven't yet been invoicing customers, let me give you a quick rundown on the prerequisites for recording cash sales and receipts:

✔ You have installed QuickBooks, of course (as described in Appendix A).

✔ You have set up a company and a chart of accounts (as described in Chapter 1).

✔ You have set up lists — particularly an Item List and a Customer List (as described in Chapter 2).

✔ You have entered a starting trial balance or have talked your accountant into entering it for you (as described in Chapter 3).

✔ You have set up a printer to use for printing invoices (by using the File⇨Printer Setup⇨Invoice Printer command, as described in Chapter 4).

Recording a Cash Sale

Cash sales work very similarly to regular sales. In fact, the big difference between the two types of sales is that cash sales are recorded in a way that changes your cash balance instead of your accounts receivable balance. (For you accountants, this means that the debit is to cash instead of to accounts receivable.) Here is the abridged procedure:

Display the Enter Cash Sales window by choosing Activities⇨Enter Cash Sales, and then fill in this window.

The following unabridged steps describe how to record cash sales for products, which are the most complicated type of cash sale. Recording cash sales for services works basically the same way, however. You just fill in fewer fields.

1. Display the Enter Cash Sales window.

Choose Activities⇨Enter Cash Sales to have QuickBooks display the Enter Cash Sales window shown in Figure 5-1.

Don't forget — the Macintosh version of QuickBooks doesn't have as many keystroke shortcuts as the Windows version has. Nearly all the Mac shortcuts are in the File, Edit, Lists, and Activities menus.

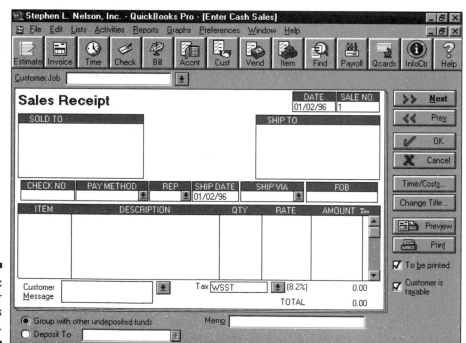

Figure 5-1:
The Enter
Cash Sales
window.

2. Identify the customer and, if necessary, the job.

Activate the Customer: Job drop-down list by clicking the down arrow at the right end of the box. Scroll through the Customer: Job list until you see the customer or job name and then click it.

3. Give the cash sale date.

Press Tab to move the cursor to the Date text box. Then enter the correct date in MM/DD/YY format. You can change the date by using any of the date-editing codes. (Chapter 4 and the Cheat Sheet at the front of the book describe these codes.)

4. (Optional) Enter a sale number.

QuickBooks suggests a cash sale number by adding 1 to the last cash sale number you used. Use this number or tab to the Sale No. text box and change it to whatever you want.

5. Fix the Sold To address if necessary.

QuickBooks grabs the billing address from the Customer List and uses it as the Sold To address. You can change the address for the cash sale, however, by replacing the appropriate part of the usual billing address.

6. Fix the Ship To address if necessary.

I feel like a broken record. QuickBooks also grabs the shipping address from the Customer List. So if you want to change the shipping address for just this one sale, replace the relevant information or add to it in the Ship To address block.

7. Record the check number.

Enter the customer's check number in the Check No. text box.

8. Specify the payment method.

To specify the payment method, activate the Pay Method drop-down list and select something from it: cash, check, VISA, MasterCard, or whatever. If you don't see the payment method that you want to use, you can add the method to the payment methods list. Choose Lists⇨Other Lists⇨Payment Methods to display the Payment Methods List window. Click New to display the New Payment Method dialog box. Enter a description of the payment method in the dialog box's only text box.

9. (Optional) Name the sales representative.

If you want to track sales by sales representative, use the Rep drop-down list box. Just activate the list — for example, by clicking its arrow — and then select the initials of the sales representative.

10. Specify the shipping date if it's something other than the sale date.

To do this, just move the cursor to the Ship Date text box and then type the date in MM/DD/YY fashion. (You can use one of the secret date-editing codes to edit the date. Refer to the Cheat Sheet at the front of the book or to Chapter 4 for more information.)

11. Specify the shipping method.

To specify the shipping method, move the cursor to the Ship Via drop-down list box, activate the list, and then select a shipping method. If need be, you can add new shipping methods to the list by choosing Lists⇨Other Lists⇨Ship Via to display the Ship Via List window, clicking its New button, and filling out the cute little dialog box that QuickBooks displays.

12. Specify the FOB point.

FOB stands for *free-on-board.* The FOB point determines when the transfer of ownership occurs, who pays freight, and who bears the risks of damage to the goods during shipping.

If a shipment is free-on-board at the shipping point, the ownership of the goods that are being sold transfers to the purchaser as soon as the goods leave the seller's shipping dock. (You are the seller, remember.) This means that the purchaser pays the freight and that the purchaser bears the risk of shipping damage. FOB shipping point can be specified either as FOB Shipping Point or by using the name of the city. If the shipping point is Houston, for example, FOB Houston is the same thing as FOB Shipping Point. Most goods are shipped as FOB Shipping Point, by the way.

If a shipment is free-on-board at the destination point, the ownership of the goods that are being sold transfers to the purchaser as soon as the goods arrive on the purchaser's shipping dock. (Remember, the purchaser is your customer.) This means that the seller pays the freight and that the seller bears the risk of shipping damage. FOB destination point can be specified either as FOB Destination Point or by using the name of the city. If the destination point is Omaha, for example, FOB Omaha is the same thing as FOB Destination Point.

13. Describe each item that you're selling.

Move the cursor to the first row of the Item/Description/Qty/Rate/Amount/Tax list box. When you do, QuickBooks turns the Item field into a drop-down list box. Activate the Item drop-down list of the first empty row in the list box, and then select the item. When you do, QuickBooks fills in the Description and Rate text boxes with whatever sales description and sales price you entered in the Item List. (You can edit this information if you want, but it probably won't be necessary.) Enter the number of items sold in the Qty text box. (QuickBooks then calculates the amount by multiplying the quantity by the rate.) Describe each of the other items you're selling by filling in the next empty rows of the list box.

Note: Telling you this again makes me feel like a broken record, but just in case you haven't already read this in another chapter, you can put as many items on a cash sales receipt as you want. If you don't have enough room on a single page, QuickBooks just adds as many pages as you need to the receipt. The cash sales receipt total, of course, goes on the last page.

14. Describe any special items that should be included on the cash sales receipt.

If you didn't set up the QuickBooks item file, you have no idea what I'm talking about. But here's the scoop: QuickBooks thinks that anything that you stick on a receipt (or an invoice, for that matter) is something that you're selling. If you sell blue, yellow, and red thingamajigs, you obviously need to add descriptions of each of these items to the Item List. But if you add freight charges to your receipt, QuickBooks thinks that these charges are just another thingamajig, so it requires you to enter another item in the list box. The same is true for a volume discount that you want to stick on the receipt. And if you add sales tax to your receipt, well, guess what? QuickBooks thinks that the sales tax is just another item that needs to be included in the list box. If you checked the Taxable check box when you added the item to the Item List, a small *T* appears in the Tax column to indicate that the item will be taxed.

To include one of these special items, move the cursor to the next empty row in the Item box, activate the drop-down list by clicking the arrow on the right side of the box, and then select the special item. After QuickBooks fills in the Description and Rate text boxes, edit this information if necessary. Enter each of the other special items — subtotals, discounts, freight, and so on — that you're itemizing on the receipt by filling in the next empty rows of the list box.

If you want to include a discount item, you need to stick a subtotal item on the receipt after the inventory items or other items you want to discount. Then stick a discount item directly after the subtotal item. In this way, QuickBooks calculates the discount as a percentage of the subtotal.

15. (Optional) Add a customer message.

Click the Customer Message box, activate its drop-down list, and select a clever customer message. To add customer messages to the customer message list, choose Lists⇨Other Lists⇨Customer Messages to have QuickBooks display the Customer Message List window. Then click New and fill in the dialog box that QuickBooks displays.

16. Specify the sales tax.

If you specified tax information when you created your company — remember how QuickBooks asked whether you charge sales tax? — QuickBooks fills in the default tax information by adding together the taxable items (which are indicated by the little *T* in the Tax column) and multiplying by the percentage you indicated when you created your company file. If the information is okay, move on to Step 17. If not, move the cursor to the Tax box that's to the right of the Customer Message box, activate the list box, and select the correct sales tax.

17. (Truly optional and probably unnecessary for cash sales) Add a memo.

You can include a memo description with the cash sale information. This memo isn't for your customer. It doesn't even print on the cash receipt, should you decide to print a cash receipt. It's for your eyes only. Memo descriptions give you a way to store information that's related to a sale with the cash sales receipt information.

18. Decide how you want to handle the resulting payment.

The option buttons in the lower-left corner enable you to designate whether to group the payment with other undeposited funds or deposit it directly to an account. To decide how to handle the payment, look at a previous bank statement. If your bank lists deposits as a transaction total, you should probably click the Group With Other Undeposited Funds button. If it lists them individually, by check, you should probably click the Deposit To option button and use the drop-down list box to designate the account to which you want to deposit the payment. (By the way, I describe how to handle deposits later in this chapter, in the section titled "In the Bank.")

19. Decide whether you're going to print the receipt.

If you're not going to print the receipt, make sure that the To Be Printed check box is empty — just click it to remove the check.

Figure 5-2 shows a completed Enter Cash Sales window.

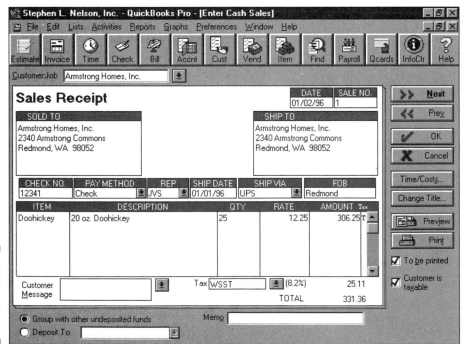

Figure 5-2:
A completed
Enter Cash
Sales
window.

20. Save the cash sales receipt.

You can save the cash sales receipt in one of several ways:

- Click Next. QuickBooks saves the cash sales receipt shown on the screen and then redisplays an empty Enter Cash Sales window so that you can enter another cash sale. If you click Next, you're done with this receipt.

- If you don't want to enter additional cash sales, click OK. QuickBooks saves the cash sales receipt and closes the Enter Cash Sales window. If you click OK, you're done with this receipt.

- If you want to save the cash sale information and print a receipt for the cash sale immediately, click the Print button. After you click it, QuickBooks displays the Print One Sales Receipt dialog box shown in Figure 5-3. The next section describes how to complete this dialog box.

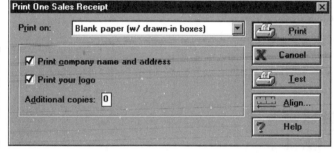

Figure 5-3:
The Print
One Sales
Receipt
dialog box.

Printing a Sales Receipt

To print a cash sales receipt as you save the information, you click the Print button. The following steps tell you how to complete the Print One Sales Receipt dialog box that QuickBooks displays.

Note: To print a batch of receipts that you've saved, choose Files⇨Print Forms⇨ Print Sales Receipts. After displaying a window that allows you to choose which receipts to print — you just choose them by putting a check in the first column — the dialog box that appears resembles the Print One Sales Receipt dialog box in just about every way, and the instructions work in exactly the same manner.

1. Select the type of cash receipt form.

If you're using a different sales receipt form type than you described for the invoice/PO printer setup, activate the Print On drop-down list box. Then select the type of form that you want to print on: Blank paper, Blank paper (w/drawn-in boxes), Letterhead paper, or Letterhead (w/drawn-in boxes). The "What am I printing on?" sidebar in Chapter 4 describes these choices.

2. **Add the company name to the top of the sales receipt.**

If you're printing the sales receipt on blank paper and not on a preprinted form or on letterhead, check the Print Company Name and Address check box to add the company name and address to the top of the cash sales receipt.

3. **Add the company logo to the cash sales receipt.**

If, during setting up the invoice printer, you described a logo that will sometimes go on invoice, credit memo, and purchase order forms, you can tell QuickBooks to place the logo on this cash sales receipt by checking the Print Your Logo check box.

4. **Specify any extra copies.**

If you want additional copies of the sales receipt, enter the number of additional copies that you want in the Additional Copies text box.

Note: You shouldn't have to worry about printing test receipts or fiddling with form alignment problems if you addressed these issues during the invoice/PO printer setup, so I'm not going to talk about the Test and Align buttons here. If you want to print a test receipt or need to change the alignment, refer to Chapter 4 for information on how to proceed.

5. **Print that puppy!**

Click the Print button to send the form to the printer. QuickBooks prints the sales receipt (see Figure 5-4). Then it displays a message box that asks whether the form printed correctly (see Figure 5-5).

6. **Review the sales receipt and reprint the form if necessary.**

Review the cash sales receipt to see whether QuickBooks printed it correctly. If the form looks okay, just click OK in the message box. If the form doesn't look okay, enter the form's number — its sales number — in the message box. Then fix whatever problem fouled up the printing; perhaps you forgot to include the company name and address, for example. Reprint the form by clicking the Print button again in the Print One Sales Receipt dialog box.

By the way, if you decide you want to print the whole batch of sales receipts at once instead of one at a time, just process the receipts without printing them out. Then, after you finish processing everything, choose Files⇨Print Forms⇨ Print Sales Receipts. The procedure after that is similar to all the others when you're printing a bunch of something at once — make sure that the receipts you want to print have a check by them, click OK, and print those puppies!

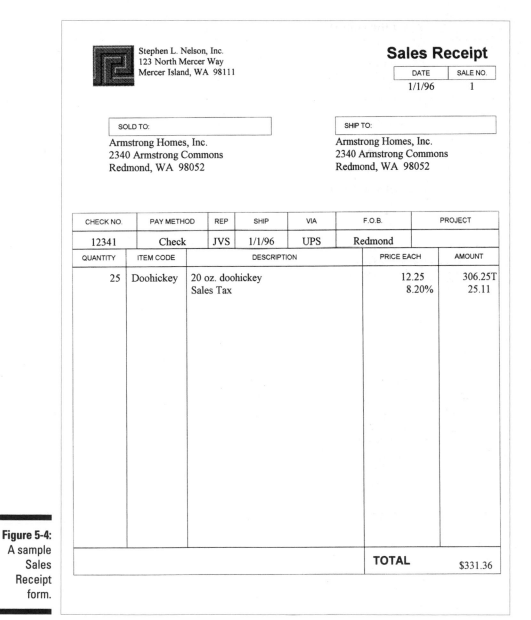

Stephen L. Nelson, Inc.
123 North Mercer Way
Mercer Island, WA 98111

Sales Receipt

DATE	SALE NO.
1/1/96	1

SOLD TO:

Armstrong Homes, Inc.
2340 Armstrong Commons
Redmond, WA 98052

SHIP TO:

Armstrong Homes, Inc.
2340 Armstrong Commons
Redmond, WA 98052

CHECK NO.	PAY METHOD	REP	SHIP	VIA	F.O.B.	PROJECT
12341	Check	JVS	1/1/96	UPS	Redmond	

QUANTITY	ITEM CODE	DESCRIPTION	PRICE EACH	AMOUNT
25	Doohickey	20 oz. doohickey	12.25	306.25T
		Sales Tax	8.20%	25.11

	TOTAL	
		$331.36

Figure 5-4:
A sample
Sales
Receipt
form.

Correcting Cash Sale Mistakes

If you make a mistake in entering a cash sale, don't worry. Fixing it is easy.

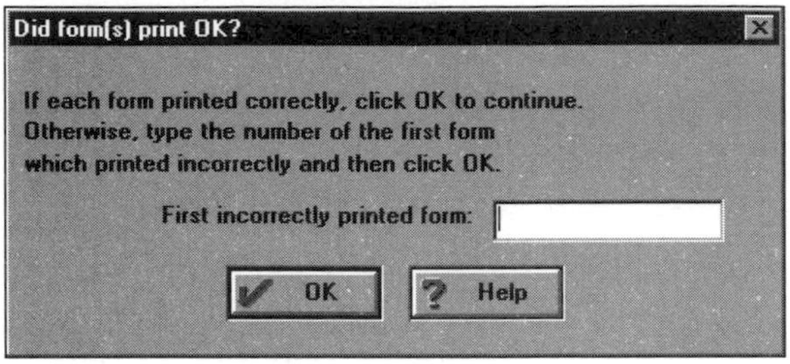

Figure 5-5:
The Did
Form(s) Print
OK?
message
box.

Did form(s) print OK?

If each form printed correctly, click OK to continue.
Otherwise, type the number of the first form
which printed incorrectly and then click OK.

First incorrectly printed form: [   ]

[✔ OK]   [? Help]

If the cash sales receipt is still displayed on the screen

If the cash sales receipt is still displayed on the screen, you can just move the cursor to the box or button that's wrong and then fix the mistake. Most of the bits of information that you enter in the Enter Cash Sales window are fairly short or are entries that you've selected from a list. You can usually just replace the contents of some field by typing over whatever is already there or by making a couple of quick clicks. To save a correction, click OK, Next, or Prev.

If the cash sales receipt isn't displayed on the screen

If the cash sales receipt isn't displayed on the screen but you haven't yet printed it, you can use the Next and Prev buttons to page through the cash sales receipts. When you get the one with the error, just fix the error as described in the preceding section.

If you have printed the customer's receipt, you also can make the sort of change that I have previously described. For example, you can page through the cash sales receipts until you find the one (now printed) that has the error. And you can change the error and print the receipt again. I'm not so sure that you want to go this route, however. Things will be much cleaner if you void the cash sale by displaying the cash sales receipt and choosing Edit⇨Void Cash Sale. Then enter a new, correct cash sales transaction.

If you don't want the cash sales receipt

You usually won't want to delete cash sales receipts, but you can delete them. (You'll almost always be in much better shape if you just void the cash sales receipt.) To delete the receipt, you just display it in the Enter Cash Sales window (choose Activities⇨Enter Cash Sales and page through the cash sales receipts by using the Next and Prev buttons until you see the cash sale that you want to delete), and then choose Edit⇨Delete Cash Sale. When QuickBooks asks you to confirm the deletion, click Yes.

If you want to see a list of all your cash sales, choose Edit⇨Find from the menu, change the Type drop-down list box to Cash Sale, and then press the Find button. QuickBooks gives you a list of your cash sales.

Recording Customer Payments

You also need to record the cash payments that customers make to pay off or pay down their invoices. To record the payments, of course, you need to first record invoices for the customer. (Chapter 4 describes how to record them.) The rest is easy.

All you do is choose Activities⇨Receive Payments to display the Receive Payments window and then describe the customer payment and the invoices paid. If you want the gory details, just read through the following steps:

1. **Display the Receive Payments window.**

   Choose Activities⇨Receive Payments to have QuickBooks display the Receive Payments window shown in Figure 5-6.

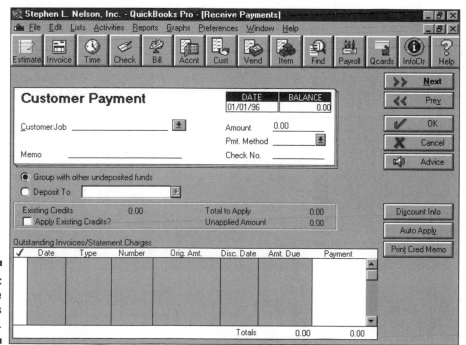

Figure 5-6: The Receive Payments window.

2. Identify the customer and, if necessary, the job.

Activate the Customer:Job drop-down list. Then select the customer or job by clicking it. QuickBooks lists the open, or unpaid, invoices for the customer in the big Outstanding Invoices/Statement Charges list box at the bottom of the window.

3. Give the payment date.

Press Tab to move the cursor to the Date text box. Then enter the correct date in MM/DD/YY format. To edit the date, you can use the secret date-editing codes that are described on the Cheat Sheet at the front of the book.

4. Enter the amount of the payment.

Move the cursor to the Amount line and enter the customer payment amount.

5. (Optional) Specify the payment method.

Activate the Pmt. Method drop-down list and select the payment method.

6. (Optional) Give the check number.

Oh, shoot. You can guess how this works, right? You move the cursor to the Check No. line. Then you type the check number from the customer's check. Do you need to do this? Naw. But this bit of information may be useful if you or the customer later have questions about what checks paid for what invoices. So I would go ahead and enter the check number.

7. (Optional) Add a memo description.

Use the memo description for storing some bit of information that will help you in some way.

8. Decide how you want to handle the payment.

The option buttons under the Memo field should look somewhat familiar because they were also in the Enter Cash Sales screen. These options enable you to designate whether to group the payment with other undeposited funds or deposit it directly to an account. The section that describes how to handle a deposit is even closer than before, but it's still called "In the Bank."

9. (Optional) If the customer has any outstanding credits, decide whether to apply them in this payment.

QuickBooks lists the amounts of any of the customer's existing credits. They could be anything from an overpayment on a previous invoice, to a return credit, to anything else. If you want to include these credits in the current transaction, click the Apply Existing Credits? check box to have the amount added to the Total To Apply amount. If a credit remains on the account, it will show in the Unapplied Amount total.

10. Identify which open invoices the customer is paying.

QuickBooks automatically applies the payment to the open invoices, starting with the oldest open invoice. You can change this application by entering amounts in the payment column. Just click the open invoice's payment amount and enter the correct amount.

You can leave a portion of the payment unapplied if you want to. You also can create a credit memo for the unapplied portion of a customer payment by clicking the Print Cred Memo button. (For information on what steps you need to follow next to print a credit memo, refer to Chapter 4.)

If you want to apply the customer payment to the oldest open invoices automatically, click the Auto Apply button. If you want to unapply payments that you have already applied to open invoices, click the Clear Payments button. Clear Payments and Auto Apply are the same button. QuickBooks changes the name of the button depending on whether you have already applied payments.

11. (Optional) Adjust the early payment discounts if necessary.

If you offer payment terms that include an early payment discount, QuickBooks reduces the open invoice original amount (shown in the Orig. Amt. column) by the early payment discount to calculate the adjusted amount due (shown in the Amt. Due column). If this discount is incorrect — or, more likely, if the customer takes the early payment discount even though the payment isn't early — you may need to adjust the early payment discount.

To adjust it, select the open invoice that has the early payment discount you want to change. Then click the Discount Info button. QuickBooks, with little or no hesitation, displays the Discount Information dialog box shown in Figure 5-7. Enter the dollar amount of the discount in the Amount of Discount text box. Then specify the expense account that you want to use to track early payment discounts by activating the Discount Account drop-down list and selecting one of the accounts. (Interest Expense is probably a good account to use unless you have set up a special early discounts expense account. After all, early payment discounts amount to interest.)

Figure 5-7:
The
Discount
Information
dialog box.

12. **Record the customer payment information.**

    When you have identified which invoices the customer is paying — the unapplied amount should probably show as zero — you're ready to record the customer payment information. You can record it in two ways:

    - If you want to record more payments, click Next. QuickBooks saves the customer payment shown on the screen and then redisplays an empty Receive Payments window so that you can enter another payment. (Note that you can return to customer payments you've recorded earlier by clicking the Prev button.)

    - If you don't want to record additional payments, click OK. QuickBooks saves the customer payment information and closes the Receive Payments window.

Correcting Mistakes in Customer Payments Entries

You can correct mistakes that you make in entering customer payments basically the same way that you correct mistakes that you make in entering cash sales. First, you display the window you used to enter the transaction. In the case of customer payments, you choose Activities⇨Receive Payments to display the Receive Payments window. Then you use the Next and Prev buttons to page through the customer payments you have entered previously until you see the one you want to change. And then you make your changes. Pretty straightforward, right?

In the Bank

Whenever you record a cash sale or a customer payment, QuickBooks adds the cash to its list of undeposited funds. These undeposited funds could be a bunch of checks that you haven't yet deposited or currency and coins. (I wanted to use the word *coinage* here, because that's what your bank deposit slip probably uses. My long-suffering editor, however, overruled me, saying *coinage* is a crummy word and overly complex.)

Eventually, though, you'll want to deposit the money in the bank. Follow these steps:

1. **Display the Payments To Deposit dialog box.**

    Choose Activities⇨Make Deposits. QuickBooks displays the Payments To Deposit dialog box, shown in Figure 5-8. This window lists all the payments, regardless of the payment method.

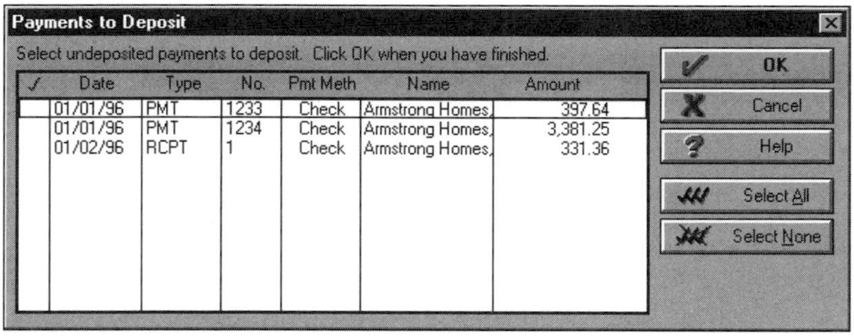

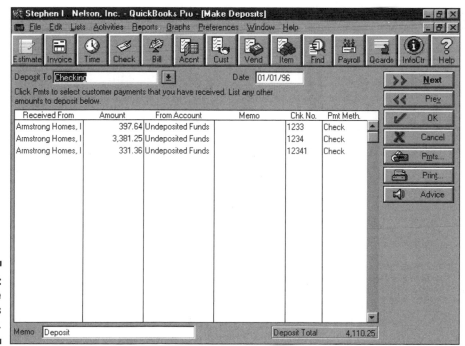

Figure 5-8:
The
Payments
To Deposit
dialog box.

2. Select the payments that you want to deposit.

QuickBooks figures, "Hey, the bank is the place for cash." So it initially marks all the undeposited payments for deposit by placing a little check mark in front of the payment description. If you want to uncheck (or later check) a payment, click it. To uncheck all the payments, click the Select None button. To check all the payments, click the Select All button.

3. Click OK.

After you have indicated which payments you want to deposit, click OK. QuickBooks displays the Make Deposits window shown in Figure 5-9.

Figure 5-9:
The Make
Deposits
window.

4. **Tell QuickBooks into which bank account you'll deposit the money.**

   Activate the Deposit To drop-down list, and select the bank account in which you want to place the funds.

5. **Give the deposit date.**

   Press Tab to move the cursor to the Date text box. Then enter the correct date in MM/DD/YY format. Use the secret date-editing codes if you need to edit it. (Get these codes from the Cheat Sheet at the front of the book if you don't know them.)

6. **(Optional) Add a memo description if you want.**

   I don't know what sort of memo description you would add for a deposit. Sorry. A bank deposit is a bank deposit. At least to me.

   If you want to redisplay the Payments to Deposit dialog box, click the Pmts button. Note, though, that QuickBooks won't display the Payments To Deposit dialog box unless the undeposited funds list has payments on it.

7. **Record the deposit.**

   Click OK or click Next. (Click Next if you want to record another deposit. When you click Next, QuickBooks leaves the Make Deposits window displayed on the screen.)

Improving Your Cash Inflow

I'm not going to provide a lengthy discussion on how to go about collecting cash from your customers. I know that you might be tired of reading, particularly if you have been with me since the start of the chapter. I do, however, want to quickly tell you a couple more things. You need to know how to monitor what your customers owe you and how to assess finance charges. Don't worry, though. I'll explain these two things as briefly as I can.

Tracking what your customers owe

You can track what your customers owe in a couple of ways. Probably the simplest method is to display the Customer:Job List window (by clicking the Cust button, for example), click the customer, and then choose the QuickReport button. QuickBooks whips up a quick, on-screen report that shows the invoices you've billed a customer for and the payments the customer has made. Figure 5-10 shows one of these QuickReports.

You also should be aware that QuickBooks provides several nifty accounts receivable, or A/R, reports. You get to these reports by choosing Reports⟹A/R Reports. QuickBooks then displays a list of about half a dozen reports that

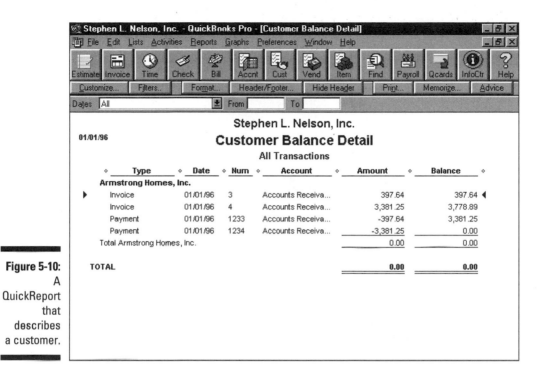

Figure 5-10:
A
QuickReport
that
describes
a customer.

describe how much money customers owe you. Some reports, for example, organize open invoices into different groups based on how old the invoices are. (These reports are called *agings.*) Some reports summarize just invoices or payments. And some reports show each customer's open, or unpaid, balance.

Chapter 13 describes in general terms how you go about producing and printing QuickBooks reports. So refer to Chapter 13 if you have questions. Let me also say that you can't hurt anything or foul up your financial records just by printing reports. So go ahead and noodle around.

Assessing finance charges

I wasn't exactly sure where to stick this discussion of finance charges. But finance charges seem to relate to collecting the cash your customers owe, so I figure that it's okay to talk about assessing finance charges here. (I also suspect that most people won't use this information.)

To assess finance charges, follow these steps:

1. **Choose Activities⊃Assess Finance Charges.**

   After you choose Activities⊃Assess Finance Charges, QuickBooks displays a message box that asks whether you want to assess finance charges now.

2. Click OK.

If you have never before tried to assess finance charges, QuickBooks displays the Finance Charge Preferences dialog box shown in Figure 5-11.

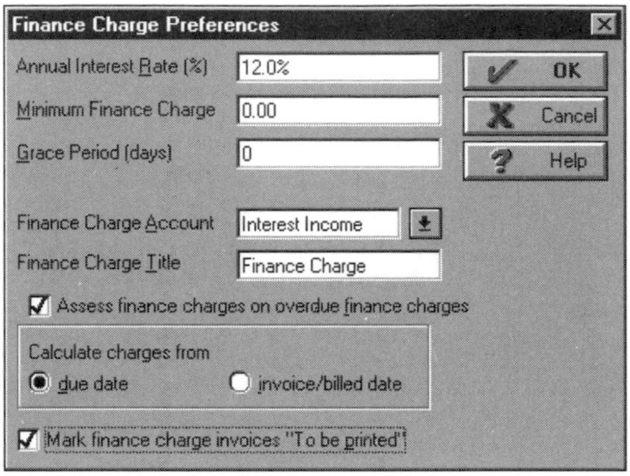

Figure 5-11:
The Finance
Charge
Preferences
dialog box.

3. Enter the annual interest rate that you want to use to calculate finance charges.

Move the cursor to the Annual Interest Rate text box, and enter the annual interest rate.

4. (Optional) Enter the minimum finance charge — if one exists.

Move the cursor to the Minimum Finance Charge text box, and enter the minimum charge. If you will always charge at least $.50 on a past due invoice, for example, type **.5**.

5. Enter the number of days of grace that you will give.

Days of Grace. That sounds kind of like an artsy movie or serious novel, doesn't it? Basically, this number is how many days of slack you'll cut people. If you enter 3 in the Grace Period (Days) text box, QuickBooks won't start assessing finance charges until three days after the invoice is past due.

6. Specify which account you want to use to track the finance charges.

Activate the Finance Charge Account drop-down list and select an account. Finance charges are, essentially, interest that you charge your customers. So unless you have some other account that you want to use, you may just want to use the Interest Income account that appears on most of the standard charts of accounts.

7. Indicate whether you want to charge finance charges on finance charges.

Does this make sense? If you charge somebody a finance charge and they don't pay the finance charge, eventually it becomes past due, too. So then what do you do the next time you assess finance charges? Do you calculate a finance charge on the finance charge? If you want to do this — and state and local laws let you — check the Assess Finance Charges On Overdue Finance Charges check box.

8. **Tell QuickBooks whether it should calculate finance charges from the due date or the invoice date.**

   Just select either the due date or invoice/billed date option button. As you might guess, you calculate bigger finance charges if you start accruing interest on the invoice date.

9. **Tell QuickBooks whether it should print finance charge invoices.**

   Check the box for Mark Finance Charge Invoices "To be Printed" if you want to print invoices later for the finance charges that you calculate.

10. **Click OK.**

    After you have used the Finance Charge Preferences dialog box to spell out to QuickBooks how the finance charges should be calculated, click OK. QuickBooks displays the Assess Finance Charges window, shown in Figure 5-12. This window shows all the finance charges that QuickBooks has calculated, organized by customer.

11. **Give the finance charge assessment date.**

    Move the cursor to the Assessment Date text box and enter the date as of when the finance charges should be calculated. (This date is also the invoice date that will be used on the finance charge invoices if you create them.)

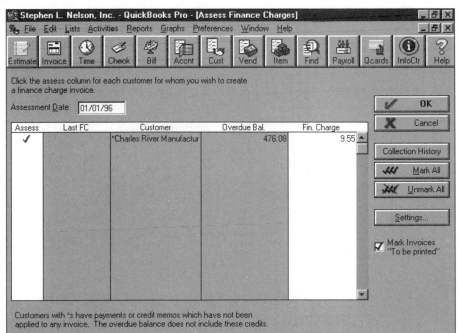

Figure 5-12:
The Assess Finance Charges window.

12. **Confirm which customers you want to be assessed finance charges.**

    QuickBooks initially marks all the finance charges, which means that it sets up a new invoice for each finance charge. (QuickBooks marks finance charges with a little check mark.) If you want to unmark (or later mark) a finance charge, click it. To unmark all the charges, click the Unmark All button. To mark all the charges, click the Mark All button.

    You can produce a collections report for any of the customers or jobs listed in the Assess Finance Charges dialog box by selecting the customer name and then clicking the Collection History button.

13. **Indicate whether you want finance charge invoices printed.**

    If you do, check the Mark Invoices "To Be Printed" check box.

14. **Click OK.**

    When the Assess Finance Charges dialog box correctly describes the finance charges that you want to assess, click OK. You're finished with the finance charge calculations and assessments.

    I'm not going to describe how to print invoices containing finance charges because I already slogged through invoice printing in painstaking detail in Chapter 4. If you have questions about how to print the invoices, you might want to visit that location again.

A word of advice from an accountant

While I'm on the subject of tracking what your customers owe you, let me share a thought about collecting this money. You should have firm collection procedures that you follow faithfully. For example, as soon as an invoice is past due a week or so, I think that it's very reasonable to place a friendly telephone call to the customer's accounts payable department and verify that the customer has received the invoice and is in the process of paying. You have no reason to be embarrassed because some customer is late in paying you! What's more, you may learn something surprising and essential to your collection. You may learn, for example, that the customer didn't receive the invoice. Or you may learn that something was wrong with the gizmo you sold or the service you provided.

As soon as an invoice is a month or so past due, I think that it's time to crank up the pressure. A firm letter asking that the customer call you to explain the past due amount is very reasonable — especially if the customer assured you only a few weeks ago that payment was forthcoming.

When an invoice is a couple of months past due, it's probably time to get pretty serious. You will probably want to stop selling the customer anything more because it's unclear whether you'll be paid. And you may want to start a formal collection process. (Ask your attorney about starting such a process.)

Chapter 6

Paying Bills

● ●

In This Chapter

▶ Paying bills by using the Write Checks – Checking window

▶ Using the Accounts Payable method to pay bills

▶ Deleting and editing bill payments

▶ Reminding yourself when to pay bills

▶ Paying sales taxes

● ●

Mark Twain said, "Nothing is certain except death and taxes and bills." Actually, I added the bills part. Hardly a day goes by that most people don't get at least one bill in the mail. I've been told to look on the bright side: If my business gets a lot of bills, it means that I have a lot of activity and I'm doing pretty well. Okay, looking on the bright side is my specialty, but that still doesn't mean that I like paying bills.

QuickBooks gives you a couple of different ways to pay and record your bills. And you have many options when it comes to deciding when to pay your bills, how to pay your bills, and how to record your bills for the purposes of tracking inventory and expenses.

This chapter explains not only how to pay vendor bills but also how to pay that all-important bill that so many businesses owe their state and local governments. I'm talking, of course, about sales taxes.

Pay Now or Pay Later?

When it comes to paying bills, you have a fundamental choice to make. You can either record and pay your bills as they come in, or you can delay when payments are recorded and made in order to hang on to your money longer. The second method, called the *accounts payable* method, gives you more leeway for managing your cash flow. If push comes to shove and you can't cover all your bills, using the accounts payable method enables you to pick and choose which bills to pay. It also gives you a better understanding of how much cash you have on hand and how much you owe.

If you have a small business with little overhead, you might just as well record and pay bills as they arrive. But if you need to juggle cash, I strongly recommend the accounts payable method of paying bills. And besides, using the accounts payable method with QuickBooks is not as difficult as it may seem at first.

The next section of this chapter describes how to pay bills by writing checks. A little later in the chapter, in a section called "Recording Bills the Accounts Payable Way," I explain how to pay bills by using the accounts payable method.

Recording Your Bills by Writing Checks

You've just come back from lunch to discover the day's mail waiting on your desk. Naturally, there is a bill. You open it, fire up your computer, and load QuickBooks. Now what? How do you write a check for the bill and then record your payment? Better read on . . . .

Note: When you record bills by writing checks, you're doing *cash-basis accounting*.

The slow way to write checks

You can write checks either from the register or from the Write Checks – Checking window. Using the Write Checks – Checking window is the slow way, but it enables you to record your expenses and the items (if any) that you're purchasing. Using the Write Checks window is the best choice in the following situations:

- You're paying for something for which you have a purchase order.
- You plan to be reimbursed for the bill that you're paying.
- You want to record what job or class this bill falls under.

Follow these steps to use the Write Checks – Checking window to write checks:

1. **Either click the Check button on the iconbar or choose Activities⟹ Write Checks.**

   The Write Checks – Checking window appears on-screen (see Figure 6-1). Notice that this dialog box has three parts:

   - The check part on the top, which you no doubt recognize from having written thousands of checks in the past.
   - The buttons on the right.

- The E<u>x</u>penses and Ite<u>m</u>s part of the dialog box on the bottom. This part is for recording what the check is for, as I explain a little later in the chapter.

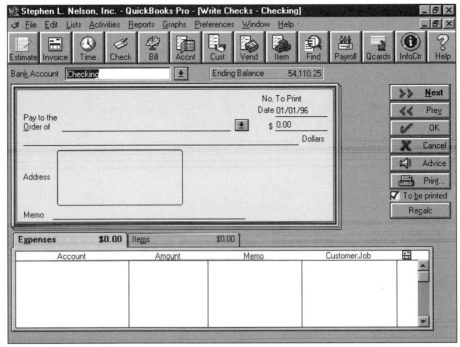

Figure 6-1:
The Write
Checks –
Checking
window.

2. **Click the Ban<u>k</u> Account drop-down list and choose the account from which you want to write this check.**

3. **Fill in the Pay To The Order Of line.**

   If you've written a check to this person or party before, the AutoFill feature fills in the name of the payee in the Pay To The Order Of line for you. (AutoFill does this by comparing what you typed with names shown in the Customer, Employee, and Other Names lists.) AutoFill also puts the payee's address in the Address box. In fact, the AutoFill feature fills out the entire check for you, based on the last check that you wrote to this vendor.

   Does the check look all right? Maybe all you need to do is tab around, adjusting numbers. If that is the case, go for it! Otherwise, read the next 12 steps (another 12-step program?). The next 12 steps explain how to record information on a new vendor and pay a check to that vendor in one fell swoop.

   If you've never paid anything to this person before, the program displays a Name Not Found message box after you enter the name on the Pay To The Order Of line. You can either <u>Q</u>uick Add or <u>S</u>et Up the payee name.

To Quick Add or to Set Up?

If you click Quick Add in the Name Not Found message box, you see a Select Name Type message box, asking whether the payee is a Vendor, Customer, Employee, or Other. Most likely, the payee is a vendor, in which case you click Vendor (but you can click one of the other three options). The address information that you write on the check goes in the Vendor List — or Customer, Employee, or Other Names List, depending on what you clicked. Look at Chapter 2 if you're in the dark about what lists are.

Choosing Set Up in the Name Not Found message box is a little more interesting. When you choose this option, you also see the Select Name Type box. Click Vendor, Customer, Employee, or Other. Click OK, and then you see the New whatever dialog box that you may remember from Chapter 2, where you initially entered your vendors, customers, and so on. Fill in the information as you would if you were describing a customer, vendor, employee, or other for the first time.

4. **Enter the amount of the check.**

   Now comes my favorite part. I've always found it a big bother to write out the amount of checks. I mean, if you're writing a check for $1,457.00, how do you spell one thousand four hundred and fifty-seven dollars and no cents? Where do you put all those hyphens, anyway?

   All you have to do with QuickBooks is enter the amount next to the dollar sign and press Tab. When you press Tab, QuickBooks writes out the amount for you on the Dollars line. At moments like this, I'm grateful to be alive in the late twentieth century when computer technology can do these marvelous things for me.

5. **Fill in the Address text box.**

   Filling in this box is optional. You need to fill it in only if the address isn't there already and you intend to send the check by mail.

6. **Fill in the Memo line.**

   Filling in the Memo line is optional too. You can put a message to the payee on the Memo line — a message such as "Quit bleeding me dry." But usually you put an account number on the Memo line so that the payee can record your account number.

   If you try to click OK and close the dialog box now, QuickBooks tells you that it's not possible and tries to bite your leg off. Why? Because you cannot write a check unless you fill out the Expenses and Items tabs. You use these tabs to describe what the check pays.

7. **Move the cursor down to the Account column of the Expenses tab and enter an expense account name.**

Chances are, you want to enter the name of an account that is already on the chart of accounts. If that is the case, move the cursor to a field in the Account column, and then QuickBooks turns the field into a drop-down list box. Click the down arrow to see a list of all your accounts. You'll probably have to scroll down the list to get to the expense accounts. Click the one that this check applies to (most likely it is Supplies or Rent or something like that). If you need to create a new expense account category for this check, type the name and press Tab to see the New Account dialog box. Fill in the information and click OK.

What if the money that you're paying out with this check can be distributed across two, three, or four expense accounts? Simply click below the account that you just entered. The down arrow shoots down next to the cursor. Click the down arrow, and enter another expense account, and another, and another if you want to.

8. **Tab over to the Amount column, if necessary, and change the numbers around.**

If you're distributing this check across more than one account, you want to make sure that the numbers in the Amount column add up to the total of the check. Well, do they?

9. **If you want, enter some words of explanation or encouragement in the Memo column.**

Someday you may have to go back to this check and try to figure out what these expenses mean. The Memo column may be your only clue. Enter some wise words here.

10. **(Optional) Assign the expense to the Customer:Job column.**

If you plan to be reimbursed for these expenses, enter the name of the customer who will reimburse you here. Click the downward-pointing arrow to find the customer. Enter an amount for each account if necessary.

11. **(Optional) Assign the expense to a class.**

You also can track expenses by class, by making entries in the Class column. Notice the usual down arrow, which you click to see a list of classes. You won't see the Class column, however, unless you told QuickBooks that you wanted to use classes when you created the company.

You have to set QuickBooks up to track expenses by Class and by Customer:Job. Choose Preferences⇨Transactions. In the Transaction Preferences dialog box, check the Track Expenses By Customer and Use Class Tracking check boxes.

12. Use the Items tab to record what you're purchasing.

You may already have filled out a purchase order for the items for which you are paying. If so, click the Select PO button to see a list of purchases on order with this vendor. Check the ones for which you are paying and click OK.

If you don't have a purchase order for the items, perform lucky Step 13.

13. Move to the Item column and enter a name for the item.

Notice the down arrow here. Click it to see the Items List. Does the item that you're paying for appear on this list? If so, click it. If not, enter a new item name to see the Item Not Found dialog box. Click Set Up and fill out the New Item dialog box as you learned to do in Chapter 2.

14. Fill in the rest of the Items columns.

You can enter all the items you're purchasing here. Make sure that the Items tab accurately shows the items that you're purchasing, the cost, and the quantity.

15. Click Next or OK to finish writing the check.

Well, that's over with. For a minute there I thought that it would never end . . . .

What are all those buttons and that box for?

In addition to the OK and Cancel buttons, which you know about (at least I hope that you know about them), the Write Checks – Checking window has a number of strange buttons and a To Be Printed check box. What do they do?

✔ Click Next or Prev when you're finished writing a check. If you write check 101, for example, clicking Next takes you to check 102 so you can write that one. Clicking Prev moves you to check 100 in case you need to edit a check you've written earlier.

✔ The Advice button appears only if you have the multimedia version of QuickBooks on CD-ROM. Clicking this button opens the SoundAdvice window, which provides spoken information regarding the available options.

✔ Clicking the Print button prints the check in the Write Checks – Checking window. It does not print all the checks that you are currently writing, however. (I explain how to print more than one check at a time in Chapter 10.)

✔ QuickBooks put a check in the To Be Printed check box by default — to show whether the check has been printed. Unless you removed the check mark manually, the check hasn't been printed yet when it has a check mark in the check box.

✔ The Recalc button totals the items and expenses in the dialog box and puts the total on both the numeric and text amount lines of the check.

The fast way to write checks

If you want to pay a bill that you won't be reimbursed for or you don't need to track in any way, shape, or form, you can write your check directly from the Checking register. This method is the fast and easy way to write checks.

1. **Open the chart of accounts.**

   To open it, click the Accnt button on the iconbar or choose Lists⇨Chart of Accounts. You can skip this step and open the register directly by clicking the Check button on the iconbar, if that's easier for you.

2. **Open the Checking register.**

   Highlight the checking account that you want to write this check against. After you select it, either double-click the account or click the Use Register button. You see the Checking window that shows the Checking register (see Figure 6-2). The cursor is at the end of the register, ready and waiting for you to enter check information.

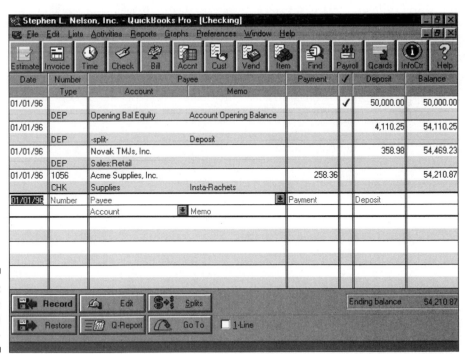

Figure 6-2:
The Checking register.

3. **Fill in the information for the check.**

Notice that the entries that you make here are the same ones that you would make on a check. You need to note a couple of things about the register.

If you enter a Payee name that QuickBooks does not recognize, you see the Name Not Found message box, and you are asked to give information about this new, mysterious vendor. Go back to Step 3 in the instructions on how to write a check the slow way, earlier in the chapter, to see what to do next.

You have to choose an Account name. Chances are, you can find the right one in the Account drop-down list, but if you can't, enter one of your own. You see the Account Not Found message box and are asked to fill in the information about this new account.

If you decide as you fill out the register that you do want to be reimbursed for this check or that you want to track expenses and items, choose the Edit button. You see the Write Checks – Checking window that you know from Figure 6-1. Follow Steps 3 through 14 in the instructions on how to write a check the slow way, earlier in this chapter, to fill in the Write Checks – Checking window. When you're done filling it in, click OK. You'll be back where you started from, in the Checking window.

4. **When you're finished filling in the check information, click Record.**

By the way, that Restore button is there in case you fill out the register but decide that you want to go back to square one. Clicking Restore blanks out what you just entered so you can start all over again.

If you want to print the check (or checks) that you just entered, I'm afraid that you'll have to flip to Chapter 10. In the meantime, Chapter 8 gives you the lowdown on keeping your checkbook — so turn to that chapter if this discussion of checks has you really excited.

Recording Bills the Accounts Payable Way

The accounts payable, or A/P, way of paying bills involves two steps — the first a trifle on the difficult side and the second as easy as pie. First, you record your bills. If you've read the section earlier in this chapter on writing checks the slow way, you're already familiar with using the Expenses tab and the Items tab to record bills. You need to fill out those tabs for the A/P method as well if you want to distribute a bill to accounts, customers, jobs, classes, and items. If you read the first half of this chapter, some of what follows will be old hat.

After you record your bills, you can go on to Step 2. All you have to do is tell QuickBooks which bills to pay. QuickBooks will write the checks. You print them. You mail them.

To make the A/P method work, you have to record your bills as they come in. That doesn't mean that you have to pay them right away. By recording your bills, you can keep track of how much money you owe and how much money your business really has. QuickBooks will remind you when your bills are due, so you don't have to worry about forgetting to pay a bill. Also, by recording bills as they arrive, you can take advantage of early payment discounts. Or, if the vendor allows 60 days for payment, for example, you can hang onto your money for the full 60 days.

When you record bills the accounts payable way, you're using accrual-basis accounting.

Recording your bills

When a bill comes in, the first thing to do is record it. You can record bills through the Enter Bills window or the Accounts Payable register. If you plan to track bills by expense and item, you have to use the Enter Bills window. I'll describe that method first. If you have a simple bill to pay that doesn't need to be reimbursed or tracked, skip ahead to the "Paying Your Bills" section later in this chapter.

Follow these steps to record a bill through the Enter Bills dialog box:

1. **Choose Activities⇨Enter Bills.**

   Figure 6-3 shows the Enter Bills dialog box. You no doubt notice that the top half of this dialog box looks a great deal like a check — that's because much of the information that you put here will end up on the check that you write to pay your bill. (If you see "Credit" in the upper-left box instead of "Bill," click the Bill option button at the top of the dialog box. You also can use this screen to enter credit from vendors.)

2. **Fill in the Bill part of the dialog box.**

   If you want to pay this bill to a vendor who is already on the Vendor List, just click the down arrow at the end of the vendor line and choose the vendor. (QuickBooks will then automatically fill the dialog box with as much information as it can remember.) But if this vendor is new, QuickBooks asks you to Quick Add or Set Up some information about the vendor — the address, credit limit, payment terms, and so on. You provide this information in the New Vendor dialog box. You should be familiar with this dialog box from Chapter 2 (and if you're not, take a brief return visit to that chapter).

   In the Terms line, open the drop-down list and choose the payment terms that describe when the bill is due (if the information is not already there from when you set up the Vendor List). If you receive a discount for paying this bill early, QuickBooks calculates the discount automatically.

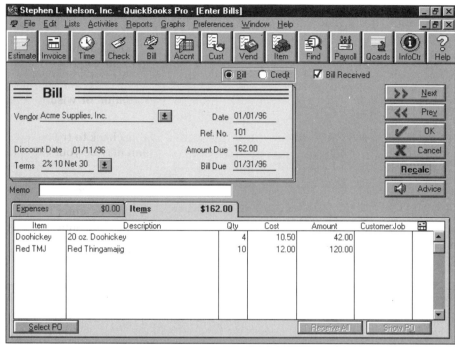

Figure 6-3:
The Enter
Bills dialog
box.

You can enter a note in the Memo box. The note that you enter will appear on the A/P register.

3. **Move the cursor down to the Account column of the Expenses tab and enter an expense account name.**

Chances are, you want to enter the name of an expense account that is already on the chart of accounts. If that is the case, click the down arrow to see a list of all your accounts. You'll probably have to scroll down the list to get to the expense accounts (a fast way to move down the list is to start typing the account name — you'll go straight down the list). Click the account that this check applies to (most likely it is Supplies or something like that).

If you need to create a new expense account category for this check, type the name and press Tab. You see the New Account dialog box. Fill in the information, and click OK.

What if the money that you're paying out with this check can be split between two, three, or four expense accounts? Simply click below the account that you just entered. The down arrow will shoot down next to the cursor. Click the arrow, and enter another expense account, and another, and another if you want to.

4. Tab over to the Amount column, if necessary, and change the numbers around.

If you're splitting this check between several accounts, make sure that the numbers in the Amount column add up to the total of the check. Well, do they?

5. If you want, enter some words of explanation or wisdom in the Memo column.

Someday you may have to go back to this check to try to figure out what these expenses mean. The Memo column may be your only clue. Enter some wise words here.

6. (Optional) Assign the expense to a Customer:Job.

If you plan to be reimbursed for these expenses, enter the customer who will reimburse you. Enter an amount for each account, if necessary. You can use the down arrow to find customers and then click them.

7. Assign the expense to a class.

You also can track expenses by class, by making entries in the Class column. Notice the usual down arrow here. Click that thing to see a list of classes. (You won't see a Class column unless you've told QuickBooks you want to use classes this way.)

If you want, click the Recalc button to total the expenses.

You have to set up QuickBooks to track expenses by Class and by Customer:Job. Choose Preferences⇨Transactions from the menu. In the Transaction Preferences dialog box, check Track Expenses By Customer and Use Class Tracking.

8. Use the Items tab to record the various items that you're purchasing with the check.

Click the Items tab. You should see the Items tab now instead of the Expenses tab.

9. (Optional) Identify the purchase orders that you're paying on.

Use the Items tab to record the various items that you're purchasing with your check.

At this point, you have to ask yourself, "Did I fill out a purchase order for this bill?" If you did, you don't have to fill out the Items tab (or do Steps 10 and 11). Why? Because you already filled out a list of items for this purchase. Click the Select PO button in the lower-left corner of the dialog box to see the Open Purchase Orders dialog box shown in Figure 6-4. From the Vendor drop-down list, click the name of the vendor who sent you this bill.

In the Purchase Order List, click in the column on the left to put a check next to the purchase order (or orders) for which you are paying. Easy enough? Click OK when you're done, and QuickBooks fills the Items tab out for you automatically.

If you don't have a purchase order for the items, go on to Step 10.

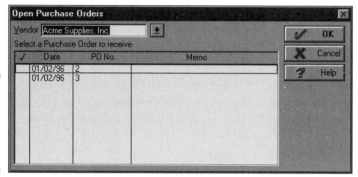

Figure 6-4:
The Open
Purchase
Orders
dialog box.

10. Move to the Item column and enter a name for the item.

Notice the down arrow here. Click it to see the Item List. Does the item that you're paying for appear on this list? If so, click it. If not, enter a new item name, and then you see the Item Not Found message box. Click Set Up and fill out the New Item dialog box as you learned to do in Chapter 2.

11. Fill in the rest of the Items columns.

You can enter all the items you're purchasing here. Make sure that the Items tab accurately shows the items that you're purchasing, their cost, and their quantity. If you want, click the Recalc button to total the items.

When you're finished, your Enter Bills window should look something like Figure 6-3.

12. Click Next, Prev, or OK.

Click Next if you want to enter information on another bill. Clicking OK closes the dialog box and puts all the information that you just entered in the Accounts Payable register. Prev just takes you to the previous bill you entered in case you want to change something there.

Entering your bills the fast way

You also can enter bills directly in the Accounts Payable register. This method is faster, but it makes tracking expenses and items harder. Follow these steps if you want to enter bills directly in the Accounts Payable register:

1. **Open the chart of accounts.**

   Either click the Accnt button on the iconbar or choose Lists➪Chart of Accounts.

2. **Open the Accounts Payable register.**

   Double-click the Accounts Payable account in the list of accounts. Or select the Accounts Payable account and click the Use Register button. You see the Accounts Payable register window, shown in Figure 6-5. The cursor is at the end of the register, ready and waiting for you to enter the next bill.

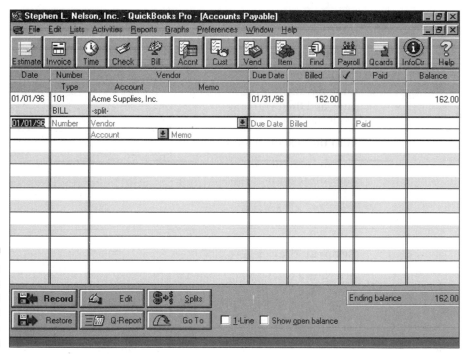

Figure 6-5: The Accounts Payable register.

3. **Fill in the information for your bill.**

Enter the same information you would if you were filling in the Enter Bills window. In the Vendor text box, click the down arrow and choose a name from the Vendor List. If you enter a vendor name that QuickBooks does not recognize, you see the Vendor Not Found message box, and you are asked to give information about this new, mysterious vendor. Either click Quick Add to have the program collect the information from the register as you fill it out, or click Set Up to see the New Vendor dialog box.

You have to choose an Account name. You can probably find the right one in the Account drop-down list, but if you can't, enter one of your own. You see the Account Not Found message box, and QuickBooks asks you to fill in information about this new account.

If you decide as you fill out the register that you want to be reimbursed for this check or that you want to track expenses and items, choose the Edit button to see the Enter Bills window that you know from Figure 6-3. Follow Steps 2 through 11 from the "Recording your bills" section, earlier in this chapter, to fill in the Enter Bills window. When you've filled it in, click OK. You'll be back where you started from — in the Accounts Payable window.

4. **When you've filled in the information, click Record.**

By the way, that Restore button is there in case you fill out the register but decide that you want to go back to square one. Clicking Restore blanks out what you just entered so that you can start all over again.

All right, so you've entered your bills and you want to pay them. Not so fast. You should know a couple of important things first. Read on to find out how to delete a bill and, more important, how to have QuickBooks remind you when bills are due and need to be paid.

Deleting a bill

Suppose that you accidentally enter the same bill twice or enter a bill that was really meant for the business next door. (Just because you're tracking bills by computer doesn't mean that you don't have to look over the things carefully anymore.) Here's how to delete a bill that you entered in the A/P register:

1. **Locate the bill in the Accounts Payable register by using one of the following methods:**

   • If you know roughly what day you entered the bill, you can scroll the list to find it. The entries are listed in date order. (Click the 1-Line check box to display each bill on one line instead of two and make the scrolling go faster.)

   • If you don't remember the date, use the Find command.

Using the Find dialog box

When you can't quite remember the information that you need in order to find a particular entry or transaction, you can search for it by using the Find dialog box. For example, if you can't recall when you entered the bill, choose Edit⇨Find to open the Find dialog box, as shown in the following figure. Choose a filter (the category to search by). The box to the right changes to include drop-down list boxes or text boxes that you can use to specify what you'd like to search for. Choose as many filters as you like, but be careful to enter information accurately, or QuickBooks looks for the wrong information.

Also, try to strike a balance, choosing only as many filters as you really need to find your information. The more filters you choose, the more searching QuickBooks will have to do, and the longer the search will take. After you finish choosing filters, click the Find button, and then the transactions that match all your filters appear in the list at the bottom of the window. Click the transaction that you want to examine more closely and then click Go To. QuickBooks opens the appropriate window and takes you right to the transaction. Very snazzy, I do believe.

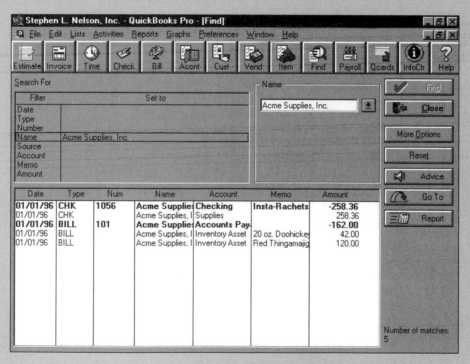

We now go back to the Accounts Payable register window in progress . . . .

2. **Select the bill that you want to delete.**

   Just put the cursor anywhere in the bill.

3. **Choose Edit⇨Delete Bill.**

   QuickBooks deletes the bill from the A/P register.

Remind me to pay that bill, will you?

You can tie a string around your finger, but the best way to make sure that you pay bills on time is to have QuickBooks remind you. In fact, you can make the Reminders message box the first thing that comes on-screen when you start QuickBooks. Choose Preferences⇨Reminders, and the window, appropriately named Reminder Preferences, appears (see Figure 6-6). See the seventh item down the list, Bills to Pay? Click it and give yourself five or six days' notice before you need to pay bills by typing 5 or 6 in the Remind Me dialog box.

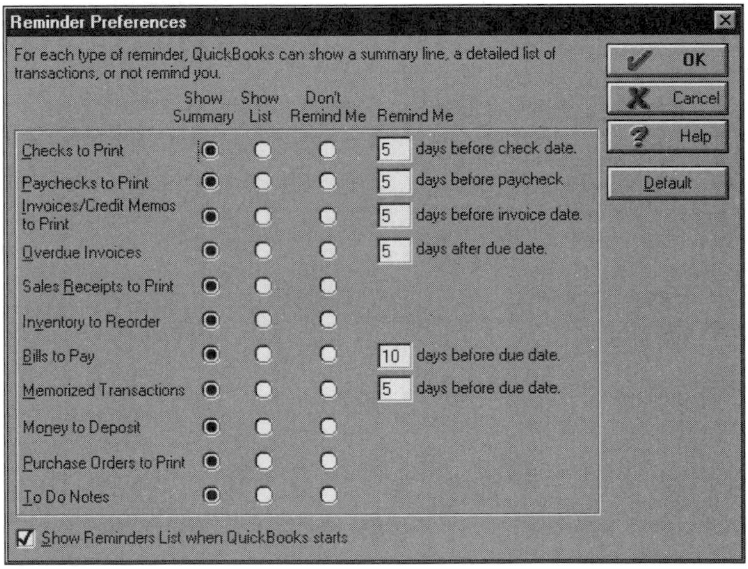

Figure 6-6:
The Reminder Preferences dialog box.

If you click Show Summary, you'll get a summary of the bills you owe each time you start QuickBooks, and if you choose Show List, you'll get the details about each bill.

Which reminds me, be sure to check the Show Reminders List When QuickBooks Starts check box. The list pops up whenever you start QuickBooks and tells you which unpaid bills you're supposed to pay. Or you can see the Reminder list at any time by choosing Lists⇨Reminders. How can you fail to pay your bills now?

Paying Your Bills

If you've done everything right and recorded your bills correctly, writing checks is a snap.

1. Choose Activities⇨Pay Bills.

You see the Pay Bills dialog box (see Figure 6-7).

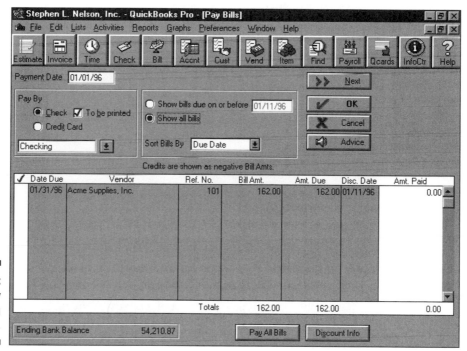

Figure 6-7: The Pay Bills dialog box.

2. **Change the Payment Date to the date that you want to appear on the checks.**

   This box should show today's date. If you want another date on the payment check — for example, if you are postdating the check — change this date. (See the Cheat Sheet for some secret date-editing codes.)

3. **Choose a payment method.**

   Click Check or Credit Card. If you choose Check and you have more than one checking account, click the down arrow by the drop-down list box, and choose the account that you want to use.

4. **If you plan to print the check, put a check mark in the To Be Printed check box.**

   Many businesses use QuickBooks to keep track of checks, but instead of printing the checks, they write them by hand. If your business uses this method, click the To Be Printed check box, and remove the check mark.

5. **Set a cutoff date for showing bills.**

   In the Show Bills Due On Or Before date box, tell QuickBooks which bills to show by entering a date. If you want to see all of them, click the Show All Bills option button.

6. **Use the Sort Bills By drop-down list box to tell QuickBooks how to sort the bills.**

   In the dialog box, you can arrange bills by Due Date, with the oldest bills listed first; arrange them alphabetically by vendor; or arrange them from largest to smallest.

7. **Identify which bills to pay.**

   If you want to pay all the bills in the dialog box, click the Pay All Bills button. But if you want to pick and choose, click to the left of the bill's due date to pay the bill. A check mark appears where you click. Note that after you've applied a payment, the Clear Payments button replaces the Pay All Bills button. For this reason, you can't see a Clear Payments button in Figure 6-7.

8. **Change the Amt. Paid figure if you want to pay only part of a bill.**

   That's right, you can pay only part of a bill by changing the number in the Amt. Paid column.

9. **Get the early payment discount rate on your bills, if any.**

   You may be eligible for an early payment discount on some of your bills. To find out how much of a discount you get, place the cursor on the line where the bill is and click the Discount Info button to see the Discount Information dialog box shown in Figure 6-8. Whether you get a discount depends on the payment terms you entered when you gave QuickBooks information about this vendor. If you do get a discount, this dialog box will tell you how much (and you can change the amount if it isn't correct). Choose an account for recording the discount in the Discount Account box. Then click OK. The discount amount appears in the Amt. Paid column of the Pay Bills dialog box.

Figure 6-8:
The
Discount
Information
dialog box.

10. **Click OK to close the Pay Bills dialog box.**

You hear that pinball-machine sound, and then QuickBooks does two things — it goes into the Accounts Payable register and notes that you paid these bills, and it goes into the Checking register and "writes" the checks. Figures 6-9 and 6-10 show what I mean.

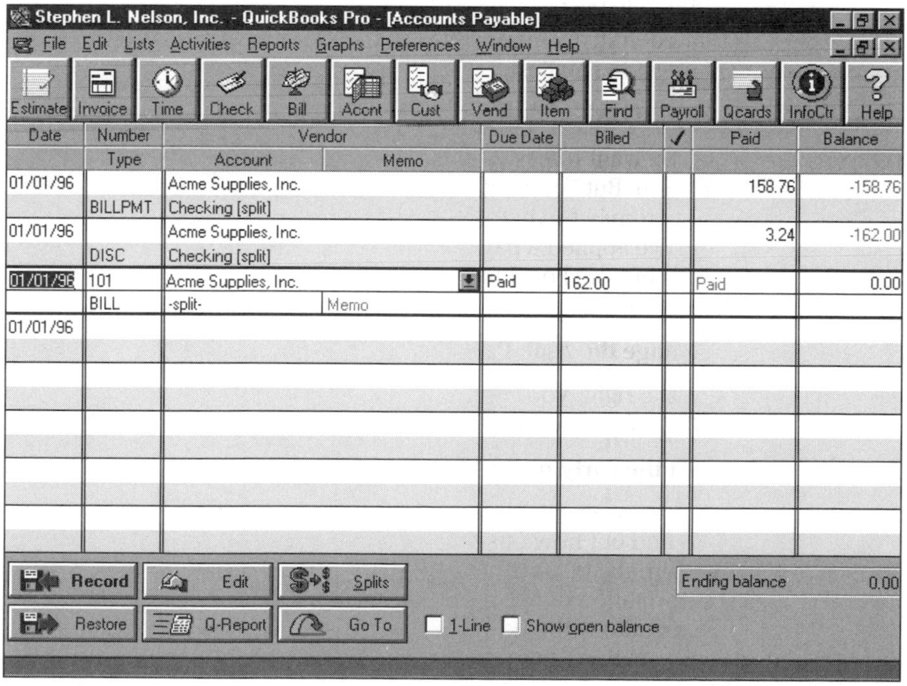

Figure 6-9:
Bills paid in
the A/P
register.

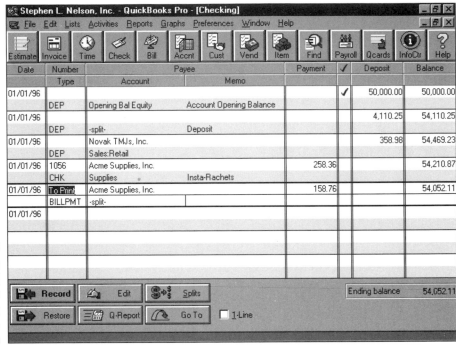

Figure 6-10:
Bills paid
in the
Checking
register.

Note: QuickBooks shows the original bill amount as the amount that's paid, not the original bill amount minus the early payment discount. It needs to use this method to completely pay off the bill.

In the Accounts Payable register, you see BILLPMT in the Type column and the amount paid in the Paid column. The Due Date and Billed columns are now empty.

In the Checking register, you again see BILLPMT in the Type column.

But don't kid yourself; these bills are not really paid yet. Sure, they are paid in the mind of QuickBooks, but the mind of QuickBooks extends only as far as the metal box that holds your computer. You still have to write or print the checks and deliver them to the payee.

If you're going to write the checks by hand, enter the check numbers from your own checkbook into the QuickBooks Checking register's Number column. You want these numbers to jibe, not jive. (I know, a pun is the lowest form of humor.)

If you plan to print the checks, see Chapter 10.

Paying the Sales Tax

In order to ingratiate itself with your retailers, QuickBooks includes a special dialog box for paying sales taxes. However, to make use of this dialog box, you have to have set up sales tax items or a sales tax group. See Chapter 2 for a thorough explanation of items and groups.

To see how much sales tax you owe and write a check to government agencies in one fell swoop, choose Activities⇨Pay Sales Tax to see the Pay Sales Tax dialog box shown in Figure 6-11.

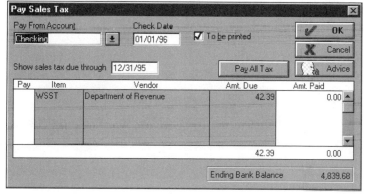

Figure 6-11:
The Pay
Sales Tax
dialog box.

The box is similar to the Pay Bills dialog box shown in Figure 6-7. The buttons basically work the same way — the only major difference is that this box has a Pay All Tax button. Click it to put check marks next to all the taxing agencies.

Put a check mark in the Pay column next to all the agencies that you want to pay by clicking in the Pay column. Checks will be written automatically in the Checking register. Your payments will likewise be recorded in the Sales Tax Payable register.

Chapter 7

Inventory Magic

● ●

In This Chapter

▶ The Item List and inventory

▶ Keeping inventory as you purchase items

▶ Keeping inventory as you sell items

▶ Using purchase orders to help track inventory

▶ Adjusting inventory records to what's really there

● ●

*H*ow many times have you, as a business owner, thought that you had some important item on hand only to discover that you didn't have it after all? How many times have you had to sprint to a hardware store or a stationery shop to get some item that you could have sworn was sitting on the back shelf just a moment ago? Did elves take it?

One of the worst things that can happen to a business is to have customers ask for something and be told, "Sorry, we're all out. But can you check with me next Thursday?" You can bet that those customers will go elsewhere the next time that they need something.

The reason that many businesses don't know what they have in stock is that keeping track of inventory is one of the biggest headaches of running a business. But here comes QuickBooks to the rescue. Keeping track of inventory with QuickBooks is a chore — but not a monumental chore.

QuickBooks keeps track of your inventory by tracking your sales and purchase orders. The program can tell you what you have on hand and what you need to order, the value of your inventory, and the income from items you've sold.

Setting Up Inventory Items: A Refresher Course

Before you can track your inventory, you need to create an Item List. This list is simply a description of all items that you might conceivably put on an invoice. In other words, all items that you order and sell belong on the Item List.

If you read Chapter 2, you already know how to set up an Item List. To put an item on the list, choose Lists⇨Items or choose the Item icon on the iconbar, and fill in the Item List window. If you don't know what I'm talking about, go to Chapter 2 and get it straight from the horse's mouth. (Wait a second. Did *I* just say that?)

And that reminds me, you can't track your inventory unless you tell QuickBooks that you want to track inventory. Choose Preferences⇨Inventory/PO's to see the Inventory/Purchase Order Preferences dialog box shown in Figure 7-1. Do you see a check mark in the check box for Inventory And Purchase Orders Are Active? If not, better put one there.

Figure 7-1:
The
Inventory/
Purchase
Order
Preferences
dialog box.

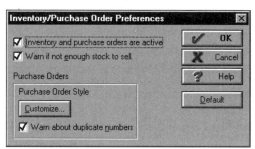

And while you're at it, make sure that the second box is checked. If you're going to the trouble of keeping track of inventory, you may as well have QuickBooks warn you when your stock is running low. If you check this box and you try to fill out a sales receipt or invoice for an item that you don't have enough of, QuickBooks warns you not to do that and bites your leg off. (Or at least nibbles at your toes.)

After you set up the Item List, you can proceed to track those items — that is, track your inventory.

When You Buy Stuff

As you unload items from a truck, receive them in the mail, or just buy them from a peddler, you have to record the items so that QuickBooks can track your inventory. How you record the items and pay for them depends on whether you are paying cash on the barrel, receiving a bill along with the items, or receiving the items without a bill (in which case you'll pay for the items later).

And you may have filled out a purchase order for the items that you are receiving. If that is the case, receiving the items gets a little easier. If you are receiving items and you have already filled out a purchase order for them, see "How Purchase Orders Work," later in this chapter. I strongly recommend filling out a purchase order when you order items that you're going to receive and pay for later.

Recording items that you pay for up front

Okay, you just bought three thingamajigs in the bazaar at Marrakech, and now you want to add them to your inventory and record the purchase. How do you record inventory you paid for over the counter?

You just follow the steps you learned in Chapter 6:

1. **Either click the Check button on the iconbar or choose Activities⇨Write Checks.**

   The Write Checks – Checking window appears before your eyes (see Figure 7-2). If you don't know how to fill out the top of this window, turn to Chapter 6. What you're mainly interested in is the Items tab at the bottom of the screen because this is where you record the items you just purchased.

2. **Click the Items tab, move to the Item column, and enter a name for the item.**

   Notice the down arrow here. (This arrow appears when you move the cursor to the Item column.) Click it to see the Item List. Does the item that you're paying for appear on this list? If so, click it. If not, enter a new item name. After you enter it, you see the Item Not Found message box. Click Set Up, and fill out the New Item dialog box as you learned to do in Chapter 2.

3. **Fill in the rest of the Items columns.**

   You can enter all the items you're purchasing here. Make sure that the Items tab accurately shows the items you're purchasing, their cost, and their quantity.

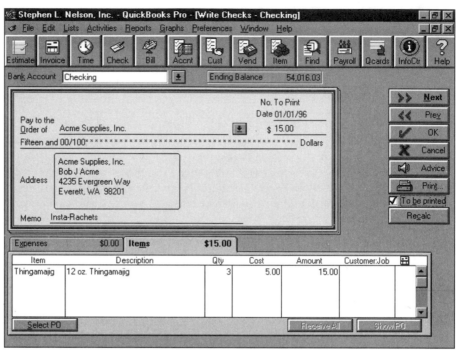

Figure 7-2:
The Write
Checks –
Checking
window.

4. Click OK to finish recording the check.

Now the items you just paid for are added to the Item List. QuickBooks knows that you have them.

Recording items that don't come with a bill

What happens if the items come in a big box with a red ribbon around it, and no bill is attached? Lucky you, you've got the stuff, and you don't have to pay for it yet. However, you do have to record the inventory you just received so that you know you have it on hand. You can't do that in the Write Checks – Checking window because you won't be writing a check to pay for the stuff — at least not for a while. How do you record items that you received without paying for them? Read on. . . .

1. Choose Activities⇨Inventory⇨Receive Items.

You see the Create Item Receipts window shown in Figure 7-3. If this window looks familiar, that's because it is very similar to the Enter Bills window that you may remember from Chapter 6. (You see the Enter Bills window again when you pay the bill for the receipt that you're filling out.)

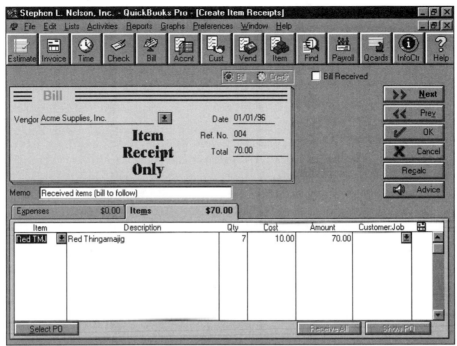

Figure 7-3:
The Create
Item
Receipts
window.

2. Fill in the top part of the window.

If you want to pay this bill to a vendor who is already on the Vendor List, just click the down arrow, and choose the vendor. But if the vendor is a new vendor, QuickBooks asks you to Quick Add or Set Up information about the vendor — the address, credit limit, payment terms, and so on. You enter the information in the New Vendor dialog box.

3. Click the Items tab.

You need to click the Items tab only if it isn't already displayed. It probably is. But the computer book writers' code of honor and a compulsive personality require me to tell you that there's another tab — the Expenses tab — and it's just possible that it could be displayed instead.

4. Move to the Item column, and enter a name for the item.

Notice the down arrow in the Item column. Click it to see the Item List. Does the item that you're paying for appear on this list? If so, click it. If not, enter a new item name, and then you see the Item Not Found message box. Click Set Up, and fill out the New Item dialog box.

You may just as well go down the packing slip, entering the items in the Items tab. Make sure that the Items tab accurately shows what is on the packing slip. And put a brief description of the items in the Memo field because that description may prove useful later when you want to match up your item receipt with the bill. When you're finished, the Create Item Receipts window should look something like Figure 7-3.

5. Click OK to enter the items you just received on the Item List.

Now the items are officially part of your inventory. The item receipt has been entered on the Accounts Payable register. And not only that, but you're all ready for when the bill comes.

Paying for items when you get the bill

The items arrive, and you fill out an item receipt. Three weeks pass. What's this in your mailbox? Why, it's the bill, of course! (You didn't think that you'd escape, did you?) Now you have to enter a bill for the items that you received three weeks ago. This job is easy.

1. Choose Activities⇨Inventory⇨Enter Bill for Rec'd Items.

You see the Select Item Receipt dialog box shown in Figure 7-4.

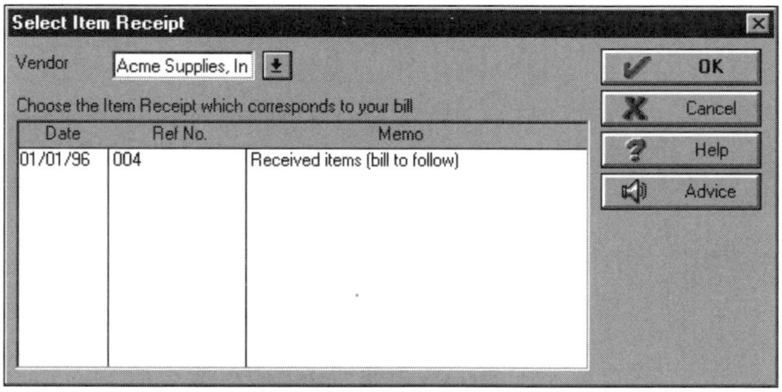

Figure 7-4:
The Select
Item Receipt
dialog box.

2. Click the Vendor drop-down list, and choose the name of the vendor who sent you the bill.

You see one or more item receipts in the box, with the date you put on the receipt, its reference number, and the memo that you wrote on the receipt.

3. Select the item receipt for which you want to enter a bill, and click OK.

After a bit of bumping and grinding, the Enter Bills window shown in Figure 7-5 appears on your screen. Does this information look familiar? It should. It's the same information that you put in the Create Item Receipts window, only now you are working with a bill, not a receipt.

4. Compare the Items tab in the window with the bill.

Are you paying for what you received earlier? Shipping charges and sales tax may have been added to your bill. If so, add them to the Items tab (you can click the Recalc button to add the new items).

How many days do you have to pay this bill? Is it due now? Click the Terms drop-down list to see what this vendor's payment terms are. Remember, you want to pay your bills at the best possible time, but to do this, the terms in the Enter Bills window must match the vendor's payment terms.

5. Click OK to record the bill and close the window.

Of course, you still need to pay the bill to the vendor. Fair enough. I suggest that you read Chapter 6 if you need help.

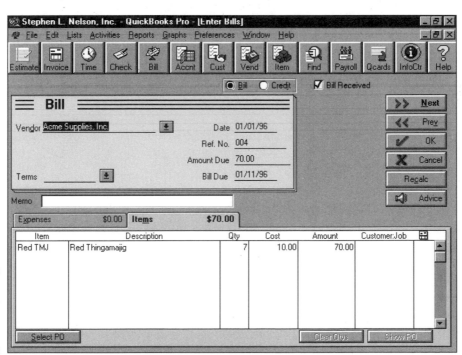

Figure 7-5:
The Enter Bills window.

Recording items and paying the bill all at once

Suppose that you receive the bill when you receive the goods. The items are unloaded from the elephant's back, and the elephant driver, with a bow, hands you the bill.

1. **Choose Activities➪Inventory➪Receive Items And Enter Bill.**

   You see the Enter Bills window (see Figure 7-5 again). If you've been reading this chapter from its beginning, you're thoroughly sick of this window, and you know exactly what it is and does. If you landed cold turkey on this page of the book by way of the index, then you need to know for inventory purposes how to record the items for which you are paying.

2. **Fill out the top part of the window.**

   This stuff is pretty basic. Choose a vendor from the drop-down list and make sure that the vendor's terms for paying this bill are shown correctly. If this vendor is new, QuickBooks asks you to fill in an information dialog box about the vendor. Do it. See that you fill out the Bill Due line correctly.

3. **Click the Items tab and list all the items that you're paying for.**

   To see the Item List, move the cursor to the Item column and click the down arrow that appears. Make sure that the quantity and cost of the items are listed correctly on the Items tab.

4. **Click OK.**

   QuickBooks adds the items you listed to the Item List and makes them an official part of your inventory.

When You Sell Stuff

Chapter 4 tells you how to list the items on the invoice. Maybe you noticed how similar the Items tab in the Enter Bills window and the Item/Description/Qty/Rate/Amount box at the bottom of an invoice are. Both are used for keeping inventory.

When you sell stuff, QuickBooks automatically adjusts your inventory. In other words, if you buy 400 doohickeys and sell 350 of them, you have only 50 on hand. QuickBooks updates records for this change. No muss, no fuss. Gosh, isn't this great? No more lying awake at night, wondering whether you've got enough doohickeys or thingamajigs.

The same thing happens when you make cash sales. When you list the items on the sales receipt, QuickBooks assumes that they are leaving your hands and subtracts them from your inventory.

The moral of this story is: Keep a good, descriptive Item List. And the other moral is: Enter items carefully on the Items tab of checks and bills and in the Item/Description/Qty/Rate/Amount box of sales receipts and invoices.

How Purchase Orders Work

If you have to order stuff for your business, consider using purchase orders. Create QuickBooks purchase orders even if you order goods by phone or by telegraph or even via the World Wide Web — that is, if you're not requesting the goods in writing.

Filling out purchase orders enables you to tell what items you have on order and when the items will arrive. All you'll have to do is ask QuickBooks, "What's on order, and when's it coming, anyway?" Never again will you have to rack your brain to remember whether you ordered those thingamajigs and doohickeys.

And when the bill comes, you will already have itemized it in the purchase order form. Guess what? Having written out all the items on your purchase order, you won't have to fill out an Items tab on your check when you pay the bill. Or, if you're paying bills with the accounts payable method, you won't have to fill out the Items tab in the Enter Bills window. (Look at Chapter 6 if you don't know what I'm talking about here.)

When the items arrive, all you have to do is let QuickBooks know — they are added immediately to your inventory list.

Use purchase orders for items that you're *ordering* — that is, for items that you'll receive and pay for in the future. If you're buying items over the counter or if you're receiving items that you didn't order, you obviously don't need a purchase order. What you need to do is just pay the bill and inventory the items you just bought, as explained in the first half of this chapter.

Choosing a purchase order form just for you . . .

The first thing to do when you use purchase orders is design a purchase order form for your business. Choose Preferences⇨Inventory/PO's to see the Inventory/Purchase Order Preferences dialog box. You may remember this dialog box from Figure 7-1, and if you don't remember the box, it doesn't matter because the only thing that you're interested in now is the Customize button.

Click the Customize button to see the Customize Purchase Order window shown in Figure 7-6. This window has four tabs for determining what your purchase orders should look like.

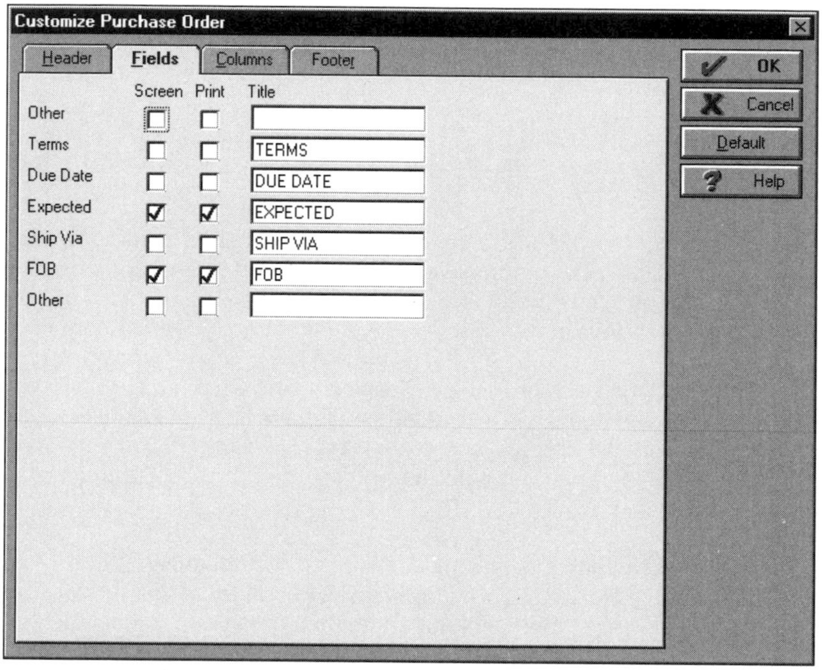

Figure 7-6:
The
Customize
Purchase
Order
window.

Click the different tabs to see what you can customize. Some of the options that are listed on the left side will apply to the purchase orders for your business; some won't. If you would like to use an option on your screen, click the Screen check box next to that option. Likewise for printed purchase orders. Click the Print check box if you want an option to appear on the order when you print it. In the Title text boxes, type the word or words that you want to see on purchase orders. The Other options on the Columns and Fields tabs are for putting a field or column of your own on the purchase order.

Play around with this window for a while until your purchase order comes out just right. To see how your choices look on a real purchase order, click OK to close the window, click OK again to close the Inventory/Purchase Order Preferences dialog box, and choose Activities⇨Create Purchase Orders. There it is! You see what your purchase order looks like on-screen.

button in the Customize Purchase Order window to go back to the default headers, fields, columns, and footers that were there originally.

When your purchase order looks magnificent, click OK in the Customize Purchase Order window.

You then return to the Inventory/Purchase Order Preferences dialog box (refer to Figure 7-1). Make sure that all the boxes are checked if you want to track inventory and create purchase orders. Checking the Warn If Not Enough Stock To Sell check box tells QuickBooks to let you know if you are trying to sell more inventory than you have on hand. Click OK when you're finished.

Filling out a purchase order

Perhaps you are running low on gizmos, or doohickeys, or some other item on your Item List, and it's time to reorder these things — whatever they are.

1. **Choose Activities⇨Create Purchase Orders.**

   You see the Create Purchase Orders window, which is similar to what is shown in Figure 7-7. Note that the exact details of this window depend on how you customize your purchase order form.

2. **Choose a vendor from the Vendor drop-down list.**

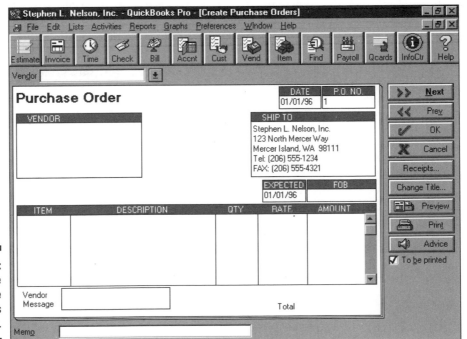

Figure 7-7:
The Create
Purchase
Orders
window.

2. Choose a vendor from the Vendor drop-down list.

Click the down arrow to see a list of your vendors. Click a vendor to see its name and address in the Vendor box. If you enter the name of a vendor that QuickBooks doesn't recognize, it asks you to Quick Add or Set Up a new vendor. Click Set Up, and fill in the information about the vendor in the New Vendor dialog box.

3. If you're tracking your inventory by class, choose a class from the Class drop-down list.

The Create Purchase Orders window may not have a Class drop-down list. If it doesn't and you want it to have one, choose Preferences⇨Transactions, and check the Use Class Tracking box.

4. (Optional) Choose a Rep, Expected date, and FOB, if you're using them on your purchase order.

You may have to fill in other fields before you get to the item-by-item descriptions at the bottom. Again, these fields may not appear if you haven't indicated you want them on your form.

5. Move to the Item column, and start entering the items you're ordering.

Entering the items is the most important part of creating a purchase order. When you move into the Item column, it turns into a drop-down list box. Click its down arrow to see the Item List. You may need to scroll to the item that you want to enter. A fast way to scroll to the item is to type the first couple of letters in the item name. If you type the name of an item that is not on the Item List, QuickBooks asks whether you want to set up this item. Click Set Up and fill in the New Item dialog box.

Enter as many items as you want in the Item column. In the QTY column, indicate how many of each item you need.

6. If you want, fill in the Message field — and definitely fill in the Memo field.

The Message field is where you put a message to the party receiving your order. You could write, "Get me this stuff pronto!"

No matter what you do, be sure to fill in the Memo field. What you write here will appear in the Open Purchase Orders dialog box and will be the surest way for you to identify what this purchase order is. Write something meaningful that you will understand two weeks, three weeks, or a month from now when you pay for the items that you are ordering.

By now you must have noticed the army of buttons deployed along the right side of the window. Below the buttons is the To Be Printed check box that tells you whether you've printed this purchase order. When you first create the purchase order, QuickBooks assumes that you want to print it

after you're done, and puts a check in the box. When you print it, the
check disappears from the box. (If you don't want to print it right away,
you can remove the check by clicking the check box.)

7. **Print the purchase order.**

   Click Print to print the purchase order. If this purchase order is one of
   many purchase orders that you've been filling out and you want to print
   several at once, you have to go to the File menu, choose Print Forms,
   choose Print Purchase Orders, and fill in the dialog box. Before you print
   the purchase order, however, click the Preview button to see what the
   purchase order will look like when you print it. QuickBooks shows you an
   on-screen replica of the purchase order. I hope that it looks okay.

   Change Title is an intriguing button. When you click it, QuickBooks gives
   you a chance to change the title of the order from "Purchase Order" to
   "Wuthering Heights," or whatever else you want to change it to.

   You use the Receipts button after you receive the items you're so carefully
   listing on the purchase order. After you receive the items and record their
   receipt, clicking this button tells QuickBooks to give you the entire history
   of an item — when you ordered it and when you received it.

   As for the top four buttons, I think that you know what those are, and if
   you don't, go to Step 8.

8. **Click Next, Prev, Cancel, or OK to record the purchase order.**

   The OK button closes the Create Purchase Orders window. The Next
   button takes you to a new purchase order screen where you can enter
   another order. Click Prev if you need to see or change the previous order.
   Click Cancel if you get cold feet and decide not to purchase this stuff
   after all.

Checking up on purchase orders

You record the purchase orders. A couple of weeks go by, and you ask yourself,
"Did I order those doohickeys from Acme?" Choose Lists⇨Purchase Orders to
see the Purchase Orders window with a list of outstanding purchase orders (see
Figure 7-8). Double-click one of the orders on the list, and it will magically
appear on-screen.

You can use this window to change the information on a purchase order. Just
highlight the order that you want to change and click Edit. You can even enter a
new purchase order from this window by clicking the (what else?) New button.

Do you want to delete a purchase order? Just keep the Purchase Orders window
open, highlight the purchase order that you want to delete, and choose
Edit⇨Delete.

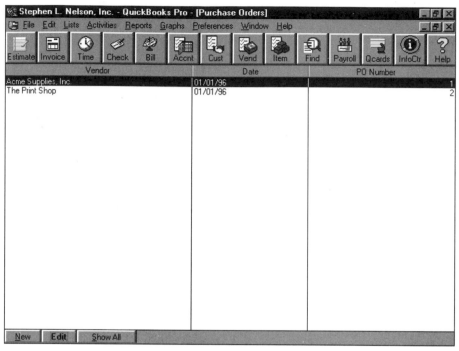

Figure 7-8:
The
Purchase
Orders
window.

Receiving purchase order items

Now the doohickeys and gizmos have arrived by camel train. It's time to record the receipt of the items and add them to your Item List.

The first thing to do is note whether the stuff came with a bill and decide how you want to pay for it. These decisions are the same ones you would have to make if you'd received the goods without having first filled out a purchase order.

Paying with a check

If the goods came with a bill attached and you pay your bills by check, follow these steps to record your purchase order:

1. Either click the Check button on the iconbar, or choose Activities⇨Write Checks.

The Write Checks – Checking window shows up on-screen.

2. **In the Pay To The Order Of drop-down list, click the name of the vendor who sent you the items.**

   The Open PO's Exist message box appears to inform you that you wrote purchase orders to this vendor (see Figure 7-9). Do you want to "receive against" one of these orders? Of course you do.

Figure 7-9:
The Open
PO's Exist
message
box.

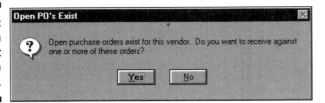

3. **Click Yes.**

   You see the Open Purchase Orders dialog box with all the purchase orders filed for this vendor.

4. **Click the purchase order you need (to put a check mark in the column on the left), and then click OK.**

   The Write Checks – Checking window appears, and both it and its Items tab are filled out. Do you recognize these items from when you filled out the purchase order? Look at the packing slip and compare what's in the package to what is on the Items tab. Does everything match up? If it doesn't, you may need to change what's on the Items tab.

5. **Click OK.**

   There's that pinball sound again. Now the items you ordered are a part of your inventory, the check is entered in the register, and all you have to do is print it and send it.

Receiving the items and recording the bill

If the items you ordered came with a bill, you can record the bill and the inventory items at the same time.

1. **Choose Activities⇨Inventory⇨Receive Items And Enter Bill.**

   You see the Enter Bills window.

2. **From the Vendor drop-down list, choose the name of the company that sent you the items.**

   The Open PO's Exist message box appears, telling you to click Yes if you want to receive against these items. Accountants use funny words, don't they? *Receive against* simply means to compare what you ordered to what you received.

3. Click Yes.

You see the Open Purchase Orders dialog box (see Figure 7-10).

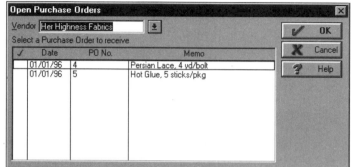

Figure 7-10:
The Open
Purchase
Orders
dialog box.

4. Click the purchase order associated with the bill and the items.

When the Enter Bills window appears, the Items tab is filled out. Make sure that you received what you ordered.

5. Click OK.

The bill is entered in the Accounts Payable register. QuickBooks will remind you when to pay it.

Receiving the goods and saving the bill for later

In the final purchase order scenario, the stuff comes, and no bill is attached. You'll record the bill when it comes, but in the meantime you want to add the items to your inventory records.

1. Choose Activities⇨Inventory⇨Receive Items.

You see the Create Item Receipts window.

2. From the Vendor drop-down list, choose the name of the party who sent you the items that you want to record.

The Open PO's Exist message box comes on-screen, urging you to click Yes to receive against a purchase order.

3. Click Yes.

You see the Open Purchase Orders dialog box (refer to Figure 7-10). This dialog box lists the purchase orders you've written for the particular vendor.

4. Click a purchase order and then click OK.

Again, click in the check mark column to choose the purchase order(s) that the items are to be charged against. When you do, the Items tab in the receipt now shows all the stuff you ordered. Is it what you received? If not, you may have to make adjustments.

5. Click OK.

You hear the pinball sound, and then the items are recorded in your inventory.

When the bill comes, choose Activities⇨Inventory⇨Enter Bill for Rec'd Items. You see the Select Item Receipt dialog box. In the Vendor drop-down list, choose the name of the vendor who sent you the bill, select the item receipt for which you want to enter a bill, and click OK. Your screen shows the Enter Bills window. Compare the Items tab in the dialog box with the bill to make sure that everything adds up. Click OK to record the bill and close the dialog box.

Of course, you still need to pay the bill to the vendor. Read Chapter 6 if you need help.

Time for a Reality Check

QuickBooks does a pretty good job of tracking inventory, but you're still going to have to make that complete annual inventory of what you have in stock. What I'm saying here is, you're going to have to go over everything and count it. Sorry. You just can't avoid that chore.

And when you've made your count, what happens if your inventory figures differ from those QuickBooks has? First, you have to decide who's right — you or a computer program. You're right, probably. Things get dropped. They break. And that means that you have to adjust the QuickBooks inventory numbers.

Choose Activities⇨Inventory⇨Adjust Qty/Value On Hand. The Adjust Quantity/ Value On Hand window appears (see Figure 7-11).

The first thing to do here is choose an account for storing your inventory adjustments. Choose it from the Adjustment Account drop-down list. You also can choose a class from the Class drop-down list.

Go down the Item column, entering numbers in the New Qty column where your count differs from the QuickBooks totals. Click OK when you're done.

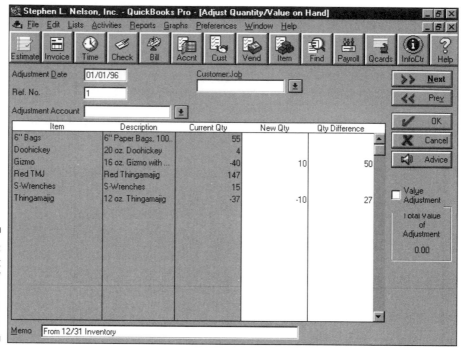

Figure 7-11:
The Adjust
Quantity/
Value on
Hand
window.

Chapter 8
Keeping Your Checkbook

• •

In This Chapter
▶ Writing checks from the Write Checks – Checking window
▶ Writing checks from the Checking register
▶ Recording deposits
▶ Recording transfers
▶ Searching for transactions
▶ Voiding and deleting transactions

• •

This is it. You're finally going to do those everyday QuickBooks things: entering checks, deposits, and transfers. Along the way, you also learn about some of the neat tools that QuickBooks provides for making these tasks easier, faster, and more precise.

Writing Checks: A Refresher Course

Back in Chapter 6, you learned about the two ways to write checks: from the Write Checks – Checking window and from the Checking register. In case you were asleep in the back row of the class, or your locker got jammed and you couldn't make it in, here is the Cliff Notes version of the instructions for writing checks.

Writing checks from the Write Checks — Checking window

You can record manually written checks and other checks that you want to print with QuickBooks by describing the checks in the Write Checks — Checking windows. Ah, it all sounds so complicated. But, really, it's not.

To write a check from the Write Checks – Checking window, follow these steps:

1. **Either click the Check button on the iconbar or choose <u>A</u>ctivities⇨<u>W</u>rite Checks.**

   You see the Write Checks – Checking window (see Figure 8-1).

2. **Click the Ban<u>k</u> Account drop-down list at the top of the window and choose the account from which you want to write this check.**

3. **Fill in the check.**

   If you've written a check to this person or party before, the AutoFill feature fills in the name of the payee in the Pay To The Order Of line for you. How QuickBooks does this may seem akin to magic, but it's really not that tough. QuickBooks just compares what you've typed so far with names on your lists of customers, employees, and other names. When it can match the letters you've typed so far with a name on one of these lists, it grabs the name. If you haven't written a check to this person or party before, by the way, QuickBooks asks you to <u>Q</u>uick Add or <u>S</u>et Up the payee name. Do that.

   Enter the amount of the check next to the dollar sign and press Tab. QuickBooks writes out the amount for you on the Dollars line. It also writes out the address.

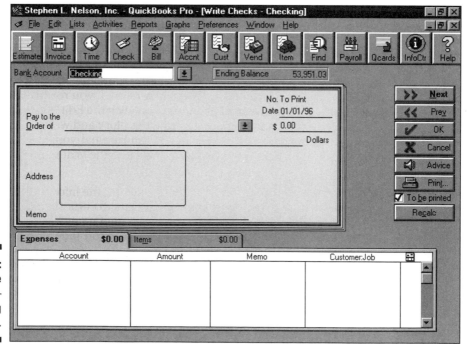

Figure 8-1:
The Write
Checks –
Checking
window.

4. **Fill in the Expenses and Items tabs, if necessary.**

   Don't know what these are? Chapter 6 explains them in minute detail. Start turning those pages.

5. **Click Next or OK to finish writing the check.**

   There you have it. Your check is written, is entered in the Checking register, and is ready to be printed and mailed.

Writing checks from the Checking register

People who have grown accustomed to Quicken, a cousin product of QuickBooks, may want to use the register window to write checks. (Quicken users like the register metaphor better, I guess.)

To write a check from the Checking register, follow these steps:

1. **Open the chart of accounts.**

   Click the Accnt button on the iconbar or choose Lists⇨Chart of Accounts.

2. **Open the Checking register.**

   Highlight the checking account you want to write this check against and then double-click the account or click the Use Register button. You see the Checking register window (see Figure 8-2). The cursor is at the end of the register, ready and waiting for you to enter check information. (QuickBooks automatically fills in today's date.)

3. **Fill in the information for your check.**

   Notice that the entries you make here are the same ones that you would make in the Write Checks – Checking window. If you're more comfortable entering checks in that window, you can click the Edit button to see the Write Checks – Checking window in all its glory and write a check there. In fact, if you want to enter expenses or itemize what you're paying for with the check, you have to click Edit and get into the Write Checks – Checking window.

   Otherwise, just go from field to field and enter the information in the register. Once again, use the drop-down lists to enter the Payee and Account name. If you enter a Payee or Account name that QuickBooks does not recognize, it asks you to give more information.

4. **When you're finished filling in the check information, click Record.**

   Or click the Restore button if you decide that you want to go back to square one and start all over again. Clicking Restore blanks out what you just entered.

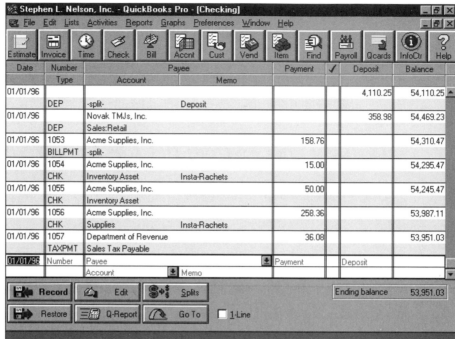

Figure 8-2:
The
Checking
register
window.

If you are writing checks by hand, make sure that the check numbers in the
Checking register and the check numbers in your personal checkbook match
up. You may need to go into the QuickBooks Checking register and change
numbers in the Number column. When your bank statement comes, reconciling
your bank statement and your checkbook will be much easier if you entered
check numbers correctly.

Changing a check that you've written

What if you need to change a check after you have already entered it? Perhaps
you made a terrible mistake, such as recording a $52.50 check as $25.20. Can
you fix it? Sure. Just go into the Checking register, and find the check that you
want to change. Put the cursor where the check is, and click Edit. QuickBooks
displays the Write Checks – Checking window with the original check in it. Make
the changes (don't forget to make changes on the Items and Expenses tabs too,
if necessary). When you're finished, click OK. You go back to the Checking
register, where you see the changes to the check. Click the Record button or
press Enter when you finish.

Packing more checks into the register

Normally, QuickBooks displays two rows of information about each check you enter. It also displays two rows of information about each of the other types of transactions that you enter. If you want to pack more checks into a visible portion of the register, check the 1-Line check box at the bottom of the Checking register window. When you check this box, QuickBooks uses a single-line format to display all the information in the register except the Memo field.

Compare Figure 8-2 with Figure 8-3 to see what the 1-line display looks like. Checking registers can get awfully long, and the 1-line display is helpful when you're looking through a long register for a check or transaction.

Depositing Money into a Checking Account

You can't write checks unless you deposit some money in your checking account. You didn't know that? Well, the next time you're taking your exercise in the prison yard, give it some serious thought. From time to time, you must deposit money in your checking account and record those deposits in the Checking register.

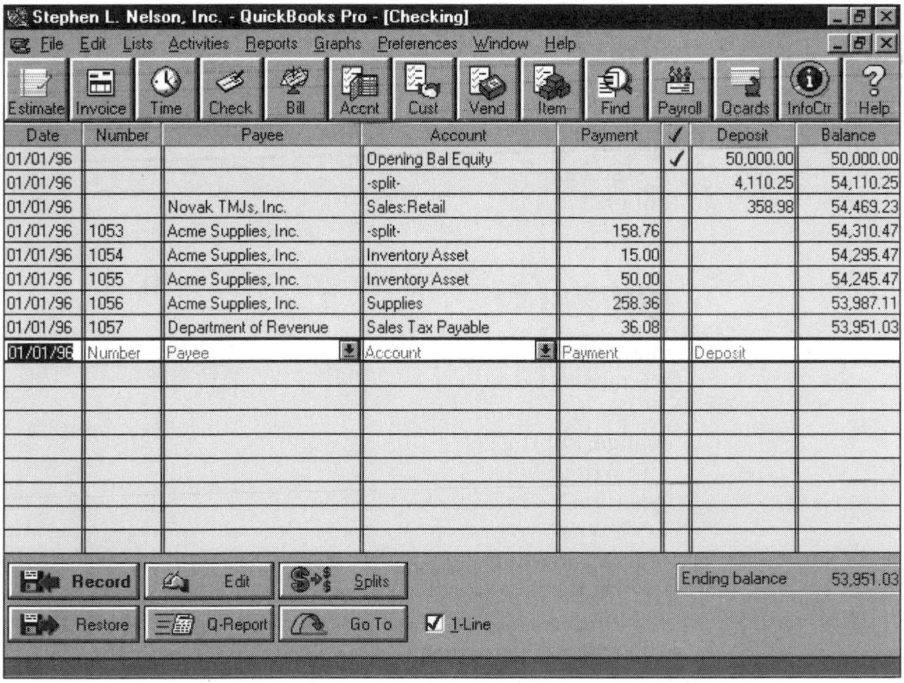

Figure 8-3:
The Checking register window with a display of one transaction per line.

You can record deposits in two ways. If you have a simple deposit to make — a sum of money that did not come from one of your customers — just make the deposit directly in the Checking register. For example, suppose that your elderly Aunt Enid sent you $100 with a note explaining how, more than 80 years ago, Great-uncle Bert started his hammock manufacturing business with only $100, and for good luck she is sending you $100 to help you along.

Recording simple deposits

Recording a simple deposit is pretty, well, simple. Follow these steps:

1. **Open the Checking register.**

   Click the Accnt button on the iconbar or choose Lists⇨Chart of Accounts. Highlight the checking account to which you want to make the deposit and click the Use button. You see the Checking register window (refer to Figure 8-2).

2. **Enter the amount that you're depositing.**

   Move the cursor to the Deposit column, and enter the amount.

3. **Enter an account for this deposit.**

   Move to the Account field, click the down arrow, and choose an account from the list. Most likely, you will choose an account such as Uncategorized Income.

4. **Click the Record button.**

   Your deposit is entered, and your checking account's balance is fattened accordingly. Note that all entries in the Checking register are made in chronological order, with deposits first and checks next.

Depositing income from customers

Depositing income from customers is a little more complicated because it involves the Payments To Deposit window. Have you been recording customer payments as they come in? (You do this with the Receive Payments command on the Activities menu.) If you have been recording customer payments, QuickBooks has placed these payments in your Undeposited Funds account. Now all you have to do is transfer the undeposited funds to your checking account.

1. **Choose Activities⇨Make Deposits.**

   Because you have undeposited funds, you see the Payments To Deposit dialog box (see Figure 8-4). This dialog box lists checks that you have received but not yet put in a checking account or other bank account.

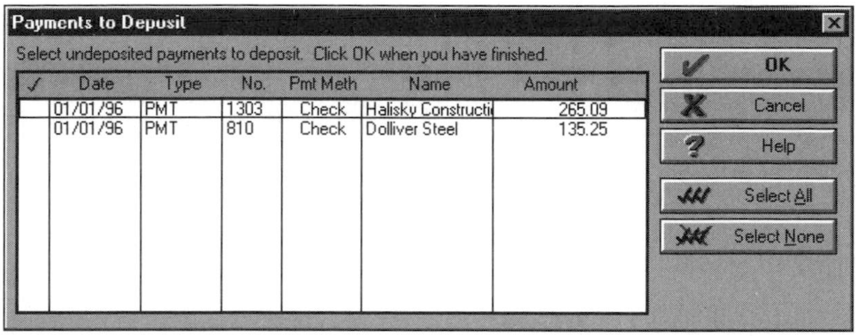

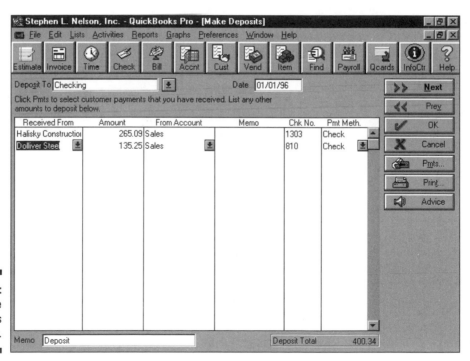

Figure 8-4:
The
Payments to
Deposit
dialog box.

2. Select the checks that you want to deposit.

Place a check mark next to the checks that you want to deposit by clicking in the column next to them. Or, if you want to deposit all the checks, click the Select All button. Click OK.

The Make Deposits window appears (see Figure 8-5). Do you recognize the information in the middle of the dialog box? It describes your undeposited checks, ready and waiting to be deposited.

Figure 8-5:
The Make
Deposits
window.

3. Select the checking account to receive these deposits.

Select the account from the Deposit To drop-down list at the top of the dialog box. And while you're at it, check the Date text box to make sure that it shows the date you will deposit these checks in your checking account. In other words, if you're not going to make it to the bank or the ATM machine until tomorrow, put tomorrow's date in the Date text box.

4. Add any other deposits to include on the deposit slip.

If one of your customers gave you 1,000 pennies in ten rolls, for example, that's ten extra dollars that you can record on this deposit slip. At the bottom of the slip, enter the customer's name who gave you the cash, the amount, the account, a memo, the payment method (cash in this case), and a class if you so desire.

5. Write a note to yourself in the Memo box to describe this deposit, if you want to, and click the Print button to get a hard copy of the deposit slip.

Many banks will accept this deposit slip, so you can print it and put it in the envelope with your ATM deposit or hand it to the bank clerk. Whatever you write on the memo will appear on the Checking register. (You should probably write a memo to yourself in case you need to know what this deposit is years from now when you're old and dotty.)

6. Click OK.

Now the deposit is recorded in QuickBooks. It will appear in your Checking register next to the letters *DEP*, which stand for *Deposit*.

Transferring Money between Accounts

Account transfers occur when you move money from one account — such as your savings account — to another account — such as your checking account. But, jeepers, why am I telling you this? If you have one of those combined savings and checking accounts, you probably do this sort of thing all the time.

Oh, now I remember why I brought this up — QuickBooks makes quick work of account transfers as long as you already have *both* accounts set up.

If you don't have the second account set up, you need to set it up first. If you don't know how to set it up, flip back to Chapter 1.

Entering an account transfer

Buckle up. The following steps speed through recording an account transfer. For the most part, recording an account transfer works the same way as recording a check or deposit.

1. **Open the Write Checks – Checking window.**

   Click the Check button on the iconbar or choose <u>A</u>ctivities⇨<u>W</u>rite Checks. You see the Write Checks – Checking window, which you may remember from Figure 8-1.

2. **Select the bank account that you're going to transfer the money from.**

   In the Ban<u>k</u> Account box at the top of the screen, choose the account from the drop-down list.

3. **On the Pay To The Order Of line, write something like** From savings to checking, Transfer, **or some other meaningful name.**

   This method enables you to keep tabs on how much money you transfer between accounts. How's that? Well, press Tab to move out of the Pay To The Order Of line. QuickBooks flashes the Name Not Found dialog box (see Figure 8-6). You see this dialog box because you haven't yet, I'm assuming, created an account name for recording money transfers. You can create one now.

Figure 8-6:
The Name
Not Found
dialog box.

Name Not Found

? Transfer From Checking to Savings is not in the Name list.

[<u>Q</u>uick Add]   [<u>S</u>et Up]   [<u>C</u>ancel]

4. **Click <u>Q</u>uick Add.**

   The Select Name Type dialog box comes on-screen. You use it to categorize the new account that you are creating for keeping track of money transfers.

5. **Click the Other option and click OK.**

   Now you're back at the Write Checks window. Just for fun, open the drop-down list on the Pay To The Order Of line and look at the account that's at the bottom of the Other Name accounts. The Other Name account that you just created should be there.

6. Enter the amount that you want to transfer and, more important, fill in the Memo line.

Someday you may go into the register for the account you're writing this check in and wonder where you transferred this money and why. Filling in the Memo line will solve this little mystery beforehand.

7. Enter the name of the account to which you're transferring the money in the Account column of the Expenses **tab.**

Go to the bottom of the Write Checks – Checking window and click the down arrow in the Account column. Up comes your list of accounts. Click the one the money will go to. It should be at the top of the list.

8. Click OK.

The transfer is recorded. If you doubt me, open the register for the account to which you transferred the money. You'll see that it's a bit richer. Figure 8-7 shows a $1,000 transfer payment made from an account named Checking to an account named Savings.

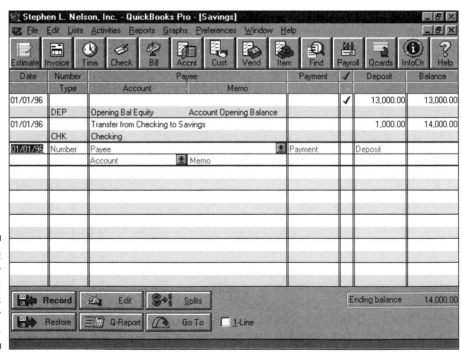

Figure 8-7: A transfer payment in a Savings register window.

About the other half of the transfer

Here's the cool thing about transfer transactions. QuickBooks automatically records the other half of the transfer for you. Figure 8-8 shows the other half of the transfer from Figure 8-7. This register is for a checking account called, oddly enough, Checking. That $1,000 deposit in Savings in Figure 8-7 came from the change that you made in the Write Checks – Checking window.

If you need to know where this $1,000 went, you can select the transaction and click the Edit button in the Checking register. You'll see where the check went — in this case, to the Savings account.

Changing a deposit that you've already entered

Big surprise here, but this works just like changing a check. First, you find the deposit in the account register, and then you click Edit. You see the Write Checks – Checking window with the Transfer check you wrote. Make changes to the check and click OK. You are returned to the register where your deposit is adjusted accordingly. Click Record.

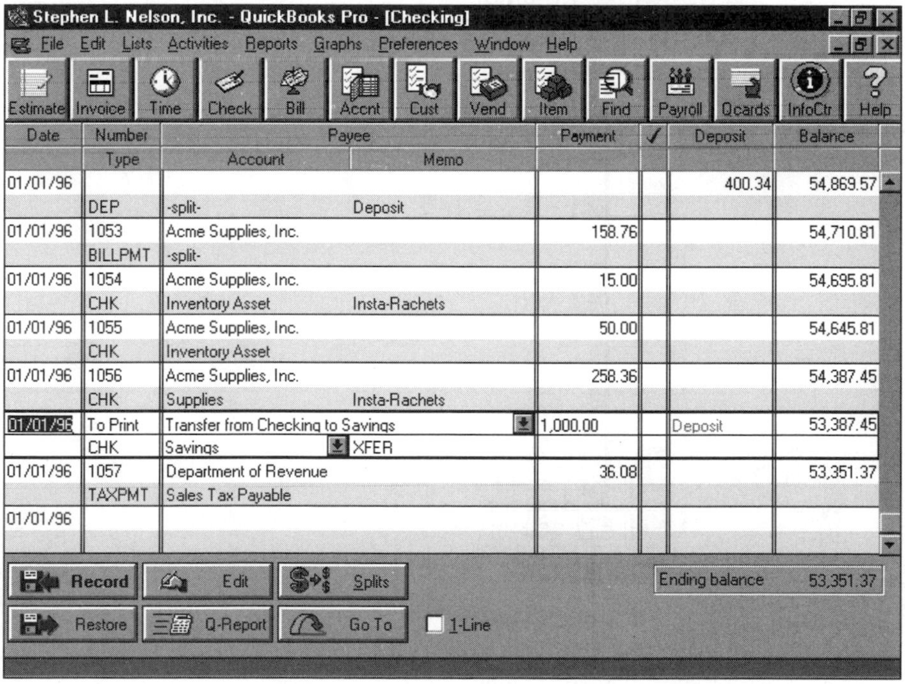

Figure 8-8: A transfer payment in the Checking register window.

To Delete or to Void?

What happens if you put a transaction — a deposit, a check, or a transfer payment — in a Checking register and later decide that it shouldn't be there? You have two ways of handling this situation. If you want to keep a record of the transaction but render it moot, meaningless, *nada,* or *kaput,* you void the transaction. But if you want to obliterate it from the face of the earth as though it never happened in the first place, then you delete it.

Decide whether you want to void or delete the transaction, and then follow these steps:

1. **Find the transaction in the register.**

   In the next section of this chapter, "The Big Register Phenomenon," I tell you some quick ways to find transactions.

2. **Choose either Edit⇨Delete Check or Edit⇨Void Check and click OK.**

   There, the deed is done. Figure 8-9 shows a Checking register window with a voided check. Notice the word *VOID.* If this check had been deleted, it wouldn't even show up in the register.

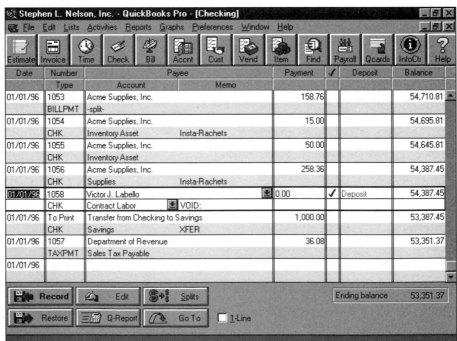

Figure 8-9: The Checking register window, showing a voided check.

The Big Register Phenomenon

If you start entering checks, deposits, and transfers into your registers, you'll shortly find yourself with registers that contain hundreds, and even thousands of transactions. You can still work with one of these big registers by using the tools and techniques that I've talked about in the preceding paragraphs. Nevertheless, let me give you some more help for dealing with . . . (drum roll, please) . . . *the big register phenomenon.*

Moving through a big register

You can use the PgUp and PgDn keys to page up and down through your register, a screenful of transactions at a time. Some people call this *scrolling*. You can call it whatever you want.

You can use the Home key to move to the first transaction in a register. Just move the cursor to the first (or Date) field in the selected transaction, and press Home.

You can use the End key to move to the last transaction in a register. Bet you can guess how this works. Move the cursor to the Memo field in the selected transaction, and press End.

Of course, you can use the vertical scrollbar along the right edge of the Checking register, too. Click the arrows at either end of the vertical scrollbar to select the next or previous transaction. Click either above or below the square scroll box to page back and forth through the register. Or, if you have no qualms about dragging the mouse around, you can drag the scroll box up and down the scrollbar.

Finding that darn transaction

Want to find that one check, deposit, or transfer? No problem. I've discussed this before, but it might be appropriate here, too. The Edit menu's Find command provides a handy way for doing just this. Here's what you do:

1. **Choose Edit⇨Find.**

   QuickBooks, with restrained but obvious enthusiasm, displays the Find window (see Figure 8-10). You use this window to describe the transaction that you want to find in as much detail as possible.

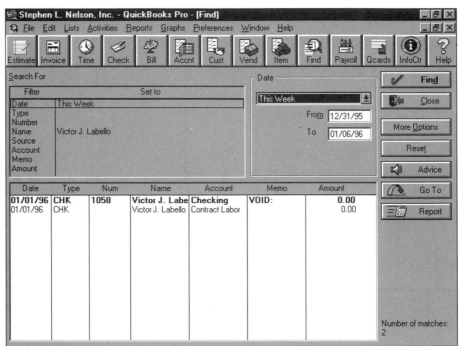

Figure 8-10:
The Find
window.

2. **Choose a filter that will describe the information that you already have.**

   In the sample, the Date filter has been chosen. As you click on different filters, the upper-right half of the dialog box changes.

3. **Enter the text or number that identifies the transaction that you want to locate.**

   In the upper-right box, which is set to Date in the figure, choose the text or number that describes the subject of your search from the drop-down list. Or just type the information in the box. If more than one field is in the box, use as many as you think will help.

   By the way, the case of the text doesn't matter. If you type **aunt**, for example, QuickBooks finds *AUNT* as well as *Aunt*.

4. **Repeat Steps 2 and 3 as needed.**

   Yes, you can filter through as many fields as you want. In fact, you can filter so much that *nothing* matches your specification. But that defeats the purpose of the whole thing, doesn't it?

5. **Let the search begin.**

   Click the Find button to begin looking.

   If QuickBooks finds transactions that match the one you described, it lists them in the bottom half of the dialog box.

Chapter 9

Credit Cards (and Debit Cards, Too)

*Y*ou can use QuickBooks to track your credit cards in much the same way that you use it to keep a checkbook. The process is almost the same, but with a few wrinkles.

Tracking Business Credit Cards

If you want to track credit card spending and balances with QuickBooks, you need to set up a credit card account. (In comparison, you use bank accounts to track things such as the money that flows into and out of a checking account.)

Setting up a credit card account

To set up a credit card account, you follow roughly the same steps that you use to set up a checking account. Here's what you do:

1. Click the Accnt icon on the iconbar or choose Lists➪Chart of Accounts.

QuickBooks displays the Chart of Accounts window, as shown in Figure 9-1.

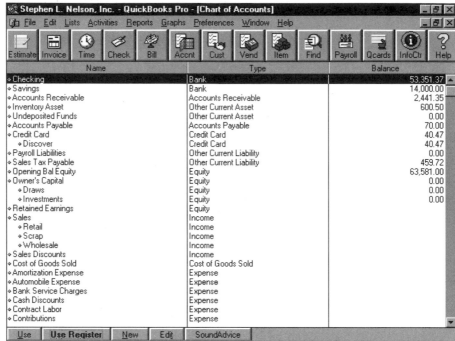

Figure 9-1:
The Chart of
Accounts
window.

2. Click the New button in the Chart of Accounts window.

QuickBooks — always sensitive to your feelings — displays the New Account window. Because I'm sensitive to your feelings too, I'm including this window as Figure 9-2.

3. Choose Credit Card from the Type drop-down list.

Choosing Credit Card tells QuickBooks that you want to set up a credit card account. I'm sure that you're surprised.

4. Name the account.

Why not do it, right? Move the cursor to the Name text box and enter the name of your credit card.

5. Enter the card number.

While you're at it, you can describe the card, too. You might type **Usury!** in the Description box, depending on the interest rate of your card.

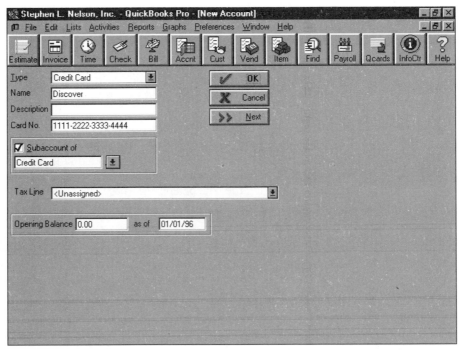

Figure 9-2:
The New
Account
window.

6. **Make this credit card account a subaccount of your all-purpose Credit Card account, if you want to.**

   Why would you want to make it a subaccount? Well, if you have three credit cards, you can call the accounts VISA, MasterCard, and Discover, or neat names like that, and all three of those accounts can be subaccounts of a generic account named Credit Card. That way, you can keep track of your total credit card payments and expenses as well as payments and expenses for individual cards.

   To create a subaccount, click the Subaccount Of check box and enter the name of the account that this credit card account will go under. QuickBooks offers a nice generic name for you in the drop-down list: Credit Card.

7. **Indicate the relationship between the expenses you will incur and your taxes.**

   Use the Tax Line drop-down list box to specify where your purchase amounts can be classified on your tax forms. Chances are, you will leave this Unassigned because you'll probably be using your credit card for a myriad of items.

8. **Enter the balance that you owed at the end of the last credit card billing period after you made your payment.**

   Move the cursor to the Opening Balance text box and use the number keys to enter the balance value. If you just got this credit card and you haven't bought anything with it, type **00.00.** Otherwise, enter the balance that you currently owe. You enter the balance as a positive number, by the way, even though you owe money.

   The only time that you should enter a credit card account balance equal to something other than zero is at the time that you start using QuickBooks and are entering your trial balance as of the conversion date. Otherwise, you'll foul up your owners equity. (Refer to Chapter 3 if you have questions about entering the trial balance or about the conversion date.)

9. **Enter the As Of date on which you will start keeping records for the credit card account.**

   You should probably use the date when you made your payment. Move the cursor to the As Of text box and type a two-digit number for the month, a two-digit number for the day of the month, and a two-digit number for the year.

10. **Click OK.**

    QuickBooks redisplays the Chart of Accounts window. Now it should look something like Figure 9-1. And you know what? This time the window lists an additional account — the credit card account that you just created.

Selecting a credit card account so that you can use it

To tell QuickBooks that you want to work with a credit card account, you use the Chart of Accounts window — the same window that you saw in Figure 9-1. Go figure!

Choose the Accnt icon from the iconbar or choose Lists➪Chart of Accounts to display the window. After you display the dialog box, select the account you want to use. You know how this works: You put the cursor on the account you want by moving to it with the arrow keys or by clicking the account name with that long-tailed plastic rodent that sits on your desk. Then you click the Use button or press Enter. QuickBooks selects the account and displays the Credit Card register so that you can begin recording transactions.

Entering Credit Card Transactions

After you select a credit card account, QuickBooks displays the Credit Card register (see Figure 9-3). It looks a lot like a Checking register, doesn't it?

The Credit Card register works like the regular register window that you use for a checking account. You enter transactions into the rows of the register. When you record a charge, QuickBooks updates the credit card balance and the remaining credit limit.

You can use the same icons and commands that you use for your regular ol' bank account register. Earlier chapters cover the icons and commands, so I won't regurgitate them here. Old news is no news.

Recording a credit card charge

Recording a credit card charge is similar to recording a check or bank account withdrawal. For the sake of illustration, suppose that you charged $40.47 for a

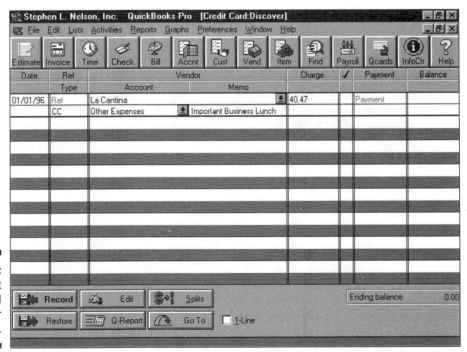

Figure 9-3:
The Credit
Card
register
window.

business lunch at your favorite Mexican restaurant, La Cantina. After you open the register, here's how you record this charge:

1. **Choose Activities➪Enter Credit Card Charges.**

   You see the Enter Credit Card Charges window (see Figure 9-4).

2. **Choose the credit card that you charged the expense against.**

   Click the down arrow next to the Credit Card box and choose a card from the drop-down list.

3. **Record the name of the business that you paid with a credit card.**

   Move the cursor to the Purchased From line and click the down arrow. You see a list of names. Choose one from the list.

   If you've never charged anything on this credit card at this restaurant before, QuickBooks asks you to Set Up or Quick Add the new account. Choose Quick Add and choose an account type. In this case, you choose Other because Vendor, Customer, and Employee don't fit the bill.

4. **Enter the charge date.**

   Move the cursor to the Date line (if it isn't already there) and type the date using the MM/DD/YY format. For example, type either **010496** or **1/4/96** for January 4, 1996. If you're entering this charge two or three days after

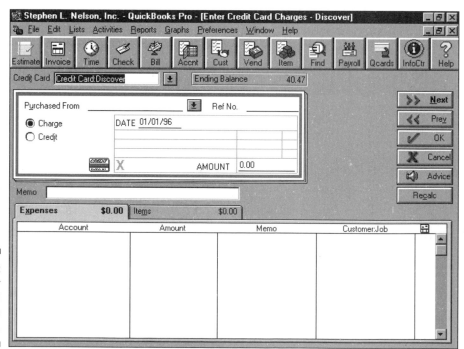

Figure 9-4:
The Enter
Credit Card
Charges
window.

the fact, don't enter today's date. Enter the date that the charge was made. Using that date will make reconciling your records with your credit card company's records easier when you get the monthly statement.

5. Enter the charge amount.

Move the cursor to the Amount line and enter the total charge amount — **40.47** in this example. Don't type a dollar sign, but do type the period to indicate the decimal place.

6. (Optional) Enter a memo description.

Move the cursor to the Memo text box and type the specific reason that you're charging the item. In this case, you could type **Important Business Lunch** or something like that.

7. Fill in the E̲xpenses tab.

I'm hoping that you read Chapters 6 and 8, that you know all about the Expenses tab, and that you are thoroughly bored by the topic. However, for those of you who opened the book right to this page, you use the Expenses tab to record business expenses.

Move to the Account column of the Expenses tab, click the down arrow, and choose an Expense account from the list (most likely Entertainment or Other Expenses, if this is a business lunch). QuickBooks asks you to set up an expense account if you enter a name here that it doesn't know already.

QuickBooks automatically fills in the Amount column when you enter an amount in the Amount line. Type something in the Memo line, and assign this expense to a Customer:Job and Class if you want to. Note that class tracking needs to be turned on if you want to assign the expense to a class.

8. Fill in the Ite̲ms tab.

Because this charge is for a meal at a restaurant, you wouldn't itemize it (although breaking down the cost of the Mexican lunch into categories might be fun — enchilada, guacamole, red hot chili pepper . . .). But if you were charging lumber, paper supplies, and so on, you would fill out the Ite̲ms tab.

If you have a purchase order on file with a vendor that you enter in the Purchased From line, QuickBooks tells you so. Click the Select PO button to see a list of your outstanding purchase orders with the vendor. If you don't know how to handle purchase orders, see Chapter 7.

Figure 9-3, in case you didn't notice, shows the charge at La Cantina recorded in the Credit Card register. Good food and reasonable prices — you can't ask for much more than that . . . except for cerveza to go with the meal.

9. Record the charge by clicking OK or N̲ext.

Click N̲ext if you want to record a second credit card charge. The charge is recorded in the Credit Card register.

Changing charges that you've already entered

Perhaps you recorded a credit card charge, and then you realize that you recorded it incorrectly. Or perhaps you shouldn't have recorded it at all because you didn't pay for the business lunch. (Someone else paid for it after one of those friendly arguments over who should pay the bill. You know the type of argument I mean: "No, I insist." "On the contrary, I insist." You get the picture.)

You have to go into the Credit Card register and either edit or delete the charge.

1. **Either click the Accnt button on the iconbar or choose Lists⇨Chart of Accounts from the menu.**

   You see the Chart of Accounts window again.

2. **Open the register.**

   Click the credit card account where the faulty charge is, and then click the Use Register button. Like magic, the Credit Card register appears on-screen.

3. **Select the credit card transaction that you want to delete or change.**

   That's easy. Just move the mouse cursor to the transaction.

4. **Delete or edit it.**

   To delete it, choose Edit⇨Delete Credit Card Charge. QuickBooks displays a message box that asks whether you really want to delete the transaction. Click OK.

   To edit it, click the Edit button on the bottom of the dialog box. You return to the Enter Credit Card Charges window. Make your changes there, and click OK. You also can make changes inside the Credit Card register and click Restore when you're done.

Reconciling Your Credit Card Statement

You know that trick where you compare your checking account records with your bank's records of your checking account? The one where you calculate the difference between what you think is your account balance and what the bank thinks is your balance? And this difference is supposed to equal the total of the transactions floating around out there in the system? You can do this same trick on your credit card account.

The actual reconciliation — neat and straight-up

To reconcile a credit card account, first get your credit card statement and then tell QuickBooks what that nasty credit card company says.

1. **Select the credit card account you want to reconcile from the Chart of Accounts window.**

2. **Choose Activities⊏⊃Reconcile Credit Card.**

   QuickBooks displays the Reconcile Credit Card window, shown in Figure 9-5. This window probably shows more charges than are on the statement because the most recent charges probably aren't on the statement.

3. **Make sure that you're reconciling the right credit card.**

   If you have more than one credit card, click the Account To Reconcile drop-down list and choose the right one, if necessary.

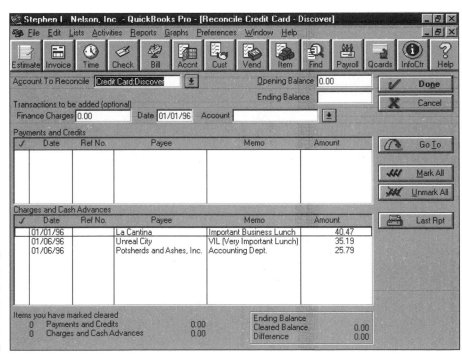

Figure 9-5: The Reconcile Credit Card window.

4. Enter the ending balance from the credit card statement.

Now I bet this is a surprise. Go ahead and enter the figure — even if you just can't believe that you charged that much.

5. Enter the finance charge.

In the Finance Charges text box, enter the finance charge from the statement. Pause for a moment of silence here if this is a sad, sad topic for you.

6. Assign the monthly interest to the appropriate account, such as Interest: Finance Charges.

Move the cursor to the Account text box and type the category name. (This is getting boring, isn't it? Move and type. . . . Move and type. . . . That's all I ever seem to say.) Remember that you can click the little down arrow at the end of the text box to see a list of categories to choose from.

7. Enter the charges and cash advances that your statement shows.

Move to the Charges and Cash Advances section and click in the far-left column next to the charges on the statement that you want to pay for. If you intend to pay for all the charges on the statement, click the Mark All button.

If you're going to pay only part of your credit card bill, click the charges that you want to pay. You can't pay an arbitrary amount, such as $8.99, because the amount that you pay has to equal the sum of specific charges in order for you to reconcile this statement and get out of the window.

8. Enter the payments and credits that your statement shows.

You know the drill: Move the cursor and type the number, tap your foot and swing your partner, do-si-do.

After you mark all the cleared charges and payments, the difference between the cleared balance for the credit card and the statement's ending balance should equal zero.

If the difference does equal zero, you're cool. You're golden. You're done. (This sort of makes you sound like chicken, doesn't it?)

9. All you need to do is click Done to tell QuickBooks that you're finished.

QuickBooks displays the Make Payment dialog box, which you can read more about later in the chapter. (Flip to the "Paying the bill" section if your statement reconciles with your register.)

Meanwhile, what do you do if your statement doesn't reconcile with the charges in the Reconcile Credit Card dialog box? Better read the next section.

When it doesn't add up

If your statement and your recorded charges are at war with each other, you can try a couple things to resolve the difference.

Fixing an incorrectly recorded transaction

As you're looking through the credit card statement, you may discover that you incorrectly recorded a transaction. In this situation, select the incorrect transaction with the mouse or arrow keys. Then click the Go To button. QuickBooks not only displays the Credit Card register so that you can make the needed fixes but also highlights the transaction that you need to fix. When you see the incorrectly recorded transaction, fix it.

Forcing the issue

If the difference still doesn't equal zero after you fix the transaction that you recorded incorrectly, you have a problem. If you click Done in spite of the problem, QuickBooks tells you that the ending balance has to equal the cleared balance. This message also offers you an opportunity to force the two amounts to agree (see Figure 9-6).

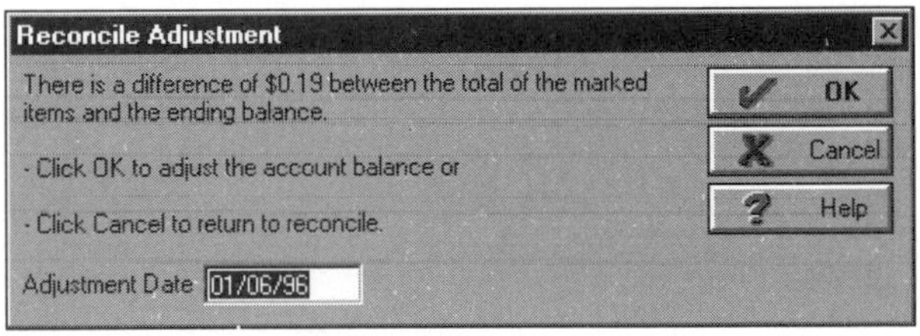

Figure 9-6:
The
Reconcile
Adjustment
dialog box.

You know what, though? Forcing the two amounts to agree isn't a very good idea. To force them to agree, QuickBooks adds a cleared transaction equal to the difference. (QuickBooks asks for an account if you choose the adjustment route.)

Despite the ease of making adjustments, a much better method is to find out why the difference exists and resolve the problem. Get out your magnifying glass and start looking again. By the way, reconciling with fictitious data is darned easy.

Chapter 11 provides some suggestions on how to figure out why a bank account that should balance won't balance. You can apply the same list of ten tips to credit card reconciliations if you're in a bad way.

Paying the bill

After you finish the reconciliation and click OK, QuickBooks politely asks whether you want to pay the bill. You see the Make Payment dialog box shown in Figure 9-7.

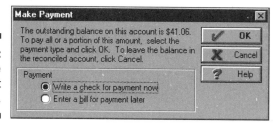

Figure 9-7:
The Make
Payment
dialog box.

From there, you can either pay by check or enter a bill to be paid later. (This would be the accounts payable method, remember?)

If you opt for writing a check, you go straight to the Write Checks – Checking window, and the Expenses tab is all filled out for you. Fill in the name of the card issuer, the date, and so on. And click OK when you're done. The payment is recorded in both the Checking register and the Credit Card register.

If you opt to enter the payment as a bill to be paid at a later date, you go to the Enter Bills window. Fill everything out just as you would if you were in the Write Checks – Checking window. When you click OK here, the transaction is recorded in the Accounts Payable register and the Credit Card register.

See Chapter 6 if you need to know more about either the Enter Bills or Write Checks – Checking window.

So What about Debit Cards?

Debit cards, when you get right down to it, aren't really credit cards at all. They're more like bank accounts. Rather than withdrawing money by writing a check, however, you withdraw money by using a debit card.

Although a debit card looks (at least to your friends and the merchants you shop with) like a credit card, you should treat it like a bank account. In a nutshell, here's what you need to do:

✔ Set up a bank account with the starting balance equal to the deposit that you make with the debit card company.

✔ When you charge something using the debit card, record the transaction just as you would record a regular check.

✔ When you replenish the debit balance by sending more money to the debit card company, record the transaction just as you would record a regular deposit.

If all this sounds pretty simple, it is. In fact, I'd go so far as to say that, if you've been plugging along, doing just fine with a bank account, you'll find that keeping track of a debit card is as easy as eating an entire bag of potato chips. (Well, maybe not *that* easy. . . .)

Part III

Stuff You Do Every So Often

The 5th Wave
By Rich Tennant

"OH BROTHER! I NEVER THOUGHT OF THIS AS A WAY TO DECIDE WHICH BUDGETS GET CUT."

In this part . . .

After you start using QuickBooks, you need to complete some tasks at the end of every week, month, or year. This part describes these tasks: printing payroll checks, backing up files, printing reports, filing quarterly and annual tax returns . . . . The list goes on and on.

Chapter 10

Printing Checks 101

● ●

In This Chapter

▶ Getting your printer ready to print checks

▶ Printing checks one at a time

▶ Printing several checks at a time

▶ Printing a register

● ●

*T*his chapter covers the reductivity of the postcolonial implications in Joseph Conrad's *Heart of Darkness*. Oops, only kidding. Guess what we're going to cover? Gee, you guessed it: how to print checks and checking registers.

Printing checks in QuickBooks is, well, quick. That is, it's quick after you set up your printer correctly. If you have a continuous-feed printer, you know by now that these printers have problems printing anything on a form. The alignment always gets screwed up.

QuickBooks has check forms that you can buy, and I recommend using them if you print checks. After all, the QuickBooks checks were made to work with this program. And all banks accept these checks.

If you want help in printing reports, refer to Chapter 13, where this topic is covered in almost too much detail.

Getting the Printer Ready

Before you can start printing checks, you have to make sure that your printer is set up to print them. You also have to tell QuickBooks what to put on the checks — your company name, address, logo, and so on. And you might try running a few sample checks through the wringer to see whether they come out all right.

Follow these steps to set up the printer:

1. **Choose File⇨Printer Setup⇨Check Printer.**

   After you choose this command, you see the Check Printer Setup dialog box shown in Figure 10-1. In this box, you tell QuickBooks about your printer and how you want checks printed.

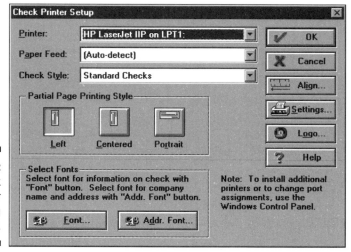

Figure 10-1:
The Check
Printer
Setup dialog
box.

2. **Tell QuickBooks what kind of printer you have.**

   In the Printer drop-down list box, click the down arrow and look at the printer names. When you installed QuickBooks, it had a frank, man-to-man talk with Windows to find out what kind of printer you have, among other things. Your printer is probably already selected, but if it's not, select the right printer.

3. **Set the correct Paper Feed option, if necessary.**

   This box is probably already filled in, too, thanks to that frank discussion I mentioned in Step 2. But if it isn't, click the down arrow and choose Continuous or Page-oriented. (The former is generally for dot-matrix printers and the latter for laser printers, but it really just depends on what kind of paper you use for your printer.)

4. **Choose a Check Style from the drop-down list.**

   Now you're cooking. This is where you get to make a real choice. Standard checks are sized to fit in a legal envelope. Voucher checks are the same width as standard checks, but they're much longer. When you choose the voucher option, QuickBooks prints voucher information as well — the items and expenses tabulations you know from the bottom of the

Write Checks – Checking window. It also provides information about the checking account that you're writing this check on. The Wallet Checks option is for printing checks that are small enough to fit in — you guessed it — a wallet.

5. Choose a Partial Page Printing Style.

Fortunately, there's a graphic in the dialog box because otherwise you wouldn't have a clue what these options are, would you? These options are for the thrifty among you. Suppose that you feed two checks to the printer, but the check sheets have three checks each. You have a leftover check.

Thanks to this option, you can use the extra check. Click one of the options to tell QuickBooks how you'll feed the check to the printer — vertically on the left (the Left option), vertically in the middle (the Centered option), or horizontally (the Portrait option). You feed checks to the printer the same way that you feed envelopes.

After you choose the Partial Page Printing Style, you're ready to click the Align button and print the extra check.

6. Customize the fonts on your checks.

When you click either the Font button or the Addr Font button in the lower-left corner of the screen, you see the Check Printing Font dialog box shown in Figure 10-2. You use the Addr Font button to designate how your company's name and address should look and the Font button to designate what all other print on your checks should look like. This is

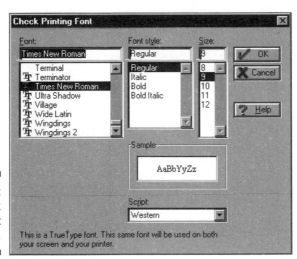

Figure 10-2:
The Check
Printing Font
dialog box.

your chance to spruce up your checks and make your company's name stand out.

Experiment for a while with the font, font style, and type size settings. For example, if you have a bookstore, choose the Bookman font (maybe using bold for your company's name and address); if you run a messenger service, choose Courier; Italian mathematicians can use Times Roman. (Just kidding.) You can see what your choices look like in the Sample box. After you're done fooling around, click the OK button to go back to the Check Printer Setup dialog box.

7. **If you're printing leftover checks on a sheet, click the Align button.**

   In the Align Partial Page dialog box, tell QuickBooks how many leftover checks you have on your sheet and click OK. In the next dialog box, you can make alignment changes and have QuickBooks remember them for later.

8. **Enter a company logo or some clip art, if you want.**

   Click the Logo button. In the Check Logo dialog box, click File and find the directory and .BMP (bitmapped) file that you want to load. Click OK. Only graphics files that are in .BMP format can be used on your checks.

9. **Click OK when you're finished.**

That setup was no Sunday picnic, was it? But your checks are all ready to be printed, and you will probably never have to go through that ordeal again.

Printing a Check

For some reason, when I get to this part of the discussion, my pulse quickens. It just seems that there's something terribly serious about actually writing a check for real money. I get the same feeling whenever I mail someone cash — even if the amount is nominal.

I think that the best way to lower my heart rate (and yours, if you're like me) is to just print the darn check and be done with it. QuickBooks can print checks in two ways: as you write them and in bunches.

First things first, however. Before you can print checks, you have to load some blank checks into your printer.

This process works the same way as loading any paper into your printer. If you have questions, refer to the printer documentation. (Sorry I can't help more on this, but there are a million different printers out there, and I can't tell which one you have even when I look into my crystal ball.)

Printing a check as you write it

If you're in the Write Checks – Checking window and you've just finished filling out a check, you can print it. The only drawback is that you have to print checks one at a time with this method.

1. **Fill out your check.**

   Yes, I strongly recommend filling out the check before printing it.

2. **Click the Print button in the Write Checks – Checking window.**

   You see the Print Check dialog box (see Figure 10-3).

Figure 10-3:
The Print
Check
dialog box.

3. **Enter a check number and click OK.**

   After you click OK, you see the similarly named Print Checks dialog box (see Figure 10-4). The settings that you see in this box are the ones that you chose when you first told QuickBooks how to print checks. If you change the settings in the Print Checks dialog box, the changes will affect only this particular check. The next time you print a check, you'll see your original settings again.

Figure 10-4:
The Print
Checks
dialog box.

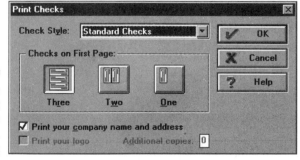

4. **Click OK to accept the default settings, or make changes in the dialog box and then click OK.**

   In the Check Style box, indicate whether you want to print a standard, voucher, or wallet-sized check. If you're printing a partial page of forms on a laser printer, indicate the number of check forms on the partial page by using one of the Checks On First Page option buttons. Mark the Three option button if there are three checks, the Two option button if there are two checks, and the One option button if there is one check.

Check the Print Your Company Name And Address check box if you want your company's name and address to appear on the check.

Note that the Print Your Logo check box and the Additional copies text box are grayed out. If you want to change these settings, you need to go back to File⇨Printer Setup⇨Check Printer.

After you click OK, QuickBooks prints the check, and you see the Did Check(s) Print OK? dialog box (see Figure 10-5). Here's your chance to start all over if the check didn't come out right. Type the number of the check in the text box and click OK. If the printing somehow got screwed up with check number 5, you would enter **5**.

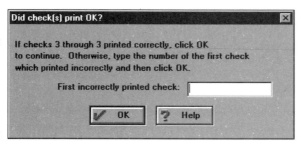

Figure 10-5:
The Did
Check(s)
Print OK?
dialog box.

5. If your check looks good, click OK.

You hear the pinball sound and return to the Write Checks – Checking window, but at least you have a good check.

Printing checks by the bushel

What if you write a mess of checks and then decide to print them? That's how it's usually done. Here's how to print a bushel of checks:

1. Go into the Checking register, and make sure that the checks that you want to print are marked To Print.

The quickest way to get into the Checking register is to click the Accnt or Reg button on the iconbar and then double-click the checking account. Do the checks that you want to print have To Print in the Number line? If not, place the cursor in the Number line, press **T**, and then click the Record button. QuickBooks automatically fills the Number field with To Print and then moves on.

2. **Choose File⇨Print Forms⇨Print Checks.**

   You see the Select Checks To Print dialog box, in which you mark which checks to print (see Figure 10-6).

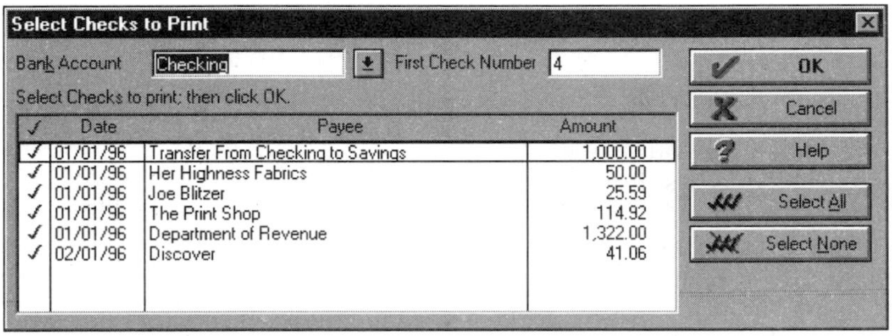

Figure 10-6:
The Select
Checks To
Print dialog
box.

✓	Date	Payee	Amount
✓	01/01/96	Transfer From Checking to Savings	1,000.00
✓	01/01/96	Her Highness Fabrics	50.00
✓	01/01/96	Joe Blitzer	25.59
✓	01/01/96	The Print Shop	114.92
✓	01/01/96	Department of Revenue	1,322.00
✓	02/01/96	Discover	41.06

Bank Account: Checking   First Check Number 4

OK / Cancel / Help / Select All / Select None

3. **Click the check marks next to the checks that you *don't* want to print, and then click OK.**

   All the checks are selected at first. If you want to print them all, fine. If not, click the check marks next to the checks that you don't want to print so that QuickBooks *removes* the check marks. Or, if you want to print only a few of the checks, click the Select None button and click next to the checks that you want to print so that QuickBooks will place a check in the column.

   When only the checks that you want to print are marked with a check mark, click OK to continue with this crazy little thing called *check printing*. QuickBooks, happy with your progress, displays the Print Checks dialog box (refer to Figure 10-4). Here you see the settings that you chose when you first told QuickBooks how to print checks.

   You can change the settings if you want them to be different. Any changes that you make for a particular batch of checks do not affect the default settings. The next time you print a check, you'll see your original settings again.

4. **Click OK to accept the default settings or make changes in the dialog box, and then click OK.**

   In the Check Style box, indicate whether you want to print standard, voucher, or wallet-sized checks. Click one of the Checks On First Page options if you are printing on a laser printer.

   Check the Print Your Company Name And Address check box if you want your company's name and address to appear on the checks.

   Check the Print Your Logo check box if you want the checks to include the .BMP company logo that you chose in Check Printer Setup dialog box.

Type a number in the Additional copies text box if you want more than one copy of the checks.

QuickBooks prints the checks, and then you see the Did Check(s) Print OK? dialog box (refer to Figure 10-5).

5. **Review the checks that QuickBooks printed.**

   If QuickBooks printed the checks correctly, answer the Did Check(s) Print OK? message box by clicking OK. (QuickBooks, apparently thinking that you now want to do nothing but print checks, redisplays the nearly exhausted Write Checks – Checking window.)

   If QuickBooks didn't print a check correctly, type the number of the first incorrectly printed check in the text box, and then click OK. In this case, repeat the steps for check printing. Note, though, that you need to reprint only the first bad check and the checks that follow it. You don't need to reprint good checks that precede the first bad check.

   If the numbers of the checks you need to reprint aren't sequential and are, in fact, spread all over creation, make it easy on yourself. Click OK to clear the list of checks to be printed, go into the Checking register, and type a **T** in the Num field of the checks you need to reprint. QuickBooks automatically fills these with To Print. Then choose File⇨Print Forms⇨Print Checks as in Step 2, and then continue on from there.

   If your checks came out all right, take the rest of the day off. And give yourself a raise while you're at it.

6. **Sign the printed checks.**

   Then — and I guess you probably don't need my help here — put the checks in the mail.

A few words about printing checks

Check printing is kind of complicated, isn't it?

For the record, I'm with you on this one. I really wish it weren't so much work. But you'll find that printing checks gets easier after the first few times.

Pretty soon, you'll be running instead of walking through the steps. Pretty soon, you'll just skate around things such as check-form alignment problems. Pretty soon, in fact, you'll know all this stuff and never have to read *pretty soon* again.

What if I made a mistake?

If you discover a mistake after you print a check, the problem isn't as big as you may think.

If you've already mailed the check, there's not a whole lot you can do. You can try to get the check back (if the person you paid hasn't cashed it) and replace it with one that's correct. (Good luck on this one.)

If the person has cashed the check, there's no way to get the check back. If you overpaid the person by writing the check for more than you should have, you need to get the person to pay you the overpayment amount. If you underpaid the person, you need to write another check for the amount of the underpayment.

If you printed the check but haven't mailed it, void the printed check. This operation is in two parts. First, write the word *VOID* in large letters across the face of the check form. (Use a ballpoint pen if you're using multipart forms so that the second and third parts also show as VOID.) Second, display the Checking register, highlight the check, and then choose Edit⇨Void Transaction. (This option marks the check as one that has been voided in the system so that QuickBooks does not use it in calculating the account balance.)

Of course, if you want to reissue the check, just enter the check all over again — only this time, try to be more careful.

Oh where, oh where, do unprinted checks go?

Unprinted checks — those you've entered using the Write Checks – Checking window but haven't yet printed — are stored in the Checking register. To identify them as unprinted checks, QuickBooks puts To Print in the Number line. What's more, when you tell QuickBooks to print the unprinted checks, what it really does is print the checks in the register that have To Print in the Number line. All this is of little practical value in most instances, but it results in several interesting possibilities.

For example, you can enter the checks that you want to print directly into the register — all you need to do is type **To Print** in the Number line. (Note that you can't enter an address anywhere in the register, so this process isn't practical if you want addresses printed on the checks.)

Another thing that you can do is to have a check that you've printed once print again by changing its check number from, for example, *007,* to *To Print.* The only reason I can think of for using this method is if you accidentally print a check on plain paper and you want to reprint it on a real check form.

Printing a Checking Register

You can print a Checking register or a register for any other account, too. Follow these steps to print a register:

1. **Select the account whose register you wish to print.**

   Open the chart of accounts window by choosing Lists⇨Chart of Accounts, and then highlight the account containing the register you want to print.

2. **Select an account.**

   Either double-click the account containing the register you want to print, or select it and click Use Register.

3. **Press Ctrl+P, or choose File⇨Print Register.**

   You see the Print Register dialog box (see Figure 10-7).

   For the Macintosh, the hot-key command for Print Register is ⌘+P.

Figure 10-7:
The Print
Register
dialog box.

Print Register	
Date Range	✓ OK
From 01/01/96	✗ Cancel
To 01/31/96	? Help
☐ Show transaction detail	

4. **Fill in the Date Range text boxes.**

   To print a register of something other than the current year-to-date transactions, use the From and To text boxes. This is pretty dang obvious, isn't it? You just move the cursor to the From and To text boxes and enter the range of months that the register should include.

5. **If you want, click the Show Transaction Detail check box.**

   As you know, a register does not show all the messy details, such as the Items and Expenses tab information. But you can click this check box to include all this stuff on your printed register.

6. **Click OK.**

   You see the standard Print Report dialog box (see Figure 10-8).

7. **If everything is copacetic, click OK.**

   You don't have to fool around with this dialog box. If you want to print a register pronto, just click OK, and QuickBooks sends the register on its merry way to your printer. Then again, if you're the sort of person who likes to fool around with this kind of stuff, carry on with the rest of these steps.

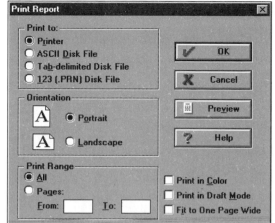

Figure 10-8:
The Print
Report
dialog box.

If you want to see the effect that the different settings in this dialog box have, just experiment. You can't hurt anything or anybody.

8. (Optional) Print the report to disk.

To print the report to disk as a text file, mark one of the following Print To option buttons:

- Click ASCII Disk File if you want to create a text file (for example, when you want to import the register into a word processing program).

- Click Tab-delimited Disk File to, for example, import the register into a database program (Oooh … fancy…).

- Click 123 (.PRN) Disk File to, for example, import the register into Lotus 1-2-3.

9. Choose the paper orientation.

The illustrations make this procedure pretty obvious. Which direction would you like the report to be printed — Portrait or Landscape? Just click the appropriate option button.

10. (Optional) Tell QuickBooks which pages to print.

Use the Print Range option buttons and text boxes to limit the pages for QuickBooks to print.

11. (Optional) Color your world.

If you have a color printer and want to print the register in color, click the Print In Color check box.

12. (Optional) Trade speed for quality.

Click the Print In Draft Mode check box to tell QuickBooks to print faster and spend less time worrying about the quality of the printing job. In other words, you can use this check box to trade print speed for print quality. Life is full of trade-offs, isn't it?

13. (Optional) One is the easiest number that you'll ever do.

If you want everything to fit on one page, click the Fit To One Page Wide check box. (If you specified a lot of transactions in the report, you're going to end up with some *tiny* type.)

14. (Optional) Check it out.

To see how your settings will affect the report before you actually print it, click Preview. QuickBooks shows you the results on the screen. This feature has probably saved more trees than can be imagined.

15. Click OK.

After you have the report exactly the way you want it (and not one moment before!), click OK, and QuickBooks finally prints the register.

The 5th Wave   By Rich Tennant

YEAH, BUT YOU SHOULD SEE HOW NICELY IT CENTERED EVERYTHING.

Chapter 11

A Matter of Balance

I want to start this chapter with an important point: Balancing a bank account in QuickBooks is easy and quick.

I'm not just trying to get you pumped up about an otherwise painfully boring topic. I don't think that balancing a bank account is any more exciting than you do. (At the Nelson house, we never answer the question, "What should we do tonight?" by saying, "Hey, let's balance an account.")

My point is this: Because bank account balancing can be tedious and boring, use QuickBooks to speed up the drudgery.

Selecting the Account You Want to Balance

This step is easy. And you probably already know how to do it, too.

To reconcile an account, make sure that all windows are closed, and then choose Activities⇨Reconcile. You see the Reconcile – Checking window, shown in Figure 11-1. Select the account that you want to balance. Use the arrow keys to highlight the account and then press Enter. Or, if you have a mouse, double-click the account. QuickBooks shows all outstanding checks or payments and all deposits to date.

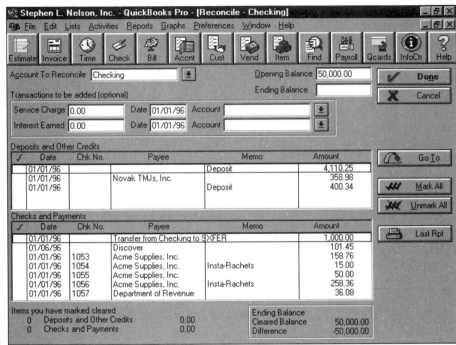

Figure 11-1:
The
Reconcile –
Checking
window.

As Figure 11-1 shows, the Reconcile – Checking window is basically just two lists — one of account withdrawals and one of account deposits. While reconciling your account, the dialog box also displays some extra information at the bottom of the screen. It shows you how many deposits and withdrawals you've marked as cleared, along with a total amount for each. It also shows the Cleared Balance (the dollar amount of the cleared checks and deposits you'll click off in the dialog box), and the Difference (the difference, if any, between what your bank says your balance is and what you say your balance is when you click off deposits and withdrawals). (You'll fill in the Ending Balance box with the balance shown on your bank statement, once we get started.)

Balancing a Bank Account

As I said, balancing a bank account is remarkably easy. In fact, I'll go so far as to say that if you have any problems, they'll stem from . . . well, sloppy record-keeping that preceded your use of QuickBooks.

Enough of this blather; let's get started.

Giving QuickBooks the information from the bank statement

As you probably know, in a reconciliation you compare your records of a bank account with the bank's records of the same account. You should be able to explain any difference between the two accounts — usually by pointing to checks that you've written but that haven't cleared. (Sometimes deposits fall into the same category; you've recorded a deposit and mailed it, but the bank hasn't yet credited your account.)

The first step, then, is to supply QuickBooks with the bank's account information. You get this information from your monthly statement. Supply QuickBooks with the figures it needs as follows:

1. **Verify the bank statement Opening Balance.**

   QuickBooks displays an amount in the Opening Balance text box. If this amount isn't correct, replace it with the correct one. You can do this because the number you enter here does not figure into any of the QuickBooks calculations. To change the Opening Balance amount, move the cursor to the text box and type over the given amount. (If this is the first time you've reconciled, QuickBooks gets this opening balance amount from your starting account balance. If you've reconciled before, QuickBooks uses the Ending Balance that you specified the last time you reconciled as the Opening Balance.)

   For more information, see the sidebar, "Why isn't my opening balance the same as the one in QuickBooks?"

2. **Enter the ending balance.**

   What is the ending, or closing, balance on your bank statement? Whatever it is, move the cursor to the Ending Balance text box and enter the ending balance.

3. **Enter the bank's service charge.**

   If the bank statement shows a service charge and you haven't already entered it, move the cursor to the Service Charge text box and enter the amount (for example, type **4.56** for $4.56).

4. **Enter a transaction date for the service charge transaction.**

   QuickBooks supplies the current system date from your computer's internal clock as the default service charge date. If this date isn't correct, enter the correct one.

   Remember that you can adjust a date one day at a time by using the plus (+) and minus (–) keys.

5. **Assign the bank's service charge to an account.**

   Enter the expense account to which you assign bank service charges in the first Account text box — the one beside the Date text box. Activate the drop-down list by clicking the down arrow, highlight the category by using the arrow keys, and press Enter. I bet anything that you record these charges in the Bank Service Charges account.

6. **Enter the account's interest income.**

   If the account earned interest for the month and you haven't already entered this figure, enter an amount in the Interest Earned text box (for example, type **.17** for $.17).

7. **Enter a transaction date for the interest income transaction.**

   You already know how to enter dates. I won't bore you by explaining it again (but see Step 4 if you're having trouble).

8. **Assign the interest to an account.**

   Enter the account to which this account's interest should be assigned in the second Account text box. I bet that you'll record this one under the Interest Income account, which is near the bottom of the Account drop-down list. To select a category from the Account list, activate the drop-down list by clicking the down arrow, highlight the category, and press Enter.

9. **Tell QuickBooks that the reconciliation is complete.**

   Just click OK.

Why isn't my opening balance the same as the one in QuickBooks?

If your opening balance isn't the same as the one shown in the Opening Balance text box, it could mean a couple of things. First, you may have mistakenly cleared a transaction the last time you reconciled. If you cleared a transaction last month that didn't go through until this month, your opening balance will be wrong. Go back to the Checking register and start examining transactions. The ones that have cleared have a check mark in the narrow column between the Payment and Deposit columns. If one of the checks that appears on this month's statement has a check mark, you made a boo-boo. From the Checking register, click the check mark to remove it. You'll be asked to confirm your actions. The check should now appear in the Reconcile – Checking window.

The other reason why the opening balance is different could be that a transaction that you cleared in the past got changed. If you deleted a transaction that occurred before this reconciliation period, for example, it threw your balance off. Why? Because the transaction that you deleted helped balance your account the last time around, but now that transaction is gone.

Whatever happens, do not fret. If worse comes to worst and you can't track down the faulty transaction, you can just have QuickBooks adjust the balance for you, as I explain later in this chapter.

Marking cleared checks and deposits

Now you need to tell QuickBooks which deposits and checks have cleared at the bank. (Refer to the bank statement for this information.)

   1. Identify the first deposit that has cleared.

   You know how to do so, I'm sure. Just leaf through the bank statement and find the first deposit listed.

   2. Mark the first cleared deposit as cleared.

   Scroll through the transactions listed in the Deposits And Other Credits section of the Reconcile – Checking window, find the deposit, and then click it. You also can highlight the deposit by using the Tab and arrow keys and then pressing Enter. QuickBooks places a check mark in front of the deposit to mark it as cleared and updates the cleared statement balance.

   If you have a large number of deposits to make and you can identify them quickly, click the Mark All button and then simply *unmark* the transactions that aren't on the bank statement. To *unmark* a transaction, click or select it. The check mark disappears.

   3. Record any cleared, but missing, deposits.

   If you can't find a deposit, you haven't entered it into the Checking register yet. I can only guess why you haven't entered it. Maybe you just forgot. In any event, go to the Control menu of the Reconcile window by clicking the little icon to the left of the menu bar and then choosing Minimize. The Reconcile window slams shut. Now open the Checking register and enter the deposit in the register in the usual way. To return to the Reconcile – Checking window, just double-click its icon at the bottom of the screen.

   4. Repeat Steps 1, 2, and 3 for all deposits listed on the bank statement.

   Make sure that the dates match and that the amounts of the deposits are also correct. If they're not, go back to the register and correct them. To get to the register, click the Go To button. You see the Write Checks or Make Deposits window where the transaction was originally recorded. Make the corrections there and click OK.

   5. Identify the first check that has cleared.

   No sweat, right? Just find the first check or withdrawal listed on the bank statement.

   6. Mark the first cleared check as cleared.

   Scroll through the transactions listed in the Reconcile – Checking window, find the first check, and then click it. You also can highlight it by pressing Tab and an arrow key and then pressing Enter. QuickBooks inserts a check mark to label this transaction as cleared and updates the cleared statement balance.

7. Record any missing, but cleared, checks.

If you can't find a check or withdrawal — guess what? — you haven't entered it in the register yet. Shrink the Reconcile – Checking window by opening its Control menu and choosing Mi<u>n</u>imize. Then display the Checking register, and enter the check or withdrawal. To return to the Reconcile – Checking window, double-click the icon for it.

8. Repeat Steps 5, 6, and 7 for withdrawals listed on the bank statement.

By the way, these steps don't take very long. Reconciling my account each month takes me about two minutes. And I'm not joking or exaggerating. By *two minutes,* I really mean two minutes.

If the difference equals zero

After you mark all the cleared checks and deposits, the difference between the Cleared Balance for the account and the bank statement's Ending Balance should equal zero. Notice that I said "should," not "will." Figure 11-2 shows a Reconcile – Checking window in which everything is hunky-dory, and life is grand.

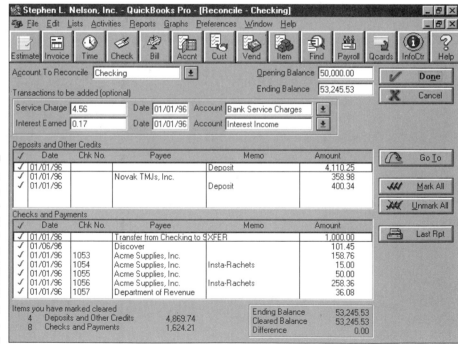

Figure 11-2: The Reconcile – Checking window filled in with the Ending Balance and Cleared Balance in agreement.

If the difference does equal zero, you're finished. Just click the Done button. QuickBooks displays a congratulatory message box telling you that the reconciliation is complete. As a reward for being such a good boy or girl, the message box asks you whether you want to print a free, all-expenses-paid Summary or Full reconciliation report. Click Summary or Full and click OK if you want to print the report. Otherwise, just click OK.

Can't decide whether to print the Reconciliation report? Unless you're a business bookkeeper or accountant who is reconciling a bank account for someone else — your employer or a client, for example — you don't need to print the Reconciliation report. All printing does is prove that you reconciled the account. (Basically, this proof is the reason why you should print the report if you are a bookkeeper or an accountant. The person for whom you're reconciling the account will know that you did your job and has a piece of paper to come back to later with any questions.)

Now the deposits, withdrawals, and checks that you just cleared are marked with a check mark in your register. If you don't believe me, open the register and find out.

If the difference doesn't equal zero

If the difference doesn't equal zero, you've got a problem. If you click Done, QuickBooks shows you the Reconcile Adjustment dialog box (see Figure 11-3). This dialog box tells you how unbalanced your account is and asks whether you want to adjust your maladjusted account.

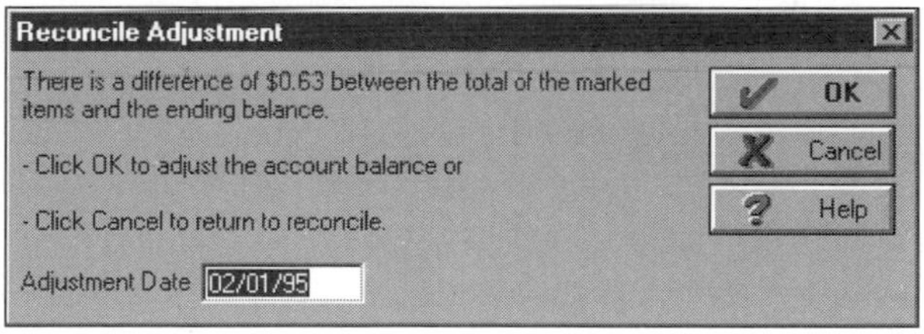

Figure 11-3:
The
Reconcile
Adjustment
dialog box.

Reconcile Adjustment

There is a difference of $0.63 between the total of the marked items and the ending balance.

- Click OK to adjust the account balance or

- Click Cancel to return to reconcile.

Adjustment Date 02/01/95

✓ OK

✗ Cancel

? Help

Click Cancel if you want to go back to the Reconcile – Checking window and start the search for the missing or incorrectly entered transaction.

If you want to force the two amounts to agree, click OK. Forcing the two amounts to agree isn't a very good idea. To do so, QuickBooks adds a cleared transaction equal to the difference. (I talk about this transaction a little later in the chapter.)

Postponing a reconciliation and not choosing to adjust the bank account balance is usually the best approach because it enables you to locate and correct problems. (The next section contains some ideas that can help you determine what the problem is.) Then you can restart the reconciliation and finish your work. (You restart a reconciliation the same way that you originate one.)

Ten Things You Should Do If Your Account Doesn't Balance

 I want to give you some suggestions for reconciling an account when you're having problems. If you're sitting in front of your computer wringing your hands, try the tips in this section.

- ✔ **Make sure that you are working with the right account.** Sounds dumb, doesn't it? If you have several different bank accounts, however, ending up in the wrong account is darn easy. So go ahead and confirm, for example, that you're trying to reconcile your checking account at Mammoth International Bank using the Mammoth International checking account statement.

- ✔ **Look for transactions that the bank has recorded but you haven't.** Go through the bank statement, and make sure that you have recorded every transaction that your bank has recorded. You can easily overlook cash machine withdrawals, special fees, or service charges (such as charges for checks or your safety deposit box), automatic withdrawals, direct deposits, and so on. If the difference is positive — that is, the bank thinks that you have less money than you think that you should have — you may be missing a withdrawal transaction. If the difference is negative, you may be missing a deposit transaction.

- ✔ **Look for reversed transactions.** Here's a tricky one. If you accidentally enter a transaction backward — a deposit as a withdrawal or a withdrawal as a deposit — your account won't balance. And the error can be difficult to find. The Reconcile – Checking window shows all the correct transactions, but a transaction amount appears positive when it should be negative or negative when it should be positive. The check that you wrote to Acme Housewreckers for the demolition of your carport appears as a positive number instead of a negative number, for example.

- ✔ **Look for a transaction that's equal to half the difference.** One handy way to find the transaction that you entered backward — *if* there's only one — is to look for a transaction that's equal to half the irreconcilable difference. If the difference is $200, for example, you may have entered a $100 deposit as a withdrawal or a $100 withdrawal as a check.

✔ **Look for a transaction that's equal to the difference.** While I'm on the subject of explaining the difference by looking at individual transactions, let me make an obvious point. If the difference between the bank's records and yours equals one of the transactions listed in your register, you may have incorrectly marked the transaction as cleared or incorrectly left the transaction unmarked (shown as uncleared). I don't know. Maybe that was *too* obvious. Naaaah.

✔ **Check for transposed numbers.** Transposed numbers occur when you flip-flop two digits in a number. For example, you enter $45.89 as $48.59. These turkeys always cause headaches for accountants and bookkeepers. If you look at the numbers, detecting an error is often difficult because the digits are the same. For example, when you compare a check amount of $45.89 in your register with a check for $48.59 shown on your bank statement, both check amounts show the same digits: *4, 5, 8,* and *9.* They just show them in different orders. Transposed numbers are tough to find, but here's a trick that you can try. Divide the difference shown on the Reconcile – Checking window by 9. If the result is an even number of dollars or cents, chances are good that there's a transposed number somewhere.

✔ **Have someone else look over your work.** This idea may seem pretty obvious, but it amazes me how often a second pair of eyes can find something that you've been overlooking. Ask one of your coworkers (preferably that one person who always seems to have way too much free time) to look over everything for you.

✔ **Be on the lookout for multiple errors.** By the way, if you find an error using this laundry list and there's still a difference, it's a good idea to start checking at the top of the list again. You may, for example, discover after you find a transposed number that you entered another transaction backward or incorrectly cleared or uncleared a transaction.

✔ **Try again next month (and maybe the month after that).** If the difference isn't huge in relation to the size of your bank account, you may want to wait until next month and attempt to reconcile your account again. Before my carefree attitude puts you in a panic, consider the following example. In January, you reconcile your account, and the difference is $24.02. Then you reconcile the account in February, and the difference is $24.02. You reconcile the account in March and, surprise, surprise, the difference is still $24.02. What's going on here? Well, your starting account balance was probably off by $24.02. (The more months you try to reconcile your account and find that you're always mysteriously $24.02 off, the more likely it is that this type of error is to blame.) After the second or third month, I think that it's pretty reasonable to have QuickBooks enter an adjusting transaction for $24.02 so that your account balances. (In my opinion, this is the only circumstance that merits your adjusting an account to match the bank's figure.) By the way, if you've successfully reconciled your account with QuickBooks before, your work may not be at fault. The mistake could be (drum roll, please) the bank's! And in this case, there's something else you should do. . . .

✔ **Get in your car, drive to the bank, and beg for help.** As an alternative to the preceding idea — which supposes that the bank's statement is correct and that your records are incorrect — I propose this idea: Ask the bank to help you reconcile the account. Hint that you think that the mistake is probably the bank's, but in a very nice, cordial way. Smile a lot. And one other thing — be sure to ask about whatever product the bank is currently advertising in the lobby. (This will encourage the staff to think that you're interested in that 180-month certificate of deposit, and they'll be extra nice to you.) In general, the bank's record-keeping is usually pretty darn good. I've never had a problem as a business banking client or as an individual. (I've also been lucky enough to deal with big, well-run banks.) Nevertheless, it's quite possible that your bank has made a mistake, so ask for help. Be sure to ask for an explanation of any transactions that you've learned about only by seeing them on your bank statement. By the way, you'll probably pay for this help.

Chapter 12

Payroll

. . . .

In This Chapter

▶ Creating payroll accounts

▶ Requesting an employer ID number

▶ Obtaining withholding information

▶ Computing an employee's gross wages, payroll deductions, and net wages

▶ Recording a payroll check in QuickBooks

▶ Making federal tax deposits

▶ Preparing quarterly and annual payroll tax returns

▶ Producing annual wage statements, such as W-2s

▶ Handling state payroll taxes

. . . .

*T*he publisher and I went round and round on whether this chapter should describe how to prepare payroll checks with QuickBooks or with QuickPay, an add-on payroll preparation tool that Intuit used to make and sell. It was a terrible fight. Name calling. Arm twisting. Eye scratching.

In the end, we decided to describe how you do payroll using QuickBooks for a pretty darn simple reason: If you're going to do payroll, QuickBooks is the only real way to make things easy.

Getting Ready to Do Payroll

To prepare payroll checks and summarize the payroll information that you need to prepare quarterly and annual returns, you need to set up some special accounts. You also need to do some paperwork. This section describes how to do both tasks.

Making sure that QuickBooks is ready

The very first thing you should do before starting this process is to choose Help⇨About Tax Table from the QuickBooks menu. You should get a window that looks incredibly similar to the one shown in Figure 12-1. This window tells you the tax information that QuickBooks is currently using. If, for any reason, you think that your information may not be up to date, follow the instructions in the window and call the Intuit number to check it.

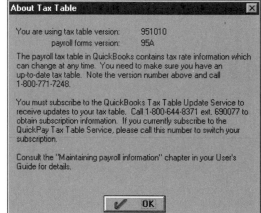

About Tax Table

You are using tax table version: 951010
        payroll forms version: 95A

The payroll tax table in QuickBooks contains tax rate information which can change at any time. You need to make sure you have an up-to-date tax table. Note the version number above and call 1-800-771-7248.

You must subscribe to the QuickBooks Tax Table Update Service to receive updates to your tax table. Call 1-800-644-8371 ext. 690077 to obtain subscription information. If you currently subscribe to the QuickPay Tax Table Service, please call this number to switch your subscription.

Consult the "Maintaining payroll information" chapter in your User's Guide for details.

✔ OK

Figure 12-1:
The About
Tax Table
window.

To do payroll in QuickBooks, you need several liability accounts, a payroll expense account, and several payroll expense subaccounts. Fortunately, none of this is particularly difficult. In fact, as long as you use a standard chart of accounts, QuickBooks sets up these accounts for you when you set up the QuickBooks company.

Figure 12-2 shows the Payroll Item List dialog box. It includes several employee wage accounts, employee withholding accounts, and employer tax accounts. To see whether your QuickBooks company has the needed payroll accounts set up, choose Lists⇨Payroll Items from the menu.

You may need to add items if any of the following apply to your business: state taxes (such as withholding tax, disability, and unemployment taxes), local taxes (county, city, and district taxes), bonuses, commissions, and so on. In other words, you need an item for anything that may appear on a paycheck. In the example here, we will only go over the federal tax items. (If this worries you, skip to the next section, "What about other taxes and deductions?" for a quick explanation, and I think you'll be comforted.)

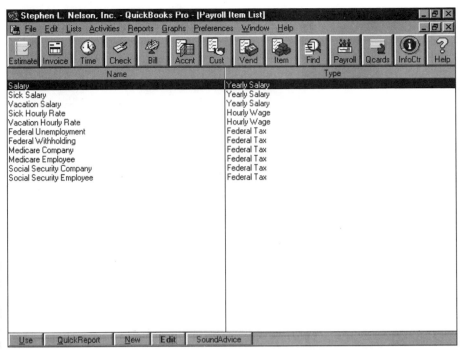

Figure 12-2:
The Payroll
Item List
dialog box.

Note that you will need a *separate* item for each category to be tracked. For example, you need separate categories for State Withholding, State Disability, and State Unemployment — you don't want to lump them all under State Expenses, or the QuickBooks tracking systems will have problems.

If you told QuickBooks that you were going to use it for your payroll while you were originally installing the program, and you didn't delete the payroll accounts, your Payroll Item List is probably ready or close to it.

What about other taxes and deductions?

If you have other payroll expense, withholding, or employer tax accounts that you need to set up and you understand the taxes shown in Figure 12-2 — and you will after you read a bit more — you'll have no trouble dealing with other employee withholding or other employer taxes. You treat local income taxes, for example, basically the same way that you treat federal or state income tax. And another employer payroll tax should be treated the same way that you treat the employer-paid portions of social security taxes.

To add a new account, open the Payroll Item List (if it isn't open already) and click the New button at the bottom of the window. Figure 12-3 shows the New Deduction Payroll Item dialog box.

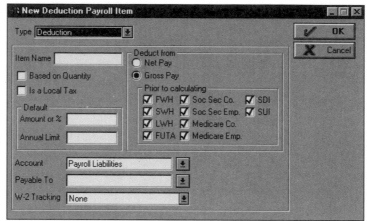

Figure 12-3:
The New
Deduction
Payroll Item
dialog box.

First, activate the Type drop-down list box, and then take a look at the different categories. When you change them, the dialog box changes, asking for different information, according to the type. Most of these are pretty self-explanatory, but you'll notice that, if you currently have someone doing your payroll, you'll have to enlist his or her help on this part. Much of the work will be in collecting the information you need for each category.

In fact, the only things you need to be careful about are those affecting employees' gross pay for income taxes but not their social security taxes — things such as 401K deductions and certain fringe benefits. If you have these kinds of things to deal with and you need help, just ask your accountant. (Providing general answers that will work for everyone who reads this book is just too difficult — and actually kind of dangerous, too. Sorry.)

Setting up the employees

No, I don't mean I'm advocating a scam. I'm talking about putting in all the applicable information so that QuickBooks can calculate their paychecks properly. (I'm shocked you even thought that! You cad!)

Choose List⇨Employees from the menu, and something akin to Figure 12-4 appears. Your first job will be to create a template containing all the defaults for inputting employees' information.

Figure 12-4:
The
Employee
List window.

Creating an employee template

1. **Bring up the Template dialog box.**

   While in the Employees List dialog box, click the Template button at the bottom of the Employees List window, and you should see Figure 12-5. Change the template to show the information that applies to most of your employees. Any changes you make to this template will show up every time you input information for a new employee. And don't worry if there are a few exceptions — you can change them on an individual basis whenever you need to.

2. **Choose the pay period that is appropriate to a majority of your employees.**

   Pretty self-explanatory, right? This information goes in the Pay Period drop-down list box. Whatever you deem appropriate for your pay period is fine with QuickBooks.

3. **(Optional) Fill in a yearly salary if most employees have the same salary.**

   Frankly, I doubt you'll need this one, but in the interest of completeness and an inappropriate desire for closure, I thought I'd mention it.

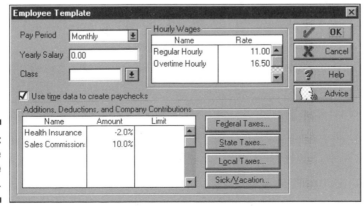

Figure 12-5:
The
Employee
Template.

4. (Optional) Have some class.

If you're using classes to track your employees, go ahead and choose a default. In order to do so, you have to check the Use Class Tracking check box in the Transaction Preferences dialog box. (You can see it by choosing Preferences⇨Transactions from the menu.)

5. (Optional) Time Tracking, twentieth century style.

Your employees may be paid by the hour, rather than annually, just to make it easier for them to pay their rent. If so, click this check box. (If it doesn't appear, choose Preferences⇨Time Tracking from the menu and complete the resulting dialog box.) Fill in the Hourly Wages table if there are standard wages you use.

6. Most of The Rest of The Story.

You can use the Additions, Deductions, and Company Contributions table for any additional items — from additional sales commissions to deductions for health insurance. The Amount column can be either an amount or a percentage, whichever is best for the situation.

The Federal Taxes button brings up a series of check boxes that you can use to describe the federal taxes your employees pay.

The State Taxes button brings up one reason why you should be sure that you have the current QuickBooks tax tables. You use the drop-down list boxes to enter the state withholding, unemployment, and disability taxes. When you indicate the state, QuickBooks automatically allows you to set up items and accounts according to the needs of your state. (If you want to play around with it, try comparing California and Washington.) Not only that, but the tax rates are automatically computed from the aforementioned tax tables.

Local taxes apply only in a few instances, mostly in New York. See the drop-down list box to see whether you're on the list or not.

7. The Rest of The Rest of The Story — The Sick & Vacation Template.

Pressing the Sick\Vacation button brings up, in a flurry of movement, the Sick & Vacation Template dialog box, as seen in Figure 12- 6. (Boy, my heart started beating faster. Didn't yours?)

First, consideration is the accrual period. Are you going to give your employees a lump amount of time at the beginning of the year or increments for every pay period? That, of course, has a distinct effect on the next two text boxes — the first indicates how many hours you want to give them for each pay period, the next indicates the maximum amount of time they can accrue. Keep them straight unless you want to give your employees 96 hours of sick time every month. (And, if you do, I'd like to apply for a position.)

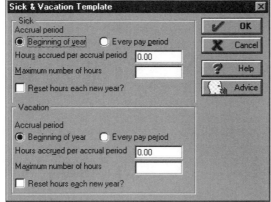

Figure 12-6:
The heart-
stopping
excitement
of the Sick
& Vacation
Template.

Finally, do the employees get to keep any sick or vacation hours they haven't used from one year to the next? If not, check the Reset Hours Each New Year? box.

8. Click OK.

QuickBooks, to no one's surprise, obeys your every bidding. You're done!

Well, the template's finished. You're ready to start inputting the actual employees. And, thanks to the legwork you've done, doing so will be a snap.

Putting employees in their place

For this step, you'll want to have the usual employee stuff handy — their W-4 forms and that kind of thing.

1. Bring up the New Employee dialog box.

Assuming that you've already chosen List⇨Employees, click the New button at the bottom of the window. Figure 12-7 appears, which shows the New Employee dialog box open to the Address Info tab, which you've already seen a couple of million times. Go ahead and fill it out, but don't click any buttons yet.

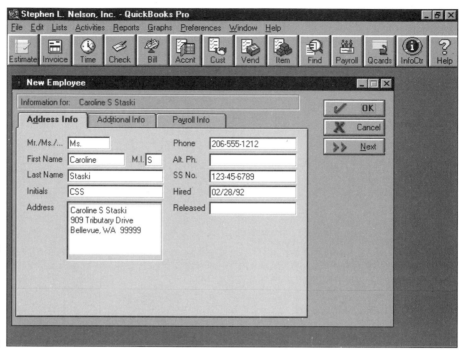

Figure 12-7:
A sample
employee's
address
info.

2. Click the Payroll Info tab.

Still another figure, this one resembling Figure 12-8, shows up on the scene. As you may have surmised, all the defaults you just input are there. By moving around to the different fields, either by clicking or using the Tab key, you can change any of the information. For example, by first clicking the Federal Taxes button, I've changed the default screen to Figure 12-9, when I added the information that Caroline may have given the company on her W-4 form when she was originally hired.

When you have gone through everything and set up the template, the rest is almost too easy. If, however, you need to change the template, just go back into the Employee List again, press the Template button, and change anything you need to change. You can fine-tune the template to your heart's content. Should you need to change an individual employee's information, go to the Employee List, highlight the employee by clicking his or her name, and then press the Edit button. Simple. Easy. Everything you could ask in payroll refreshment.

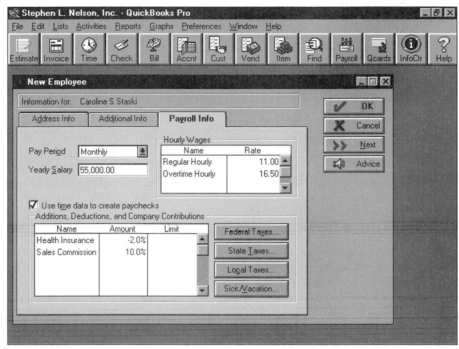

Figure 12-8:
The Payroll
Info tab
again.

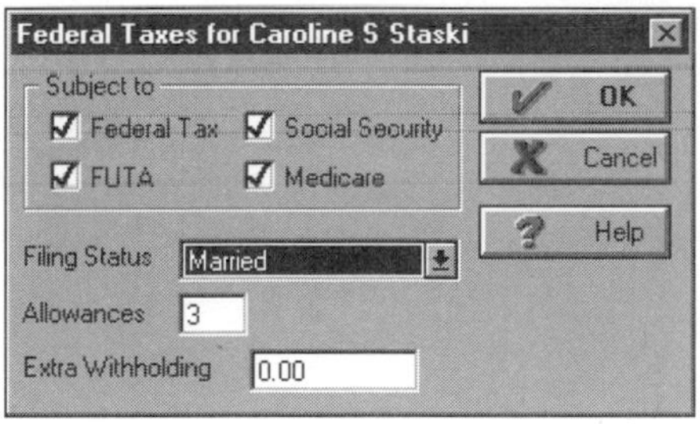

Figure 12-9:
The Federal
Taxes dialog
box again.

3. **Click OK.**

   After you've made any changes, click OK, and move on.

Doing taxes the right way

You need another thing if you want to do payroll the right way. If you want to do payroll the wrong way, you're reading the wrong book.

Getting an employer ID number

First, you need to file an SS-4, or Request for Employer Identification Number form, with the Internal Revenue Service (IRS) so you can get an employer identification number. You can get this form by calling the IRS and asking for one. Or if you have a friend who's an accountant, that person may have one of these forms. (See, there *is* a reason to invite people like me to your dinner parties.)

In one of its cooler moves, the IRS changed its ways. Now you can apply for and receive an employer identification number over the telephone. You still need to fill out the SS-4 form, however, so you can answer the questions that the IRS asks during the short telephone-application process. (You also need to mail or fax the form to the IRS after you have your little telephone conversation.)

Having employees do their part

You also need to do something else before you can know how to handle all those taxes — you need to have each of your employees fill out a W-4 form to tell you what filing status they will use and how many personal exemptions they will claim. Guess where you get blank W-4 forms? That's right . . . from your friendly IRS agent.

Paying Your Employees

After you have your payroll accounts set up and get an employer identification number, you're ready to pay someone. This section is going to blow your mind, especially if you've been doing payroll manually. It will make your whole decision to use QuickBooks to do your payroll worthwhile. Ready?

1. **Start the payroll process.**

   Either choose A̲ctivities⇨P̲ayroll⇨P̲ay Employees or just press the Payroll button on the iconbar. The Select Employees To Pay dialog box appears, as shown in Figure 12-10.

2. **Change any settings that you want to.**

   Unless you're not going to print the checks — maybe you handwrite them and just use QuickBooks to keep the books — leave the To B̲e Printed check box checked.

   Indicate the Bank Account from which the employees are paid in the appropriate drop-down list box.

   I'd suggest leaving the Enter Hours And Preview Check Before Creating option button marked, just in case.

   Set the Check Date and the Pay Period Ends dates appropriately.

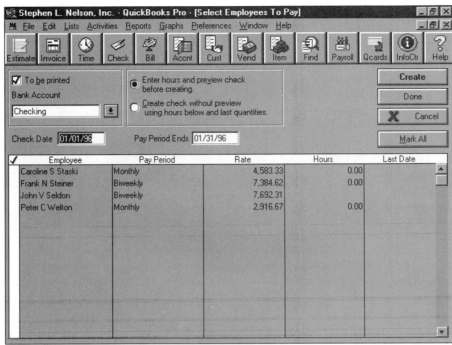

Figure 12-10:
The Select
Employees
To Pay
dialog box.

3. Select the employees whom you are paying.

If you are paying all the employees listed, just click the Mark All button on the right-hand side of the screen. If you need to mark them individually, just click in the left-hand column — the one with the check in the heading.

4. Click Create.

Watch this. QuickBooks does all the calculations and then gives you a window similar to the one shown in Figure 12-11. Everything is calculated and filled out for you. If some information is inaccurate, simply click the amount and change it, either deleting it or replacing it with the correct information.

You might also note that QuickBooks keeps totals both for the current check and for the year to date.

5. Click Create. (Yes, again.)

Once everything is set to your satisfaction, click Create. After you've checked all the employees' paychecks, QuickBooks returns to the Select Employees To Pay dialog box.

6. Click Done.

Just because you are.

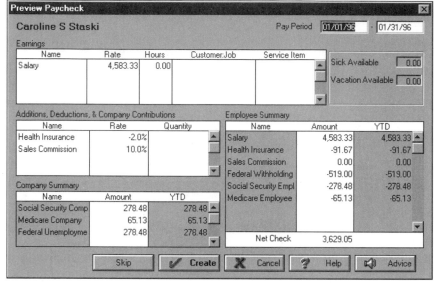

Figure 12-11:
The Preview
Paycheck
window —
what a
program,
eh?

To print the checks, just choose File⇨Print Forms⇨Print Paychecks, and the Select Paychecks To Print window appears (see Figure 12-12). Choose the checks you want to print, make sure that the printer is loaded with the forms, and then click OK. From then on, it's like printing any other check — except it pays an employee's wages and not some vendor. The same old Print Checks window appears, which you have seen many, many times by now, and so on, and so on.

Note: If you have questions about printing employee payroll checks, refer back to Chapter 10.

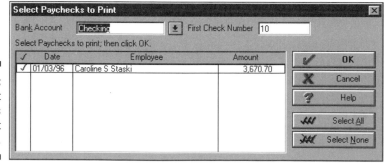

Figure 12-12:
The Select
Paychecks
To Print
window.

Making Deposits to Uncle Sam

Make no mistake. Big Brother wants the money you withhold from an employee's payroll check for federal income taxes, social security, and medicare. Big Brother also wants the payroll taxes you owe — the matching social security and medicare taxes, federal unemployment taxes, and so on. So every so often you need to pay Big Brother the amounts you owe.

Making this payment is actually simple. Just write a check equal to the account balances shown in the payroll tax liability accounts.

You do this by choosing Activities⇨Payroll⇨Pay Liabilities/Taxes from the menu, whereupon the Pay Liabilities dialog box appears, as shown in Figure 12-13.

All you have to do now is choose the liabilities or taxes that you want to pay, by clicking in the left-hand column and indicating the portion you want to pay of the amount due. Unless you've clicked the Preview Liability Check To Enter Expenses/Penalties check box at the bottom of the screen, QuickBooks automatically writes the check and puts it in your register. QuickBooks automatically gives the check the appropriate date and schedules it to pop up in your Reminders window at the right time.

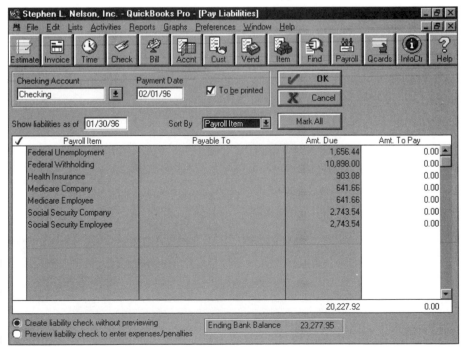

Figure 12-13: The Pay Liabilities dialog box.

When do you make payroll tax deposits? That's a question that frequently comes up. The general rule about United States federal tax deposits is this: If your accumulated payroll taxes are less than $500 for the quarter, you can just pay the taxes the following month with your quarterly return. This is called the *De Minimis* rule. (My understanding is that the law was named after Congresswoman Dee Minimis.) If you owe $500 or more, other special rules come into play that determine whether you pay deposits monthly, semi-monthly, weekly, or even immediately. The IRS tells you, by the way, how often you're supposed to make payments.

If you owe a large amount of money, you're required to deposit it almost immediately. For example, if you owe $100,000 or more, you need to make the payroll tax deposit by the next banking day. Some nuances apply to these rules, so unless you don't owe very much and, therefore, can fall back on the *De Minimis* rule, you may want to consult a real, live tax adviser (or call the Internal Revenue Service).

Paying tax deposits in QuickBooks is easy, so a good rule of thumb when you are writing payroll checks is to make the last checks you write the ones that pay your federal and state tax deposits. You'll never get into late-payment trouble if you follow this approach.

To make a payroll tax deposit, just deliver your check with a federal tax deposit coupon to a financial institution that is qualified as a depository for federal taxes or to the Federal Reserve bank that serves your geographical area. The IRS should have already sent you a book of coupons as a result of your asking for an employer ID number. And one other thing: Make your check payable to the depository or to the Federal Reserve.

Preparing Quarterly Payroll Tax Returns

At the end of every quarter, you need to file a quarterly payroll tax return. (By *quarters* here, I'm referring to calendar quarters. You don't have to file these returns four times on a Sunday afternoon as you or your couch-potato spouse watch football.)

If you're a business owner, for example, you must file a Form 941, which is just a form that you fill out to say how much you paid in gross wages, how much you withheld in federal taxes, and how much you owe for employer payroll taxes.

If you have household employees, such as a nanny, you must file a Form 942. Again, Form 942 is just a form you fill out to say how much you paid in gross wages, withheld in federal taxes, and owe in payroll taxes.

You'll find that filling out these forms is darn simple. All you really need to know is what the gross wages totals are.

To get the gross wages totals and the balances in each of the payroll tax liability accounts at the end of the quarter, print the Payroll report. Choose Reports⇨Payroll Reports⇨Employee Journal. QuickBooks displays the Employee Journal Report (see Figure 12-14). Specify the range of dates as the start and end of the quarter for which you're preparing a quarterly report.

The column totals show the gross wages upon which your employer payroll taxes are calculated. Note that the employee journal provides a bunch of different columns that detail your payroll expenses. So what you're really interested in are the columns and totals that show any payroll item that is, essentially, wages: salary, hourly pay, bonuses, commissions, and so on.

The withholding account amounts are the amounts you have recorded to date for the employee's federal income taxes withheld and the employee's social security and medicare taxes — so you need to double these figures to get the actual social security and medicare taxes owed. Choose Reports⇨Payroll Reports⇨Liabilities By Item, and QuickBooks creates a report similar to Figure 12-15.

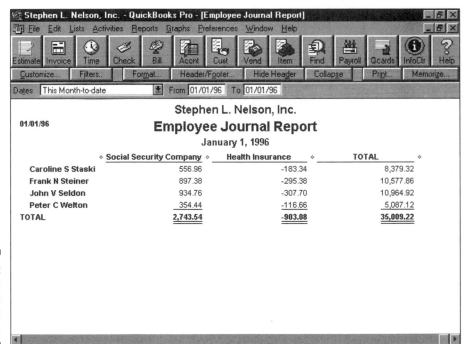

Figure 12-14:
The
Employee
Journal
Report.

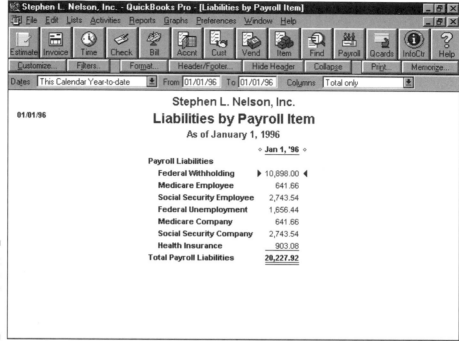

Figure 12-15:
The
Liabilities by
Payroll Item
report.

By the way, if your accountant is the person who will fill out the 941 or 942, you don't even need to read this stuff. Your accountant won't have any problem completing the quarterly payroll tax return using the QuickBooks Payroll report, and in fact — I kid you not — your accountant will probably even enjoy it.

About Annual Returns and Wage Statements

At the end of the year, you need to file some annual returns — such as the 940 federal unemployment tax return — and the W-2 and W-3 wages statements.

As a practical matter, the only thing that's different about filling out these reports is that you need to use a Payroll report that covers the entire year, not just a single quarter. So you need to enter the range of dates in the report window as January 1 and December 31.

Use the Payroll Summary by Employee report as the basis for preparing your employees' W-2s. To produce this report, choose Reports➪Payroll Reports➪ Summary by Employee.

The 940 annual return is darn easy if you've been wrestling with the 941 quarterly returns. The 940 annual return works the same basic way as those more-difficult quarterly tax returns. You print the old Payroll report, enter a few numbers, and then write a check for the amount you owe.

Note that you need to prepare any state unemployment annual summary before you prepare the 940 because the 940 requires information from the state returns.

For the W-2 statements and the summary W-3 (which summarizes your W-2s), you just print the old Payroll report and then, carefully following directions, enter the gross wages, the social security and medicare taxes withheld, and the federal income taxes withheld in the appropriate blanks.

If you have a little trouble, call the IRS. If you have a great deal of trouble, splurge and have someone else fill out the forms for you. Filling out these forms doesn't take a rocket scientist, by the way. Any experienced bookkeeper can do it for you.

Please don't construe my "rocket scientist" comment as personal criticism if this payroll taxes business seems terribly complicated. My experience is that some people — and you may very well be one of them — just don't have an interest in things such as payroll accounting. If, on the other hand, you're a "numbers are my friend" kind of person, you'll have no trouble at all after you learn the ropes.

The State Wants Some Money, Too

Yeah. I haven't talked about state payroll taxes — at least not in any great detail. I wish that I could provide this sort of detailed, state-specific help to you. Unfortunately, doing so would make this chapter about 150 pages long. It would also cause me to go stark, raving mad.

My sanity and laziness aside, however, you still need to deal with state payroll taxes. Let me say, however, that you apply to state payroll taxes the same basic mechanics that you apply to federal payroll taxes. For example, a state income tax works the same way as the federal income tax; employer-paid state unemployment taxes work like the employer-paid federal taxes; and employee-paid state taxes work like the employee-paid social security and medicare taxes.

If you've tuned in to how federal payroll taxes work in QuickBooks, you really shouldn't have a problem with the state payroll taxes — at least, not in terms of mechanics.

Chapter 13

Cool Report Options

● ●

● ●

*O*ne of the fastest ways to find out whether your business is thriving or diving is to use the QuickBooks Reports feature. The different kinds of reports in QuickBooks cover everything from invoices to missing checks, not to mention QuickReports. *QuickReports* are summary reports that you can get from the information on forms, account registers, or lists by merely clicking the mouse.

This chapter tells you how to prepare reports, how to print them, and how to customize reports for your special needs.

What Kinds of Reports Are There, Anyway?

If you are running a small business, you don't need all the reports that QuickBooks offers, but many of these reports are extremely useful. Reports can tell you how healthy or unhealthy your business is, where your profits are, and where you're wasting time and squandering resources.

To make sense of what may otherwise become mass confusion, QuickBooks arranges all its reports into categories, with two additional reports at the end of the menu. You can see what the ten categories are by pulling down the Reports menu (see Figure 13-1). The names of the reports read a bit like PBS documentary names, don't they? "Tonight, Joob Taylor explores the mazelike federal budget in 'Budget Reports.'" (The last two menu items, QuickReport and Memorized Reports, are explained later in this chapter.) You select a report category to see a list of actual report names. Figure 13-2 shows the Profit & Loss reports submenu.

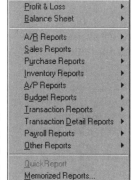

Figure 13-1:
The Reports
menu.

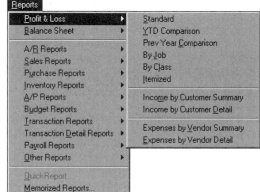

Figure 13-2:
The Profit &
Loss
Reports
submenu.

Table 13-1 describes reports by category, along with a short description of the major reports in each category. To get a thorough description of a particular report, go to the Help feature. To find out what a Standard report does, for example, start with a clear QuickBooks screen — no lists or windows open. Press F1 to open Help and click the Reports, Graphs, and Budgets button. Click Creating Reports, Types of Reports, and finally Profit and Loss Reports. You see a description of each profit-and-loss report type, beginning with the Standard report.

Table 13-1	QuickBooks Report Categories
Report Category	**Description**
Profit & Loss	These reports give you a bird's-eye view of the health of your company. They show income, expenses, and net profit or loss over time. You can group the expense and income data by job, class, item, or customer.
Balance Sheet	These reports give you a snapshot of your assets, liabilities, and equity. You can compare your present financial condition with your past financial condition and group information by account type.
A/R Reports	These Accounts Receivable reports are great for finding out where you stand in regard to your customer invoices. You can list unpaid invoices and group them in various ways, including by customer, job, and aging status.
Sales Reports	These reports show what you have sold and who your customers are. You can see your sales by item, by customer, or by sales representative.
Purchase Reports	These reports show from whom you bought, what you bought, and how much you paid. You can list purchases by item or by vendor. One handy report shows any outstanding purchase orders.
Inventory Reports	These reports help answer the all-important question, "What do I have in stock?" You can get an enormous amount of detail from these reports. For example, you can find out how much of an item you have on hand and how much you have on order. You can group inventory by vendor or by item. If you need price lists, you can print them using a special report from your QuickBooks file.
A/P Reports	These Accounts Payable reports tell you everything you need to know about your unpaid bills. You can list bills in a variety of ways, including by vendor and by aging status. This category also includes a report for determining sales tax liability.
Budget Reports	These reports show you once and for all whether your budgeting skills are realistic. You can view budgets by job, by month, or by balance sheet account. Then you can compare the budgets to actual income and expense totals. (You need to have a budget already set up to use this report — something I discuss in Chapter 15.)

(continued)

Table 13-1 *(continued)*

Report Category	Description
Transaction Reports	These reports list individual transactions — by date, vendor, or customer.
Transaction Detail Reports	These reports not only list the individual transactions but also add a column to give you the current balance of each entry. They can be listed by account, date, vendor, or customer.
Payroll Reports	These three reports offer ways of tracking your payroll or checking your payroll liability accounts. Believe me, these reports come in handy.
Other Reports	This catch-all category includes reports for estimating cash flow, listing missing checks, summarizing debits and credits, and showing transactions that were voided or modified. (If you're an accountant, you'll find all your favorites here.)

Creating and Printing a Report

After you decide what report you need, all you have to do is select it from the appropriate menu. To create a Standard report, for example, choose Reports⇨Profit & Loss⇨Standard.

Depending on how much data QuickBooks has to process, you may see a Building Report box before the report appears on the screen in all its glory. Figure 13-3 shows a Standard Profit and Loss report, also called an *income statement*. (If you see a Customize Report dialog box on the screen instead of a report, the check box for Display Customize Report Window Automatically is checked in the Reporting Preferences dialog box that you see when you choose Preferences⇨Reporting. For now, just click OK to see your report.)

You can't see the entire on-screen version of a report unless your report is very small (or your screen is monstrously large). Use the PgUp and PgDn keys to scroll up and down and the Tab and Shift+Tab keys to move left and right. Or, if you're a mouse lover, you can click and drag various pieces of the scrollbars.

To print a report, click the Print button under the icon bar. QuickBooks displays the Print Report dialog box shown in Figure 13-4. To accept the given specifications, which are almost always fine, just click the Print button. You'll never guess what happens next: QuickBooks prints the report!

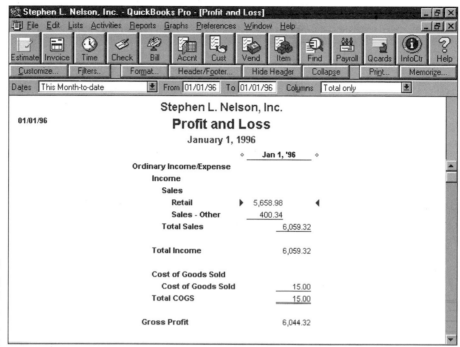

Figure 13-3:
A Standard
Profit and
Loss report.

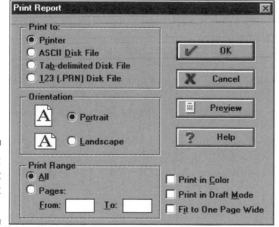

Figure 13-4:
The Print
Report
dialog box.

Before I forget, you can use the Print To option buttons to tell QuickBooks
where it should send the report it produces: to the printer or to an ASCII,
tab-delimited, or (.PRN) PRN disk file. The Orientation setting tells QuickBooks
how the report is supposed to appear on the paper. The Print Range settings
specify the pages you want to print. And I think that the three check boxes are
probably pretty self-evident.

You also can preview the report by clicking the Preview button. The next section of the chapter describes how some of the options for the preview work.

Visiting the report dog-and-pony show

You can do some neat things with the reports you create. Here is a quick rundown of some of the most valuable tricks.

QuickZooming mysterious figures

If you don't understand where a number in a report comes from, point to it with the mouse. As you point to numbers, QuickBooks changes the mouse pointer to a magnifying glass marked with a *Z*. Double-click the mouse to have QuickBooks display a list of all the transactions that make up that number.

This feature, called *QuickZoom,* is extremely handy for understanding the figures that appear on reports. All you have to do is double-click any mysterious-looking figure in a report. QuickBooks immediately tells you exactly how it arrived at that figure.

Sharing report data with spreadsheets

If you use a Windows spreadsheet program, such as Microsoft Excel for Windows 95, 1-2-3 for Windows, or Quattro Pro for Windows, you can print the report to a tab-delimited disk file by marking the Tab-delimited Disk File option button in the Print Report dialog box and then clicking OK (see Figure 13-4). This dialog box is the one that QuickBooks displays when you click the Print button at the top of the report document window. When you select the Tab-delimited Disk File button, QuickBooks displays the Create Disk File dialog box shown in Figure 13-5.

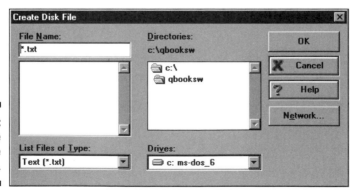

Figure 13-5:
The Create
Disk File
dialog box.

Enter a filename for the new spreadsheet file in the File Name text box. If you're using a PC, whatever name you enter must be a valid DOS name. (As long as you use eight or fewer letters or numbers, you'll be fine.)

Use the Directories and Drives list boxes to specify where you want the file located. For example, to stick the file on another disk — such as a floppy disk — activate the Drives drop-down list box and click the disk you want.

You don't have to fiddle with the List Files of Type drop-down list box, by the way. QuickBooks automatically uses the file extension, .TXT for tab-delimited disk files that you create.

To work with the new file from inside a spreadsheet program, start the spreadsheet program first. Then open or input the file. (In Excel, open the new disk file by using the File⇨Open command, and make sure that the Files of Type box is set to either Text File or All Files.)

Sharing report data with word processing programs

You can share report data with a word processing program, too. No sweat. While you're looking at the report you want to work with, click the Print button. Then, all you do is click the ASCII Disk File option button under the Print To area in the Print Report dialog box (see Figure 13-4). Then you click the OK button to "print" the report to a file and use the Create Disk File dialog box to name the file you want to print your report to (see Figure 13-5).

To work with the new file from inside a word processing program, you start the word processing program and then open the new file. (Again, watch the filename extensions. For example, Microsoft Word's default looks only for files ending with .DOC so unless the File Type is set properly, you won't find the report on the list of files.)

You can share report data with a word processing program, too. No sweat. Just follow these steps:

1. **Click the Print button at the top of the report document window.**

   The Print Report dialog box shown in Figure 13-4 appears from within the recesses of QuickBooks.

2. **Click the ASCII Disk File option button in the Print Report dialog box.**

3. **Click OK.**

   QuickBooks needs a name for the ASCII file.

4. **Name that file.**

   Use the Create Disk File dialog box shown in Figure 13-5 to name the file. You can name the file whatever you want, but don't name it after me. I don't want any more little Steve Nelsons running around this planet.

5. **To work with the new file from inside a word processing program, start the word processing program.**

6. **Choose File⇨Open.**

7. **Change the filename extension to .txt, if necessary.**

8. **Find your QuickBook file, click OK, and thar she be — your QuickBook report ready for you to use.**

Editing and rearranging reports

You may have noticed that, when QuickBooks displays the report document window, it also displays a row of buttons: Customize, Filters, Format, Header/Footer, Hide Header, Collapse, Print, and Memorize (see Figure 13-3). Below this toolbar are some drop-down list boxes that have to do with dates and a drop-down list called Columns. (Not all of these are available in every report document window. I don't know why, really. Maybe just to keep you guessing.)

You don't need to worry about these buttons. Read through the discussion that follows only if you're feeling comfortable, relaxed, and truly mellow, okay?

Customizing

The Customize button works pretty much the same no matter what report shows in the report document window.

When you click this button, QuickBooks displays the Customize Report dialog box (see Figure 13-6). From this dialog box, you change the time period that the report covers (in Report Dates), add extra columns in the report (in Columns), and choose between basing the report on expected payments (the Accrual option) or payments already made (the Cash option). I suggest marking the Accrual option so that you can use accrual-based accounting. If you're curious as to why, read Appendix B.

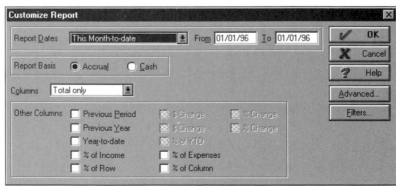

Figure 13-6:
The
Customize
Report
dialog box.

Filtering

Click the Filters button to *filter* a report. (I don't know how they came up with the term *filter*. Maybe the programmers had one of those aquarium screen savers.) Filtering is a little like sorting a database in that you use the Filter Transactions dialog box (see Figure 13-7) to tell QuickBooks what data to include and exclude in the report. You have a large number of choices here, and more power to you.

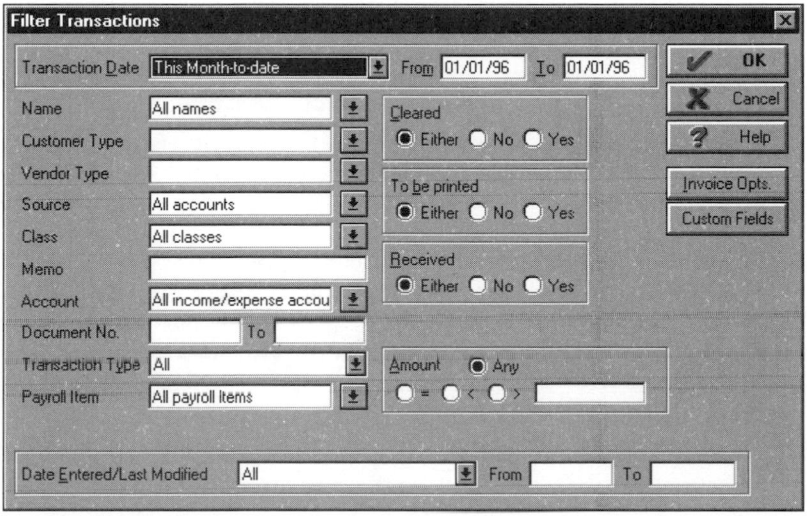

Figure 13-7:
The Filter
Transactions
dialog box.

You can use the Transaction Date and the From and To text boxes to specify the range of dates the report should cover. That makes sense, right?

Then see those drop-down list boxes along the left edge of the dialog box: Name, Customer Type, Vendor Type, Source, Class, Account, and Transaction Type. You can use these lists to select the transactions that you want to include on the report. You just activate a drop-down list box and select whatever you want to see. "Whatever" isn't very good, is it? Maybe an example will help. If you want to filter by customer type, you activate the Customer Type drop-down list box and then select the customer type you want to see.

You can use the Memo text box to filter transactions, too. You just enter whatever memo you want the included transactions to use.

The Document No. and To text boxes seem confusing at first. But they are easy to use. You use them to select a range of transactions, based on their numbers. For example, you can select a range of invoices by giving a range of invoice numbers. That makes sense, right?

You use the Cleared and To Be Printed sets of option buttons to specify when you want cleared, uncleared, printed, or unprinted transactions included.

You use the Amount option buttons and the text box to tell QuickBooks to include any transactions or just those that have an amount that is equal to (=), less than (<), or greater than (>) the amount you enter in the text box.

Note: If you click the Invoice Opts. button, QuickBooks displays a different set of buttons and boxes. You can use these other buttons and boxes to filter transactions by an invoice field, such as items, shipping date, payment terms, and so forth.

Checking out those other buttons, except Memorize

Close the Filters window by clicking the Close button (the one in the upper right-hand corner, with the X in it), and we'll go back to the regular report screen.

The Format button, between the Filters and Header/Footer buttons, gives you several options for displaying numbers and changing the fonts of the report text. If you want to see how the Header/Footer, Hide Header, Collapse, and Dates stuff works, just noodle around. You can't hurt anything.

Memorize...

If you do play around with the remaining buttons on the iconbar, you can save any custom report specifications that you create. Just click the Memorize button. QuickBooks displays a dialog box that asks you to supply a name for the customized report (see Figure 13-8). After you name the customized report, QuickBooks lists it whenever you choose Reports⇨Memorized Reports. To use your report, select your customized report in the list and click the Report button.

Figure 13-8:
The
Memorize
Report
dialog box.

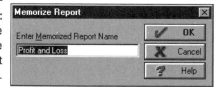

Reports Made to Order

If you intend to print a large number of reports, and more important, if you intend to print a large number of reports and show them to customers, investors, and other important people, you want your reports to look good and be easy to understand. I believe that beauty is in the eye of the beholder, so I'm not going to get into the aesthetics of report layouts. What I am going to do is explain how you can make QuickBooks reports look exactly the way *you* want them to look.

Choose Preferences⇨Reporting to see the Reporting Preferences dialog box (see Figure 13-9).

Figure 13-9:
The
Reporting
Preferences
dialog box.

Accrual is one of those cruel accounting terms that is hard to understand at first. If you choose Accrual in the Summary Reports Basis panel, you tell QuickBooks to date all your transactions, purchases, expenses, and so on from the moment they are recorded, not from the time you receive or pay cash for them. If you choose Cash, all the financial transactions in your reports are dated from the time payments are made.

Accountants follow the accrual method because it gives a more accurate picture of profits.

If you click Age From Due Date in the Aging Reports panel, QuickBooks counts your expenses and invoices from the day that they fall due. Otherwise, QuickBooks counts them from the day that they were recorded.

Check the box for Display Customize Report Window Automatically if you are an exceptionally artistic person and you want the Customize Report window to show up whenever you try to create a report. (This option gives you a chance to change the report's appearance before you produce the report rather than after you produce it.)

Click the Format button if you want to improve the look of your reports. In the Report Format Preferences dialog box shown in Figure 13-10, you can choose preferences for displaying numbers, decimal fractions, and negative numbers. You also can fool around with different fonts and point sizes for labels, column headings, titles, and other things in your reports.

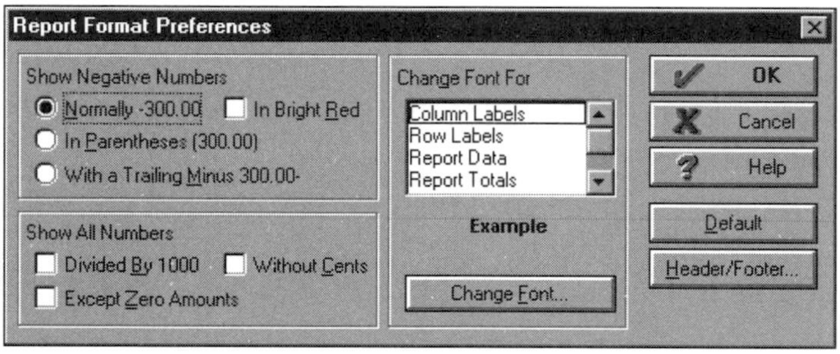

Figure 13-10:
The Report
Format
Preferences
dialog box.

You can even click the Header/Footer button and enter your company name or some other text that you want to appear on all your reports.

Click the Default buttons in the Report Format Preferences and Reporting Preferences dialog boxes after you're finished. Now the choices you just made affect all your reports. If you decide that you don't like your choices after all, you can choose Preferences⇨Reporting again and redo everything or click Customize in the report document window and customize your reports as you make them.

Last but Not Least: The QuickReport

The last kind of report is the QuickReport. QuickReports are one of the best kinds of reports, so I've saved them for last. You can generate a QuickReport from a list, from invoices and bills with names of people or items on them, and from account registers.

QuickReports are especially useful when you're studying a list and you see something that momentarily baffles you. Simply make sure that the item you're curious about is highlighted and click the QuickReport button (sometimes called the *Q-Report* button). You see a payment history, expense transaction, a list of unpaid bills, or whatever is appropriate to the open window, to satisfy your curiosity.

Figure 13-11 shows a QuickReport produced from an Accounts Receivable register. Click the QuickReport button to display this Register QuickReport with the complete invoice information about SNG, Ltd.

The QuickReport option is also on the Reports menu. You can display a QuickReport from a form, even though no QuickReport button appears, by choosing the menu option. For example, if you were writing a check to SNG, Ltd., you could enter the company name on the check and choose Reports⇨QuickReport to see a report of transactions involving SNG, Ltd.

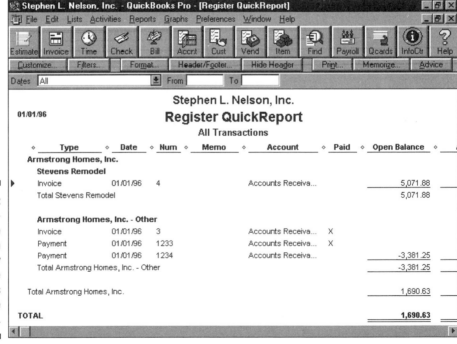

Figure 13-11:
A Quick-
Report made
from an
entry
in the
Accounts
Receivable
register.

Chapter 14

Housekeeping for QuickBooks

. . . .

In This Chapter

▶ Formatting floppy disks

▶ Backing up QuickBooks data

▶ Deciding when and how often to back up your data

▶ Restoring your QuickBooks data (if you lose it)

. . . .

*O*kay, you don't need to worry about chasing dust bunnies in QuickBooks, but you do have little housekeeping tasks to take care of. This chapter describes these chores and how do them correctly with minimal hassle.

Formatting Floppy Disks

You need a safe place to store the company information that you collect with QuickBooks — some place in addition to your computer's hard disk. No, I'm not talking about under your mattress or that secret place in the attic. I'm talking about floppy disks. So, you, my friend, need to know how to format a floppy disk.

A floppy disk needs to be formatted before you can store information on it. You can buy formatted floppy disks. (The package says "Formatted Disks.") You also can buy unformatted floppy disks. The only trick is to make sure that you buy disks that match your disk drive in terms of density (low or high) and size ($5^1/_4$ inches or $3^1/_2$ inches).

Size is easy to determine: Just get a ruler and measure one of the disks you're using. The disk is either $5^1/_4$ inches square or $3^1/_2$ inches square. Simple, huh?

Density is a little trickier because you can use both low- and high-density disks in a high-density drive. If you don't know the density of your drive, I suggest that you find the paperwork you got when you (or whoever) bought the computer. The paperwork should tell you whether the drive is high density (designated by using the code HD or by telling you the amount of storage space that you have per disk — 1.2MB on a $5^1/_4$-inch floppy or 1.44MB on a $3^1/_2$-inch floppy). You also can scrounge around to see whether you've been using low-density or high-density floppy disks. High-density floppy disks often have the HD secret code on the label. Low-density disks, however, use the DS/DD secret code (for Double-Sided/Double-Density) or give the amount of storage space — 360K on a 5^1/$_4$-inch floppy or 720K on a 3^1/$_2$-inch floppy.

Most Macintoshes use the 1.44 high-density, 3^1/$_2$-inch disk. Some of the older models use the 720K drives, but none of them use the 5^1/$_4$-inch floppies in either density, so at least you have a 50-50 chance of guessing correctly.

Anyway, after you figure out the density and size thing, you can format the disk. Just follow the steps in the following sections.

Windows 3.x

1. **Stuff a floppy disk of the correct size and density into the correct floppy disk drive.**

2. **Start the File Manager application, and then choose <u>D</u>isk⇨<u>F</u>ormat Disk.**

   The File Manager displays a Format Disk dialog box.

3. **Use the Disk In drop-down list to indicate the floppy disk drive that you're using.**

4. **Use the Capacity drop-down list to indicate the floppy disk density.**

   Before you click OK in the next step, choose <u>O</u>ptions⇨<u>C</u>onfirmation, and make sure that Disk Commands is checked. This is a potentially lifesaving option — one that keeps you from formatting over a beloved floppy disk by accident and one I'd suggest that you keep checked.

5. **Click OK.**

   The File Manager displays a message box that asks you to confirm the formatting. (The File Manager asks this question because formatting erases everything on the disk.)

6. **Click OK again to confirm the formatting.**

   The File Manager goes off and formats the disk. Next, you see a message box that tells you that the format is complete and asks whether you want to format another disk.

7. **Click No to indicate "Heck, no!" and press Enter.**

8. **Exit the File Manager application by choosing <u>F</u>ile⇨E<u>x</u>it.**

Windows 95

1. **Slip the unformatted floppy in the appropriate drive.**

   In other words, if the disk doesn't fit, don't force it — a good, general rule to follow in life.

2. **Double-click the My Computer icon.**

   It's usually the first icon in the upper-left corner of the desktop, providing that no windows are covering it.

3. **Highlight the icon for the appropriate floppy drive.**

   Just click the icon which represents the correct drive.

   Be sure that you click the correct icon! When you format a disk, you're also erasing any existing information on it. You can imagine what would happen if you clicked the wrong icon. (I'm getting chills just *thinking* about such a catastrophe. Guess why I can relate to this so well. A hint: I wasn't always this apprehensive.)

4. **Choose File⇨Format.**

   The Format dialog box opens (see Figure 14-1).

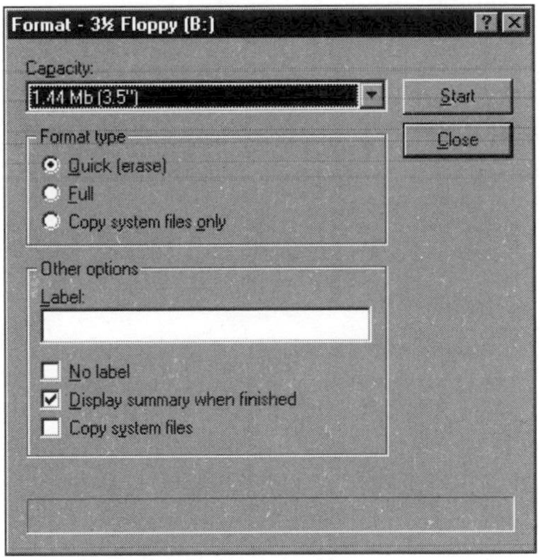

Figure 14-1:
The Format
dialog box.

Format - 3½ Floppy (B:)

Capacity:
1.44 Mb (3.5")

Start
Close

Format type
- Quick (erase)
- Full
- Copy system files only

Other options
Label:

- No label
- ☑ Display summary when finished
- Copy system files

5. **For Format Type, click Full because the disk hasn't been formatted before.**

6. **Click Start.**

   (If you want to know about the other options in the Format dialog box, feel free to look at your Windows 95 documentation.)

7. **Celebrate.**

   After Windows 95 formats your disk, you see a message box similar to the one in Figure 14-2. You're finished!

   Close the window, and *live it up*. Measure your life with coffee spoons. Have your cake and eat it, too. Spit in the eye of death. Dance in the disco of life. Whatever metaphor makes you happy.

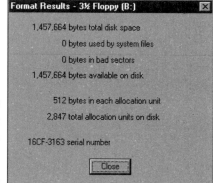

Figure 14-2:
Happy,
happy!
Joy, joy!

Macintosh

To format a Macintosh disk, follow these steps:

1. **Press ⌘-E to eject any disk you may already have in the drive.**

2. **Insert the disk that you want to format.**

   One of two things happens:

   If it hasn't been formatted before, a window appears mentioning that the Macintosh can't read the disk and asks whether you would like to initialize, or format, the disk. Of course, you want to initialize it, or you wouldn't be here. If it offers you a choice of formats, choose Macintosh, and go to Step 3.

   If it has been formatted either for a PC or a Macintosh already, a new disk icon will appear on the desktop. Because I'm assuming you want to erase the whole disk, click the icon to highlight it, and then choose Special⇨Erase Disk, and go to Step 3.

3. **Name the disk.**

   Type the name you want to give the disk in the text box.

4. **Click the Initialize button.**

   The Macintosh asks whether you realize that it will erase any information on the disk.

5. **Click Continue.**

   You'll hear the disk drive humming along while an "Initializing disk" window appears. Then the Mac disk verifies the format, creates the initial directories, and the disk appears as an icon on the desktop. At that point, the disk is ready to be used.

More is involved in this formatting business than I've described here. If you want more information and you're adventurous, flip open the *User's Guide* that came with your computer and look up the Format command in the index. Or better yet, buy the appropriate *For Dummies* book (IDG Books WorldWide), which will undoubtedly be more fun to read.

If you're not adventurous, you should probably be buying preformatted floppy disks.

Backing Up Is (Not That) Hard to Do

You should back up the files that QuickBooks uses to store your financial records. But you need to know how to back up before you can back up. Got it? So let's get to it. . . .

Backing up the quick-and-dirty way

You're busy. You don't have time to fool around. You just want to do a passable job of backing up. Sound like your situation? Then follow these steps:

1. **Insert a blank, formatted floppy disk into your floppy drive.**

   If you have two floppy drives, one is drive A, and one is drive B. I'm going out on a limb here and assuming that you're using the ol' drive A. (If not, just substitute the drive letters accordingly.)

2. **If you store data on more than one company, make sure that the company whose data you want to back up is the active company.**

Yes, all your companies are active — I'm hoping they're not dead in the water. My point is that you want to back up the right company. To find out whether the right company is active, just look at the QuickBooks application window's title bar, which names the active company. (If you don't remember setting up multiple files, don't worry. You probably have only one file — the usual case.)

3. **Choose File⇨Back Up or click the Backup icon (the floppy disk) to begin the backup operation.**

   QuickBooks displays the Back Up Company To dialog box, shown in Figure 14-3.

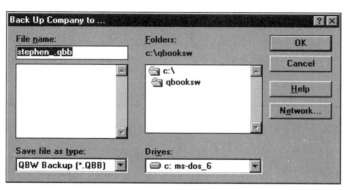

Figure 14-3:
The Back Up
Company To
dialog box.

In the Windows version of QuickBooks, if you choose the File⇨Back Up route, you'll find a submenu that gives you the option of backing up the file up in either Windows format or Macintosh format. I imagine this could come in handy any time you have to change platforms unexpectedly. (Who knows, maybe your repair shop has only a Macintosh for a loaner. Stranger things have happened.) In order to use a Windows disk in a Macintosh, however, you need to confirm that the Macintosh was built after 1990, after which Apple added a program and high-density drive that understands a PC-formatted disk.

4. **Identify the backup floppy drive.**

   Click the Drives drop-down list, and select the letter of the floppy drive that you stuffed the disk into.

5. **Click OK.**

   You see a message box on-screen that says, "Aye, Cap'n, I'm working just as fast as I can" (or something to that effect). Then you see a message box saying that the backup procedure is complete (see Figure 14-4).

Don't worry. You never see a message that says, "She's starting to break up, Cap'n. She can't take warp 9 much longer." You may see a warning message if the file you want to back up is too large. In that case, you need to shrink it. (Later in the chapter, I describe how to shrink files.)

Figure 14-4:
Congrats on
a successful
backup.

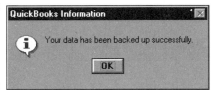

6. **Click OK again.**

   QuickBooks backs up your company file to a new file with a .QBB extension (*.QBB* stands for QuickBooks Backup, I presume).

Here's the Macintosh backup procedure.

1. **Insert a blank, formatted disk into your disk drive.**

   Macs generally only have one floppy disk drive. Use that one.

2. **Make sure that QuickBooks is the active program and that the company you want to back up is the open company; then choose File⇨ Back Up, and the Back Up Company window opens.**

3. **Choose Desktop from the pop-up menu located above the list of folders and files.**

4. **Double-click the disk name in the directory window where you want to back up the files.**

5. **Click the Save button, and QuickBooks saves the file to the disk.**

   When the file's been saved, a "QuickBooks Information" window opens to tell you that the data has been backed up successfully.

Knowing when to back up

Sure, I can give you some tricky, technical examples of fancy backup strategies, but they have no point here. You want to know the basics, right?

The guiding rule is that you back up anytime you work on something that you wouldn't want to redo. Some people think that a week's worth of work is negligible, and others think that a month's worth of work is negligible.

So here's what I do to back up my files. I back up every month after I reconcile my accounts at work. Then I stick the floppy disk in my briefcase so that, if something terrible happens, I don't lose both my computer and the backup disk with the data. (I carry my briefcase around with me — a sort of middle-age security blanket — so that it won't get destroyed in some after-hours disaster.) As I mentioned, I keep all the paperwork in a file folder through the month and do all the reconciling at one time.

I admit that my strategy has its problems, however. Because I'm backing up monthly, for example, I may have to re-enter as much as a month's worth of data if the computer crashes toward the end of the month. In my case, I wouldn't lose all that much work. However, if you're someone with heavy transaction volumes — if you prepare hundreds of invoices or write hundreds of checks a month, for example — you probably want to back up more frequently, perhaps once a week.

A second problem with my strategy is only remotely possible but still worth mentioning. If something bad does happen to the QuickBooks files stored on my computer's hard disk *and* the files stored on the backup floppy disk, I'll be up the proverbial creek without a paddle. (I should also note that a floppy disk is far more likely to fail than a hard drive.) If this worst-case scenario actually occurs, I'll need to start over from scratch from the beginning of the year.

To prevent this scenario from happening, some people — who are religiously careful — circulate three sets of backup disks to reduce the chance of this mishap. In this scenario, whenever you back up your data, you use the oldest set of backup disks. Say you back up your data every week, and your hard disk not only crashes, but bursts into a ball of flames rising high into the night. To restore your files, you use the most recent set of backups — one week old, max. If something is wrong with those, you use the next recent set — two weeks old. If something is wrong with those, you use the last set — three weeks old. This way, you have three chances to get a set that works — a nice bit of security for the cost of a few extra floppy disks. I should also add that, generally, one company account's backup file doesn't take more than one floppy disk.

You know what else? All backup files are condensed to save on disk space. If you are so inclined (I'm not), open Windows Explorer (or, if you're not using Windows 95, the File Manager) and look in the QBOOKSW directory for your company's file. (The backup file is, of course, on the disk you specified in the previous procedure.) If you set Windows Explorer to show file size — choose View⇨Details to set Windows Explorer — you'll notice that your backup file (the one with the .QBB extension) is a fraction of the size of its regular company file counterpart (the one with the .QBW extension). QuickBooks shrinks the backup file in order to keep the disk from getting too crowded.

Getting QuickBooks data back if you have backed up

What happens if you lose all your QuickBooks data? First of all, I encourage you to feel smug. Get a cup of coffee. Lean back in your chair. Gloat for a couple of minutes. You, my friend, will have no problem. You have followed instructions.

After you have gloated sufficiently, carefully do the following to reinstate your QuickBooks data on the computer:

1. **Get your backup floppy disk.**

   Find the backup disk you created, and carefully insert it into one of the disk drives. (If you can't find the backup disk, forget what I said about feeling smug — stop gloating and skip to the next section, "Trying to get QuickBooks data back if you haven't backed up.")

2. **Start QuickBooks.**

   You already know how to do this, right? By the way, if the disaster that caused you to lose your data also trashed other parts of your computer, you may need to reinstall QuickBooks. You also may need to reinstall all your other software.

3. **Choose File⇨Restore.**

   QuickBooks will need to close whatever company file you have open. Guess what happens then? QuickBooks displays the Name Of File To Restore dialog box. Figure 14-5 shows you what this box looks like.

When you choose File⇨Restore, your Macintosh automatically checks the floppy disk drive to see if it contains the backup file. When you select the file from the dialog box that appears, QuickBooks notifies you of your file-naming options. When you click OK in this window, the Name Restored File dialog box appears, showing the backup file's default name.

If the name is correct, just click Save, and you're okay. If not, you need to find the disk and folder that contain the correct backup file. If you click Save and a company already exists by that name, QuickBooks gives you the option of either canceling the whole restore routine by clicking Cancel or overwriting the existing file by clicking Replace. Make your choice, and you're done with your restoration project! Go to the next section, and leave the rest of the stuff for the Windows users.

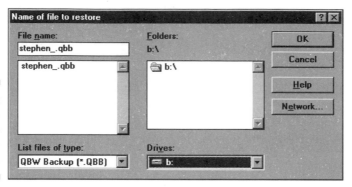

Figure 14-5:
The Name
Of File To
Restore
dialog box.

4. **In the Drives box, click the name of the drive that contains the backup floppy disk.**

   QuickBooks looks at the floppy disk in this drive and displays a list of the files stored on the floppy disk in the box under the section headed File Name, as shown in Figure 14-5. (If you have only one QuickBooks file on the disk — the usual case — only one file is listed.)

5. **Select the file that you want to restore, and click OK.**

   Use the arrow keys or the mouse to highlight the file you want to restore, and click OK or double-click the filename.

   You see the Name Restored File dialog box, shown in Figure 14-6. In the File Name box, you should see the .QBW name of the .QBB file that you want to restore. QuickBooks lists the .QBW name to let you know the name that the restored file will have and, if necessary, offers you an opportunity to give it a different name.

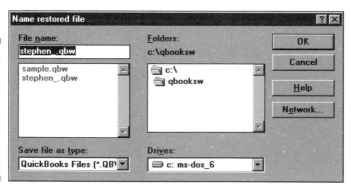

Figure 14-6:
The Name
·Restored
File dialog
box has a
funny name.
At least, I
think so.

6. Change folders and drives in the Drives and Folders boxes.

Make sure that you place the restored file in the QBOOKSW directory on the correct drive.

7. Click OK.

If the file you are trying to restore already exists, you see a message box telling you so. Either click Yes to overwrite or replace the file with the one stored on the floppy disk, or click No to keep the original copy. (If you click Yes, a message box similar to the one in Figure 14-7 appears — the QuickBooks way of saying, "Just checking, boss.")

Figure 14-7:
Just
checking,
boss.

Then, if everything goes okay, you see the message box shown in Figure 14-8. Breathe a deep sigh of relief, and give thanks.

Figure 14-8:
Whew!
Another
close
escape.

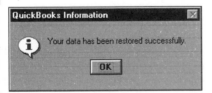

When you restore a file, you replace the current version of the file with the backup version stored on the floppy disk. Don't restore a file for fun. Don't restore a file for entertainment. Restore a file only if the current version is trashed and you want to start over by using the version stored on the backup floppy disk.

Just to be on the safe side, you should back up the file after you complete this process. I have heard that lightning never strikes the same place twice, but I'm not sure that the old saying is true. If you have hard disk problems or another recurring problem, whatever fouled up your file this time may rear its ugly head again — and soon.

I almost forgot. You need to complete one last step to finish restoring your data. You need to re-enter everything you entered since you made the backup copy. I know. You're bummed out. Hopefully, it hasn't been all that long since you backed up.

Trying to get QuickBooks data back if you haven't backed up

What do you do if you haven't backed up your files in a while and you lose all the data in your QuickBooks files? Okay. Stay calm. It may be that all is not lost.

Try restoring from the backup file on the hard drive. To restore from this file, you follow the same file-restoration steps I covered earlier in the chapter, with one minor exception. When you get to the Name Of File To Restore dialog box shown in Figure 14-5, you use the Drives and Folders list boxes to indicate that you want to see the backup files in the QuickBooks directory on the hard drive. You will probably choose drive C from the Drives list box and open the QBOOKSW directory. At this point, you'll probably see a file with a name similar to the name of the file that you lost. If the file you lost had the name STEPHEN.QBW, for example, you may see a file named STEPHEN.QBB. Select it. QuickBooks uses the file to restore the current file. This method may just work. And if this method does, you should feel very lucky. Very lucky indeed.

Okay, suppose that you've tried the approach described in the preceding paragraph. Suppose that it didn't work. What next?

All you have to do is re-enter all the transactions for the entire year. Yeah. I know — what a bummer. This method isn't quick, and it isn't pretty, but it works. (Besides, I bring this up in the interest of showing you the alternative of not backing up your files.)

If you have hard copies (printed copies) of the invoices, checks, purchase orders, and so on, you can, of course, use these sources for the information that you need to re-enter. If you don't have copies of these kinds of things, you need to use bank statements and any other paper financial records that you have.

Shrinking files that are too big for their own good

You can enter a large number of transactions in a QuickBooks company file. Even so, you may want to shrink or condense the .QBW or working set of your data file. Working with files of a manageable size means that QuickBooks runs faster because your computer has more memory and disk space available.

Condensing defined

If your company file has gotten too big for its own good, you can knock it down to size by *condensing* it. As part of condensing the file, QuickBooks lets you decide what parts should be condensed and what parts should be readily accessible. You make this decision based on a cutoff date of your choice. In other words, if you have two or three years' worth of data records and the stuff from three years ago doesn't pertain to you for the most part, you can condense it. You also can condense unused accounts, information on inactive customers and vendors, old invoices, and Audit Trail information.

Condensed information is not lost — it is merely "summarized." QuickBooks retains numeric totals and dates of the transactions but deletes other details, such as the names. In other words, if you wrote a check to Tuggey's Hardware on July 31, 1993, QuickBooks retains the amount of the check and the date it was written but loses the name of the hardware store.

Do not despair, however, about losing crucial data. In all its wisdom, QuickBooks can tell if a data item that you want to condense still bears on transactions that you enter in the future, *and QuickBooks will not condense these transactions*. If you choose to condense all information from before January 1, 1995, and you just so happen to have skipped a monthly rent payment in December 1994, for example, QuickBooks still retains all accounts payable information pertaining to your missed payment. And quit trying to pull a fast one, you rascal.

Unpaid invoices, bills and credit memos; undeposited customer payments that have been applied to invoices; unreconciled transactions in credit card and checking accounts; and anything whatsoever that has been checked To Be Printed are not condensed.

For the purposes of tax liability, QuickBooks does not condense any of your tax data. QuickBooks retains all information about taxable items and tax vendors. If you get audited, you won't be able to point to your computer and say, "There you are. Just uncondense that, Mr. Taxman."

Condensing means that you get to work with a smaller file. And that, in turn, means QuickBooks runs faster. (The memory thing comes into play again.) And a smaller file should make backing up easier because you can probably keep your file small enough to fit on a single double-density floppy disk.

 Call me a Nervous Nellie — or a Nervous Nelson — but because shrinking a file involves wholesale change, I'd really feel more comfortable about helping you through this process if you backed up the file you're about to shrink before we start. I don't think that you need to get anxious about anything, but just in case something does go wrong during the shrinking process, I know that you would like to have a backup copy of the file to fall back on.

I'll tell you what happens to your company file when you shrink it a little later in the chapter. For now, I'll tell you how to get the job finished.

Condensing made simple

To condense a QuickBooks file, follow these steps:

1. **Start from a blank QuickBooks screen.**

   Close registers, reports, or anything else on-screen.

2. **Choose File⇨Utilities⇨Condense Data.**

   You knew that the Condensing feature had to be on the Utilities menu, didn't you?

   QuickBooks displays a portrait of Barry Nelson, the first actor to portray James Bond. No, not really — I just wanted to see whether you were awake. Actually, QuickBooks displays the Condense Data dialog box, as shown in Figure 14-9.

3. **Specify a cutoff date.**

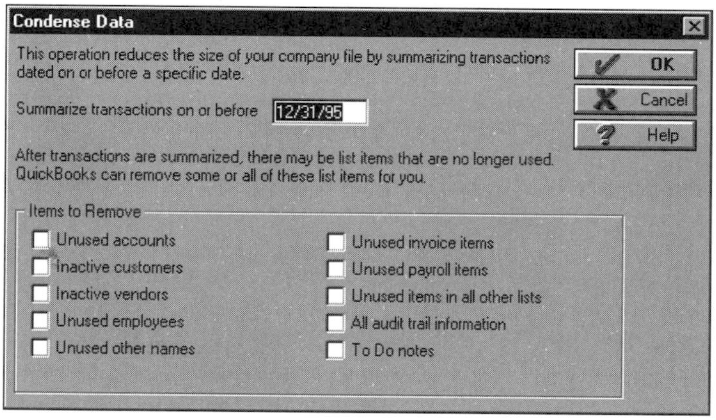

Figure 14-9: The Condense Data dialog box.

In the Summarize Transactions On Or Before line, enter a cutoff date. QuickBooks keeps all transactions with a date that falls after this cutoff date. But all transactions with a date that falls before this cutoff date are condensed (with the exceptions noted earlier in this chapter).

4. **(Optional) Select other items in the Items To Remove list.**

   Take a look at the Items To Remove list. You may see something that you can condense. Prime candidates are employees you have nothing to do with (and whose tax information you no longer need) and inactive vendors.

5. **Click OK.**

   A message box appears, telling you that transactions exist before the date you entered in Step 4. You knew that, but QuickBooks is an exceptionally courteous program, and it wants to know whether you really want to condense this stuff.

6. **Click OK (again).**

   Or click Cancel if you get nervous.

   At this point, QuickBooks gives you another chance to create a backup file. Why not? Create yet another backup to be on the safe side (I explain how to create a backup earlier in this chapter). Condensing your file may take a while, depending on how large it is. So expect a little whirring and humming from the computer. After QuickBooks condenses the file, you see the message box shown in Figure 14-10.

Figure 14-10:
This message tells you that QuickBooks condensed your file.

7. **Click OK in the QuickBooks Information message box.**

How condensing is summarized on registers

QuickBooks summarizes data on registers into the generic GENJRNL entry. So if you condense all data from 1995, your Accounts Payable register for May 1995 shows a GENJRNL entry totaling all accounts payable transactions from that month. You don't see the individual transactions that have been condensed.

Some reports are affected by condensed data. Summary reports about your total equity are not affected, but any report concerning details — classes, items, and so on — aren't as complete.

The 5th Wave   By Rich Tennant

"I just don't know where the money's going."

Chapter 15

Building the Perfect Budget

. . . .

. . . .

1 don't think that a budget amounts to financial handcuffs, and neither should you. A budget is just a plan that outlines the way you should spend your money and organize your financial affairs.

Is This a Game You Want to Play?

If you have created a good, workable chart of accounts, you're halfway to a good, solid budget. (In fact, for 99 out of 100 businesses, the only step left is to specify how much you earn in each income account and how much you spend in each expense account.)

Does everybody need a budget? No, of course not. Maybe you've got a simple financial plan that you can monitor some other way. Maybe in your business, you make money so effortlessly that you don't need to plan your income and outgo. Maybe Elvis Presley really is still alive and living somewhere in the Midwest.

For everyone else, though, a budget improves your chances of getting to wherever it is you want to go financially. It gives you a way to "plan your work and work your plan." In fact, I'll stop calling it a budget. The word has such negative connotations. I know — I'll call it *The Secret Plan.*

All Joking Aside

Before I walk you through the mechanics of outlining your secret plan, I want to give you a few tips. After that, I want to tell you a secret. A very special secret.

Some basic budgeting tips

Following are four ways to increase the chances that your secret plan will work:

- ✔ **Plan your income and expenses as a team if that's possible.**

  For this sort of planning, two heads are invariably better than one. What's more, although I don't really want to get into marriage counseling or partnership counseling here, a business's budget — oops, I mean secret plan — needs to reflect the priorities and feelings of everyone who has to live within the plan: partners, partners' spouses, key employees, and so on. So don't use a secret plan as a way to minimize what your partner spends on marketing or on long-distance telephone charges talking to pseudo-customers and relatives in the old country. You need to resolve such issues before you finalize your secret plan.

- ✔ **Include some cushion in your plan.**

  In other words, don't budget to spend every last dollar (or if you're German, every last deutsche mark). If you plan from the start to spend every dollar you make, you'll undoubtedly have to fight the mother of all financial battles: paying for unexpected expenses when you don't have any money. (You know the sort of things I mean: the repair bill when the delivery truck breaks down, a new piece of essential equipment, or that cocktail dress or tuxedo you absolutely must have for a special party.)

- ✔ **Regularly compare your actual income and outgo to your planned income and outgo.**

  This comparison is probably the most important part of budgeting, and it is what QuickBooks can help you with the most. As long as you use QuickBooks to record what you receive and spend, and to describe your budget, you'll be able to print reports that show what you planned and what actually occurred.

- ✔ **Make adjustments as necessary.**

  When there are problems with your secret plan — and there will be — you'll know that your plan isn't working. You can then make adjustments (by spending a little less on calling the old country, for example).

All these tips also apply to a family's secret plan. And that brings up another important subject. If you're a small business owner or partner who relies on the profits of the business to buy things such as groceries for your family or to pay the rent, you should also have a solid family budget. In fact, in my opinion, planning your family finances is as important as planning your business finances. If your business is like most businesses, your profits will probably bounce up and down like a yo-yo. You need to have enough slack in your personal finances that a bad, or a so-so, business year doesn't cause all sorts of trouble at home.

The QuickBooks cousin product, Quicken, is a great personal finance program. It includes record-keeping tools that you can use to track all your personal financial information. It also has some nifty planning tools that enable you to intelligently think about and plan for things such as retirement, your children's college expenses, and your income taxes.

Can I say one more thing about the relationship between your family's finances and the business's finances? If you let me say this one more thing, I'll get off my pulpit. I promise. Okay. Here's my other point. Please, please, please: Don't gear up your living and lifestyle when you have a great year in the business. When you have a good year or even a few good years, keep your living expenses modest. Stash the extra cash. Build up some financial wealth that's independent and apart from your business assets. (One great way to do this, for example, is by contributing to an IRA or by setting up an SEP/IRA.)

A budgeting secret

I also have a secret tip for business budgeting. (I'm going to write very quietly now so that no one else hears . . . .)

Here's the secret tip: Go to the library, ask for the Robert Morris & Associates Survey, and look up the ways that other businesses like yours spend money.

This survey is really cool. Robert Morris & Associates surveys bank lending officers, creates a summary of the information that these bankers receive from their customers, and publishes the results. For example, you can look up what percentage of sales the average tavern spends on beer and peanuts.

Plan to spend an hour or so at the library. Getting used to the way that the Robert Morris & Associates information is displayed takes a while. The taverns page won't actually have a line for beer and peanuts, for example. Instead, you'll see the words *cost of goods sold* or some similarly vague accounting term.

Remember to make a few notes so that you can use the information you glean to better plan your own business financial affairs.

Two things that really goof up secret plans

Because I'm talking about you-know-whats, I want to touch on a couple of things that really goof up your financial plans: windfalls and monster changes. (This stuff applies to both businesses and to families, but, because this book's about business accounting, I'm going to talk about all this stuff from a business perspective.)

The problem with windfalls

Your big customer calls and asks you to come to his office for a meeting. When the time arrives, he calls you into his office, smiles, and then gives you the good news: He's buying a huge order of your *[insert name of your product or service here],* and you'll make about $50,000 on the deal. You read right. That's $50,000. Yippee, you think to yourself. On the outside, of course, you maintain your dignity. You act grateful, but not gushy. Then you call your husband, Bob.

Here's what happens next: Bob gets excited, congratulates you, and tells you he'll pick up a bottle of wine on the way home to celebrate. (If you don't drink, tell Bob to pick up something else. Geez....)

On your drive home, you mull over the possibilities and conclude that you can use the $50,000 as a big down payment for some new machinery that you can use to make even more of *[insert name of your product or service here].* Let's say that with the trade-in of your old machinery and the $50,000, your payments will be a manageable $2,000 a month.

Bob, on his way home, stops at a travel agency and books an eight-week tour through Europe for the two of you. (Apparently, at one point in the discussion, he tells the travel agent, "If you don't spend the big money, there's no sense in making it, right?") A few minutes later, your loving husband has charged $18,000 on his credit card.

You may laugh at this scenario, but suppose that it really happened. Furthermore, pretend that you really do buy that new machinery. At this point, you've spent $68,000 on a combination of business and personal expenditures, and you've signed up for what you're guessing will be another $2,000-a-month payment.

This doesn't sound all that bad now, does it?

Here's the problem: When you finish the accounting and you take out the business and personal taxes, your net profit on the deal isn't going to be $50,000. No way. You may pay as much as $7,500 in social security and medicare taxes, maybe around $15,000 in federal income taxes, and then probably some state income taxes.

Other business expense or personal expenditure money may be taken out, too, for forced savings plans (such as a 401K plan) or for charitable giving. After all is said and done, you'll get maybe half the profit in cash — perhaps $25,000.

Now you see the problem, of course. You've got $25,000 in cold, hard cash, but, with knucklehead Bob's help, you have already spent $68,000 and signed up for $2,000-a-month payments.

In a nutshell, the two big problems with windfalls are these:

- ✔ You never get the entire windfall — yet it's easy to spend money as if you will get the entire amount.

- ✔ Windfalls, by their very nature, tend to be used for big business and personal purchases (often as down payments) that ratchet up your operating or living expenses. Boats. New houses. Cars.

My advice regarding windfalls is simple:

- ✔ Don't spend the money until you've paid all the expenses, made all the estimated tax payments, and actually hold the check in your hot little hand. (It's even better to wait, say, six months. That way Bob can really think about whether he needs the super-luxurious "Grand Continental" tour.)

- ✔ Don't spend a windfall on something that increases your monthly business (or family) expenses without redoing your budget.

About monster income changes

I have some special business-family pointers for any business owners or partners reading this book. If your business and, therefore, your personal income changes radically, it becomes *really* hard to plan.

Suppose, for example, that your income doubles. One day you're cruising along making $35,000, and the next day you're suddenly making $70,000. (Congratulations, by the way.)

I'll tell you what you'll discover, however, should you find yourself in this position. You'll find that $70,000 a year isn't as much money as you might think.

Go ahead. Laugh. But for one thing, if your income doubles, your income taxes almost certainly more than quadruple.

One of the great myths about income taxes is that the rich don't pay very much or that they pay the same percentage. Poppycock. If you make $30,000 a year and you're an average family, you probably pay about $1,500 in federal income taxes. If you make $200,000 a year, you'll pay about $45,000 a year. So if your salary increases by roughly 7 times, your income taxes increase by about 30 times. I don't bring this up to get you agitated about whether making the rich pay more is right or fair. I bring it up so that you can better plan for any monster income changes you experience.

Another thing — and I know it sounds crazy — but you'll find it hard to spend, for example, $70,000 intelligently when you've been making a lot less. And if you start making some big purchases, such as houses, cars, and speedboats, you'll not only burn through a lot of cash, you'll also ratchet up your monthly living expenses.

Monster income changes that go the other way are even more difficult. If you've been making, say, $70,000 a year and then see your salary drop to a darn respectable $35,000, it's going to hurt, too. And probably more than you think. (This factor, by the way, is the main reason that I suggested earlier in this chapter that you *not* ratchet up your living expenses to what your business makes in a good year.)

That old living-expenses ratcheting effect comes into play here, of course. Presumably, if you've been making $70,000 a year, you've been spending it — or most of it.

But, at least initially, some other reasons make having a monster salary drop very difficult. You've probably chosen friends (nice people, like the Joneses), clothing stores, and hobbies that are in line with your income.

Another thing is sort of subtle. You probably denominate your purchases in amounts related to your income. Make $35,000 and you think in terms of $5 or $10 purchases. But make $70,000 a year and you think in terms of $10 or $20 purchases. This all makes perfect sense. But if your income drops from $70,000 to $35,000, you'll probably still find yourself thinking of those old $20 purchases.

So what to do? If you experience a monster income change, redo your secret plan. Be particularly careful and thoughtful, though.

The Nelson philosophy

I keep weaving between issues related to a business's budget and issues related to a business owner's family budget. I'm sorry if this flip-flopping is confusing, but I have found the two budgets to be closely connected in small businesses. So, because of that closeness, I want to make a short philosophical digression about your family budget.

At the point that you've provided yourself and your family with the creature comforts — a cozy home, adequate food, and comfortable clothes — more stuff won't make the difference you think.

I don't mean to minimize the challenges of raising a family of four on, say, $14,000 a year. But, hey, I work with a fair number of small business people who have been very successful. What continually surprises me is that when you get right down to it, someone who makes $300,000 or $600,000 a year doesn't live a better life than someone who makes $30,000.

Sure, they spend more money. They buy more stuff. They buy more expensive stuff. But they don't live better. They don't have better marriages. Their kids don't love them more. They don't have better friends or more considerate neighbors.

But you already know all this. I know you do.

Setting Up a Secret Plan

Okay, enough metaphysical stuff. The time has come to set up your budget — er, your *secret plan*. Follow these steps:

1. Choose Activities⇨Set Up Budgets.

QuickBooks displays the Set Up Budgets dialog box (see Figure 15-1).

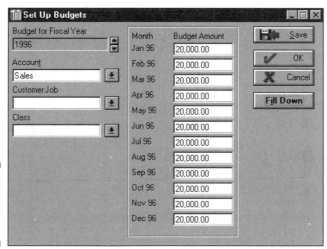

Figure 15-1:
The Set Up
Budgets
dialog box.

2. Select the fiscal year you want to budget.

Use the Budget For Fiscal Year line to specify the fiscal year. You use the up and down arrows at the end of the box to adjust the year number incrementally.

3. Choose the account that you want to budget.

See the Account drop-down list box? You use it to specify which account you're budgeting. Normally, you'll probably limit yourself to budgeting just income and expense accounts. You can, however, budget balance sheet accounts, too.

Note that I said you *can* budget balance sheet accounts. I don't *recommend* it. Here's why.

Many line items are fairly easy to anticipate. If you own a freelance writing business, for example, anticipating your sales for the month is fairly easy. Balance sheet accounts — frequently referred to as "real" accounts — are infinitely more complicated, and that makes them much harder to forecast. For example, let's take your "cash" account. In order to come up with a figure for this account properly, you probably need at least to consider income, expenses, loans taken out, loans paid off, and more. Moreover, it would help if you had figures from the previous year to use in calculating the potential amounts — but why would you want to spend all that time putting last year's figures into QuickBooks just for a budget?

Let's put it this way: assembling a budget for balance sheet accounts is usually not tackled in undergraduate accounting degree programs until the third year of studies, and even then, they use *big* spreadsheets.

4. (Optional) Specify the customer or job.

If you want to budget an account by customer or job, activate the Customer:Job drop-down list. Then select the customer or job. (If you're just starting out in your budgeting, one way to make things easier is to not budget by customer or job.)

5. (Optional) Specify the class.

If you want to budget an account by class, activate the Class drop-down list. Then select the class. (Again, if you're just starting out in your budgeting, you may want to make things easier by not budgeting by class.)

6. Enter the first month's budget amount.

To enter the budget, type the budgeted amount for the account into the first month's text box. You need to remember just two things:

- If you're budgeting an income or expense account, you need to enter the amount of income you'll earn or the expense you'll incur over the month.

- If you're budgeting an amount for a balance sheet account, you need to enter the account balance you expect at the end of the month you're budgeting.

7. Enter the budget amounts for subsequent months.

You can enter the budget amounts for subsequent months into the other text boxes manually.

If monthly budgeted amounts are the same over the year or the monthly amounts grow by a constant percentage or amount, you can use the Fill Down button. When you click Fill Down, QuickBooks displays the Fill Down dialog box (see Figure 15-2). Enter the percentage change (followed by a percent symbol) or the dollar change you want from one month to the next. If you don't want the monthly amount to change, leave the percentage change as 0.0%.

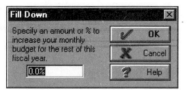

Figure 15-2:
The Fill Down dialog box.

To create a complete budget, you need to repeat Steps 6 and 7 for each of the accounts you want to budget. I know that I said this earlier, but let me repeat a couple of things: If you're budgeting some income or expense amount, enter the amount of income you'll earn or the expense you'll incur over the month; if you're budgeting some balance sheet account — an asset, liability, or owner's equity amount — enter the account balance that you expect at the end of the month you're budgeting.

After you enter your secret plan, click Save to save your work and leave the Set Up Budgets dialog box open. Or click OK to save your work but close the Set Up Budgets dialog box.

I should mention, too, that you can just click Cancel if you don't want to save your work (in case you've just been noodling around).

Using business-planning and budgeting software

You can usually create a family budget on a sheet of paper. You put down your salary. You estimate your expenses. You're done.

Unfortunately, budgeting a business is more complicated. More specifically, budgeting any of your balance sheet accounts — assets, liabilities, and owner's equity — is really tough. (Remember that cash is a balance sheet account.) To do this sort of budgeting with any degree of accuracy, you need either budgeting or business-planning software or a spreadsheet program (such as Microsoft Excel) and a fair amount of accounting knowledge. How you do this kind of budgeting is way, way beyond this book. But I did want to mention that several good packages are available.

Are you interested in more information? In the September 1994 issue of *Home Office Computing* magazine, I described and reviewed a half-dozen packages. If you're interested in more information, you can look up that article. (The article starts on page 80.) If you just want to cut to the chase, you can call Planet Corp. at 800-366-5111 and order the Destiny Business Information and Planning System (if you want a stand-alone package) or call Palo Alto Software at 800-229-7526 and order the Business Plan Toolkit (if you want a business planning tool that works with your spreadsheet program).

Part IV
The Part of Tens

In this part . . .

As a writing tool, laundry lists aren't something high school English teachers encourage. But you know what? The old laundry list format is pretty handy for certain sorts of information.

With this in mind (and, of course, with deepest apologies to my high school English teacher, Mrs. O'Rourke), this part simply provides you with almost ten-item lists of information about QuickBooks.

Chapter 16

Ten Things You Should Do If You're Audited

*B*ecause you will probably use QuickBooks to produce the reports you or your accountant uses to prepare your annual income tax returns, I want to mention some of the things you should do if your business gets audited.

Leave QuickBooks at Home

Don't bring QuickBooks with you to an IRS audit — even if you're really proud of that new laptop.

Here's the problem: The QuickBooks reporting capabilities are incredibly powerful. If you have been using QuickBooks diligently, you own a rich database that describes almost all of your financial affairs. When you bring QuickBooks (and your QuickBooks file) to the IRS, you're spilling your financial guts.

Now I'm not one who recommends sneaking stuff by the IRS. But giving an IRS agent the opportunity to go on a fishing expedition is dumb. Remember, the agent isn't going to be looking for additional deductions.

I know of a young, inexperienced CPA who took Quicken, the younger sibling of QuickBooks, to an audit. The IRS agent would ask a question, and the CPA would proudly tap a few keys on the laptop, smile broadly, and then, for example, show the agent all the individual entertainment expenses claimed by the taxpayer in question.

Funny thing, though, the IRS agent also saw some other things on-screen — such as money that should have been claimed as income, reporting require-ments that the taxpayer failed to meet, and obvious out-of-line deductions.

Print Transaction Reports for Questionable Accounts

Ol' QuickBooks can be your friend, though, if you're audited.

Before you go to the audit, find out what the IRS is questioning. Print a transac-tion report of every questioned income or expense account: supplies, travel and entertainment, yachting expenses, and so on. You will have an easy-to-understand report that explains how you came up with every number that the IRS wants to examine.

Collect All Source Documents

After you print a transaction report of every questioned deduction, collect all the source documents — usually canceled checks, invoices, and bills — that prove or indicate a transaction in question.

If you claim $600 in postage expenses, for example, the report summarizing this deduction may show 12 $50 checks written to the local postmaster. To verify this report, find the 12 canceled checks. Even better, find the 12 $50 receipts supplied by the postal clerk who sold you the stamps.

Call a Tax Attorney If the Agent Is Special

An IRS *special agent* isn't an agent endorsed by Mr. Rogers. Internal Revenue Service special agents investigate criminal tax code violations. If a special agent is auditing your return, you're in a heap of trouble. So get a tax attorney.

In my mind, being audited by a special agent is like being arrested for murder. Call me a scaredy-cat, but I'd want legal representation even If I were innocent.

Don't Volunteer Information

Loose lips sink ships. Don't volunteer any information — even if it seems innocuous. Just answer the questions you're asked.

Again, I'm not suggesting that you lie. The agent, however, is looking for income that you forgot or deductions that you overstated. The more information you provide, the more likely you'll reveal something damaging.

For example, if you offhandedly tell the agent about your other business — where you knit socks for golf clubs — you may wind up debating whether that cute little business is really a business (and not a hobby) and whether knitting golf socks entitles you to deduct those country club dues and greens fees.

Consider Using a Pinch Hitter

I don't think an audit should terrify you. And I'm someone who's scared of everything: dinner parties where I don't know anyone, stormy nights when the neighborhood seems particularly deserted, driving on bald tires. You get the idea. Nonetheless, if you used a paid preparer, think about sending that person in your place.

You pay for this service, of course. But you may benefit from having the person who prepared your return do the talking.

Understand Everything on Your Return

Be sure that you understand everything on your return. You won't help yourself if you tell an agent that you don't have a clue about some number on the return.

Be Friendly

Be nice to the IRS. Remember, the agents actually work for you. In fact, the more taxes that the agents collect from people who owe the federal government, the less the rest of us have to pay. (An article in *Money* magazine a few years ago suggested that we end up paying several hundred dollars more a year in income taxes because so many people cheat.)

Don't Worry

If you have been honest and careful, you have nothing to worry about. Sure, maybe you made a mistake. Maybe the agent will find the mistake. And maybe you'll have to pay some additional taxes.

If you haven't been honest and careful, I offer my condolences. Sorry.

Don't Lie

Don't lie; it may be perjury. You could go to jail and share a cell with someone named Skullcrusher. And develop a close relationship.

You get the picture. And it's not pretty. So don't lie.

The 5th Wave   By Rich Tennant

"WE HARDLY GET ANY COMPLAINTS FROM TAXPAYERS ANYMORE. THINK IT'S BECAUSE WE HIRED A TROGLODYTE TO RUN THE DEPARTMENT?"

Chapter 17

Ten Secret Business Formulas

1 have some good news and some bad news for you. The good news is that you can use some powerful formulas to better your chances of business success and increase your profits. No, I'm not joking. Formulas such as these do exist. You can and should use them. And in the pages that follow, I explain the formulas and how to use them.

Now for the bad news: To use these formulas, you need to feel comfortable with a bit of arithmetic. You don't need to be a serious mathematician or anything. But you do need to feel comfortable with percentages and calculators.

Even so, I want to encourage you to skim through this chapter. Even if you're not particularly fond of, or all that good at, arithmetic, you can pick up some weird insights into the world of finance.

You can use the standard Windows Calculator accessory, available from within QuickBooks, to calculate any of the secret formulas.

The First "Most Expensive Money You Can Borrow" Formula

Here's something you may not know. The most expensive money that you borrow is from vendors who offer early payment discounts that you don't take. For example, perhaps your friendly office supply store offers a 2 percent discount if you pay cash at the time of purchase instead of paying within the usual 30 days. In this case, you're paying 2 percent more by paying 30 days later. So, in effect, you're paying a 2 percent monthly interest charge. A 2 percent monthly interest charge works out to a 24 percent annual interest charge. And that's a lot of money.

Here's another example that is only slightly more complicated. Many, many vendors offer a 2 percent discount if you pay within the first 10 days an invoice is due instead of 30 days later. (These payment terms are often described and printed at the bottom of the invoice as "2/10, Net 30.")

In this case, you're paying 2 percent more by paying 20 days later. (The 20 days later is the difference between 10 days and 30 days.) Two percent for 20 days is roughly equivalent to 3 percent for 30 days, or a month. So, a 2 percent 20-day interest charge works out to a 36 percent annual interest charge. And now you're talking serious money.

Table 17-1 shows how some common early payment discounts translate into annual interest rates. By the way, I have been a bit more precise in my calculations for this table, so these numbers vary slightly from (and are larger than) those I have given in the preceding paragraph.

Table 17-1	Annual Interest Rates for Early Payment Discounts	
Early Payment Discount	*For Paying 20 Days Early*	*For Paying 30 Days Early*
1%	18.43%	12.29%
2%	37.24%	24.83%
3%	56.44%	37.63%
4%	76.04%	50.69%
5%	96.05%	64.04%

Is it just me, or do those numbers blow you away? The 2 percent for 20 days early payment discount that you always see works out (if you do the math precisely) to more than 37 percent annual interest. Man, that hurts. And if you don't take a 5 percent for 20 days early payment discount when it's offered, you're effectively borrowing money at an annual rate of 96 percent. You didn't read that last number wrong. Yes, a 5 percent for 20 days early payment discount works out to an annual interest rate of almost 100 percent.

I should make a couple more observations, too. A 1 percent discount for paying 30 days early isn't such a bad deal in many cases. Look at Table 17-1. It shows the 1 percent discount for paying 30 days early as 12.29 percent. Sure, that rate is pretty high. But that interest rate is less than for many credit cards. And it is less than for many small business credit lines.

The bottom line on all this is that early payment discounts, if not taken, represent one of the truly expensive ways to borrow money. I'm not saying that you won't need to borrow money this way at times. I can guess that your cash flow gets pretty tight sometimes. (This circumstance is true in most businesses, as you probably know.) I am saying that you should never skip taking an early payment discount unless borrowing money at outrageous interest rates makes sense.

Oh, yes. The secret formula. To figure out the effective annual interest rate that you're paying by not taking an early payment discount, you use this formula:

Discount % / (1 – Discount %) * (365 / Number of Days of Early Payment)

So, to calculate the effective annual interest rate that you're paying by not taking a 2 percent discount for paying 20 days early, you calculate this formula:

.02 / (1 – .02) * (365 / 20)

Work out the mathematics and you get .3724, which is the same thing as a 37.24 percent interest rate. (Note that the discount percents are entered as their equivalent decimal values.)

The Scientific view of the Windows calculator includes parenthesis keys that you can use to calculate this formula and the others described in the chapter. Choose View⇨Scientific to switch to the Scientific view of the calculator.

The Second "Most Expensive Money You Can Borrow" Formula

You know that "most expensive money you can borrow" stuff that I talked about in the preceding section? The very tragic flip side to that story is when you offer your customers early payment discounts and they take them. In effect, you're borrowing money from your customers. And at the same outrageous interest rates. For example, if customer Joe Schmoe gets a 2 percent early payment discount for paying 20 days early, you are, in effect, paying ol' Joe roughly 2 percent interest for a 20-day loan. Using the same formula I gave for the first "most expensive money you can borrow" formula, the rate works out to 37.24 percent.

What about cash payment discounts?

Good question. These discounts are different. My doctor, for example, offers me a 2 percent discount if I pay him in cash at the end of my visit rather than 30 days later. Is my doctor stupid or desperate? No. Here's the reason: First, if I pay him on the spot, he doesn't have to bill me or the insurance company, which saves his book-keeper time. If the $12/hour bookkeeper needs a quarter hour to prepare the invoice, send it out to both me and the insurance company, and then record and deposit the payment, my doctor has to pay $3 in real money to invoice me. So he saves $3 if he gets the cash up front.

The good doctor is too polite to bring up a more subtle reason for offering this discount. If the discount encourages patients to pay the fees up front, he'll probably have fewer uncollectible accounts receivable later on. This equation is tricky. I can't give you any formula for it. But the logic is that he'll collect at least some of the fees — 98 percent of the fees, to be precise — from deadbeats from whom he would otherwise collect nothing. And the deadbeats who pay 98 percent up front instead of stiffing him more than make up for the 2 percent discount that the nondeadbeats enjoy.

In some industries, customers expect early payment discounts. You may have to offer them. But you should never offer them willingly. You should never offer them just for fun. Borrowing money this way is just too expensive. A rate of 37.24 percent. Yikes!

Let me also offer a rather dour observation. In my experience, any time someone is offering big early payment discounts — I've seen them as big as 5 percent — they're either stupid or desperate, and probably both.

The "How Do I Break Even?" Formula

I know that you're not interested in just *breaking even*. I know that you want to make money in your business. But, that said, knowing what quantities you need to sell just to cover your expenses is often super-helpful. If you're a one-person accounting firm (or some other service business), for example, how many hours do you need to work to pay your expenses and perhaps pay yourself a small salary? Or, if you're a retailer of, say, toys, how many toys do you need to sell to pay your overhead, the rent, and sales clerks?

You see my point, right? Knowing how much revenue you need to generate just to stay in the game is essential. Knowing your *break-even point,* as it's known, enables you to establish a benchmark for your performance. (Anytime you're not breaking even, you know that you have a serious problem you need to resolve quickly to stay in business.) And considering break-even points are invaluable when you think about new businesses or new ventures. As you ponder any new opportunity and its potential income and expenses, you need to know how much income you need to generate just to pay those expenses.

To calculate a break-even point, you need to know just three pieces of information: your fixed costs (the expenses you have to pay regardless of the business's revenue, or income), the revenue you generate for each sale, and the variable costs that you incur in each sale. (These variable costs, which also are called *direct expenses* in case you care, aren't the same thing as the fixed costs.)

Take the book-writing business as an example. Suppose that as you read this book, you think, "Man, that guy is having too much fun. Writing about accounting programs . . . working day-in and day-out with buggy beta software . . . . Yeah, that would be the life."

Further suppose that for every book that you write you think that you can make $5,000, but that you'll probably end up paying about $1,000 a book for things such as long-distance telephone charges, overnight courier charges, and extra hardware and software. And suppose that you need to pay yourself a salary of $20,000 a year. (In this scenario, your salary is your only fixed cost because you plan to write at home at a small desk in your bedroom.)

Okay, here's how the situation breaks down:

Variable	Amount	Explanation
Revenue	$ 5,000	What you can squeeze out of the publisher
Variable costs	$ 1,000	All the little things that add up
Fixed costs	$20,000	You need someplace to live and food to eat

With these three bits of data, you can easily calculate how many books you need to write to break even. Here's the formula:

Fixed Costs / (Revenue – Variable Costs)

If you plug in the writing business example data, things look like this:

$20,000 / ($5,000 – $1,000)

Work through the math and you get five. So you need to write (and get paid for) five books a year to pay the $1,000 per book variable costs and your $20,000 salary. Just to prove that I didn't make up this formula and that it really works, here's how things look if you write five books:

Description	Amount	Explanation
Revenue	$25,000	Five books at $5,000 each
Variable costs	($5,000)	Five books at $1,000 each
Fixed costs	($20,000)	A little food money, a little rent money, a little beer money
Profits	0	Subtract the costs from the revenue, and there's nothing left

Accountants, by the way, use parenthesis marks to show negative numbers. That's why the $5,000 and the $20,000 are in parentheses.

But back to the game. To break even in a book-writing business such as the one described here, you need to sell and write five books a year. If you don't think that you can write and sell five books in a year, getting into the book-writing business makes no sense.

Your business is probably more complicated than book writing, but the same formula and logic apply. You need just three pieces of information: the revenue you receive from the sale of a single item, the variable costs of selling (and possibly making) the item, and the fixed costs that you pay just to be in business.

QuickBooks doesn't collect or present information in a way that enables you to easily pull the revenue per item and variable costs per item off some report. Nor does it provide a fixed costs total on some report. But if you understand the logic of the preceding discussion, you can easily massage the QuickBooks data to get the information you need.

✔ Whatever you sell — be it thingamajigs, corporate jets, or hours of consulting services — has a price. That price is your revenue per item input.

✔ Most of the time, what you sell has a cost, too. If you buy and resell thingamajigs, those thingamajigs cost you some amount of money. Sometimes the variable cost per item is zero, however. (If you're a consultant, for example, you sell hours of your time. But you may not pay an hourly cost just because you consult for an hour.)

✔ Your fixed costs are all those costs that you pay regardless of whether you sell your product or service. For example, if you have to pay an employee a salary regardless of whether you're selling anything, that salary is a fixed cost. Your rent is probably a fixed cost. Things such as insurance and legal and accounting expenses are probably also fixed costs because they don't vary with fluctuations in your revenue.

✔ Fixed costs, by the way, may change a bit from year to year or may bounce around a bit. So maybe *fixed* isn't a very good adjective. People use the term *fixed costs,* however, to differentiate these costs from variable costs, which are those costs that do vary with income.

The "You Can Grow Too Fast" Formula

Here's a weird little paradox: One of the easiest ways for a small business to fail is by being too successful. I know. It sounds crazy. But it's true. In fact, I'll even go so far as to say that by far the most common reason for business failure that I see is business success.

"Oh, geez," you're saying. "This nut is talking in circles."

Let me explain. Whether you realize it or not, you need a certain amount of financial horsepower, or net worth, to do business. (Your *net worth* is just the difference between your assets and your liabilities.) You have to have some cash in the bank to tide you over the rough times that everybody has at least occasionally. You probably have to have some office furniture and computers so that you can take care of the business end of the business. And if you make anything at all, you have to have adequate tools and machinery. This part all makes sense, right?

Okay, now on to the next reality. If your business grows and continues to grow, you're going to need to increase your financial horsepower, or net worth. A bigger business, for example, needs more cash to make it through the tough times, more office furniture and computers, and more tools and machinery. Oh sure, you may be able to have a one-time spurt in size because you have more financial horsepower (more net worth) than you need. But — and this is the key part — you can't grow and continue to grow without increasing your net worth at some point. In other words, you can't sustain business growth without increasing your net worth.

Some of you are now saying things like, "No way, man. That doesn't apply to me." I assure you, my new friend, that it does. The reality is this: Growing a business means more than just growing your sales and growing your expenses. You need to grow your financial net worth, too.

Before I give you the actual formula, I want to tell you one more thing. The most important thing that you can take away from this discussion is this bit of knowledge: The growth rate that a business can sustain has a limit.

But back to the chase. As long as your creditors will extend you additional credit as you grow your business — and they should, as long as the business is profitable and you don't have cash flow problems — you can grow your business as fast as you can grow your net worth. If you can grow your net worth by 5 percent a year, your business can grow at an easily sustained rate of only 5 percent a year. If you can grow your net worth by 50 percent a year, your business can grow at an easily sustained rate of only (only?) 50 percent a year.

You grow your business's net worth in only two ways: One way is by reinvesting profits in the business, and the other way is by getting people to invest money in the business. If you're not in a position to continually raise money from new investors — and most small businesses aren't — the only practical way to grow is by reinvesting profits in the business. (Note that any profits that you leave in the business instead of drawing them out — such as through dividends or draws — are reinvested.) So you can calculate the growth rate that your business can sustain by using this formula:

> Reinvested Profits / Net Worth

I should say, just for the record, that the formula given earlier is a very simple "sustainable growth" formula. But even so, it offers some amazingly interesting insights. For example, perhaps you are a commercial printer doing $500,000 in revenues a year with a business net worth of $100,000; your business earns $50,000 a year, but you leave only $10,000 a year in the business. In other words, your reinvested profits are $10,000. In this case, your sustainable growth is calculated as follows:

> $10,000 / $100,000

Work out the numbers and you get .1, or 10 percent. In other words, you can grow your business by 10 percent a year (as long as you grow the net worth by 10 percent a year by reinvesting profits). For example, you can easily go from $500,000, to $550,000, to $605,000 and continue growing at this 10 percent rate. But your business can't grow any faster than 10 percent a year. For example, you'll get into serious trouble if you try to go from $500,000, to $600,000, to $720,000 and continue growing at 20 percent a year.

You can convert a decimal value to a percentage by multiplying the value by 100. For example, .1 x 100 equals 10, so .1 equals 10 percent. You can convert a percentage to a decimal value by dividing the value by 100. For example, 25 (as in 25 percent) divided by 100 equals .25.

By the way, the sustainable growth formula inputs are pretty easy to get after you have QuickBooks up and running. You can get the net worth figure off the balance sheet. You can calculate the reinvested profits by looking at the net income and deducting any amounts that you pulled out of the business.

Note: I'm not going to go through the mathematical proof of why this sustainable growth formula is true. My experience is that it makes intuitive sense to people who think about it for a few minutes. If you aren't into the intuition-thing or you don't believe me, get a college finance textbook and look up its discussion of the sustainable growth formula.

I don't want to beat this sustainable growth thing to death, but let me close with a true and mercifully short story.

I have just seen another entrepreneur fail because he was successful. At first, he ignored the symptoms of fast growth. He needed another computer, so he bought it. He had to hire another person, so he just did it. Cash flow was tight and getting tighter, but he ignored the problems. After all, he was making a large number of sales, and the business was growing. Sure, things were getting awkward, but he didn't need to worry, right?

Unfortunately, vendors were getting paid later and later. This went on for a few weeks until some vendors started insisting on cash payments.

One Friday, he couldn't make his payroll. He then committed the unpardonable sin of borrowing payroll tax money — something you should never, ever do.

Finally, he had a large number of bills to pay and not only no cash to pay the bills but no cash in sight. Employees quit. Vendors said, "No more." And this is what ultimately killed the business. When the telephone company cuts off your telephone service, you're pretty much in serious trouble. When your landlord locks you out of your business location, you're pretty much out of luck.

The paradox in all this is that the guy had a successful business. He just spread his financial resources too thin by growing too fast.

The First "What Happens If . . ." Formula

One thing that's curious about small businesses is that small changes in revenue or income can have huge impacts on profits. A retailer who is cruising along at $200,000 in revenue and struggling to live on $30,000 a year never realizes that boosting the sales volume by 20 percent to $250,000 may increase his profits by 200 percent to $60,000.

In fact, if you take only one thing away from this discussion, it should be this curious little truth: If fixed costs don't change, small changes in revenue can produce big changes in profits.

The following example shows how all this works and provides a secret formula. For starters, say that you're currently generating $100,000 a year in revenue and are making $20,000 a year in profits. The revenue per item sold is $100, and the variable cost per item sold is $35. (In this case, the fixed costs happen to be $45,000 a year, but that figure isn't all that important to the analysis.)

Accountants like to whip up little tables that describe these sorts of things, so Table 17-2 gives the current story on your imaginary business.

Table 17-2		Your Business Profits
Description	*Amount*	*Explanation*
Revenue	$100,000	You sell 1,000 doohickeys at $100 a pop
Variable costs	($35,000)	You buy 1,000 doohickeys at $35 a pop
Fixed costs	($45,000)	All the little things: rent, your salary, and so on
Profits	$20,000	What's left over

Okay, Table 17-2 shows the current situation. But suppose that you want to know what will happen to your profits if revenue increases by 20 percent but your fixed costs don't change. Mere mortals, not knowing what you and I know, might assume that a 20 percent increase in revenue would produce an approximate 20 percent increase in profits. But you know that small changes in revenue can produce big changes in profits, right?

To estimate exactly how a change in revenue affects profits, you use the following secret formula:

Percentage * Revenue * (1 – Variable Cost per Item / Revenue per Item)

Using the example data provided in Table 17-2 — and I'm sorry this is starting to resemble those story problems from eighth-grade math — you make the following calculation:

.20 * $100,000 * (1 – 35 / 100)

Work out the numbers and you get 13,000. What does this figure mean? It means that a 20 percent increase in revenue produces a $13,000 increase in profits. As a percentage of profits, this $13,000 increase is 65 percent ($13,000 / $20,000 = 65 percent).

To summarize, in this case, a 20 percent increase in revenues results in a 65 percent increase in profits.

Let me stop here and make a quick observation. In my experience, entrepreneurs always seem to think that they need to grow big to make big money. They concentrate on doing things that will double, or triple, or quadruple their sales. Their logic, though, isn't always correct. If you can grow your business without having to increase your fixed costs, small changes in revenues can produce big changes in profits.

Before I stop talking about this first "What happens if . . ." formula, I should quickly describe where you get the inputs you need for the formula:

> ✔ The percentage change input is just a number that you pick. If you want to see what happens to your profits with a 25 percent increase in sales, for example, you use .25.
>
> ✔ The revenue input is your total revenue. You can get it from your Profit & Loss Statement.
>
> ✔ The revenue per item sold and variable costs per item sold figures work the same way as described for the break-even formula. Rather than repeat myself, I'm assuming that you've read that formula description or that you can read it next.

The Second "What Happens If..." Formula

Maybe I shouldn't tell you this. But people in finance, like me, usually have a prejudice against people in sales. And it's not just because people who are good at sales usually make more money than people who are good at finance. It's really not. Honest to goodness.

Here's the prejudice: People in finance think that people in sales always want to reduce prices.

People in sales see things a bit differently. They say, in effect, "Hey, you worry too much. We'll make up the difference in additional sales volume."

The argument is appealing: You just undercut your competitor's prices by a healthy chunk and make less on each sale. But because you sell your stuff so cheaply, your customers will beat a path to your door.

Just for the record, I love people who are good at sales. I think someone who is good at sales is more important than someone who is good at finance.

But, that painful admission aside, I have to tell you that a problem exists with the "Cut the prices; we'll make it up with volume" strategy. If you cut prices by a given percentage — perhaps by 10 percent — you usually have to have a much bigger percentage gain in revenue to break even.

The following example shows what I mean and how this works. Suppose that you have a business that sells some doohickey or thingamajig. You generate $100,000 a year in revenue and make $20,000 a year in profits. Your revenue per item, or doohickey, sold is $100, and your variable cost per item, or doohickey, sold is $35. Your fixed costs happen to be $45,000 a year; but, again, the fixed costs aren't all that important to the analysis. Table 17-3 summarizes the current situation.

Table 17-3	Your Current Situation	
Description	**Amount**	**Explanation**
Revenue	$100,000	You sell 1,000 doohickeys at $100 a pop
Variable costs	($35,000)	You buy 1,000 doohickeys at $35 a pop
Fixed costs	($45,000)	All the little things: rent,your salary, and so on
Profits	$20,000	What's left over

Then business is particularly bad for one month. Joe-Bob, your sales guy, comes to you and says, "Boss, I've got an idea. I think we can cut prices by 15 percent to $85 a doohickey and get a truly massive boost in sales."

You're a good boss. You're a polite boss. Plus, you're intrigued. So you think a bit. The idea has a certain appeal. You start wondering how much of an increase in sales you need to break even on the price reduction.

You're probably not surprised to read this, but I have another secret formula that can help. You can use the following formula to calculate how many items (doohickeys, in the example) you need to sell just to break even on the new, discounted price. Here is the formula:

(Current Profits + Fixed Costs) / (Revenue per Item – Variable Cost per Item)

Using the example data provided earlier, you make the following calculation:

($20,000 + $45,000) / ($85 – $35)

Work out the numbers, and you get 1,300. What does this figure mean? It means that just to break even on the $85 doohickey price — *just to break even* — Joe-Bob needs to sell 1,300 doohickeys. Currently, per Table 17-3, Joe-Bob is selling 1,000 doohickeys a year. As a percentage, then, this jump from 1,000 doohickeys to 1,300 doohickeys is exactly a 30 percent increase. (Remember that Joe-Bob is proposing a 15 percent price cut.)

Okay, I don't know Joe-Bob. He may be a great guy. He may be a wonderful salesperson. But here's my guess. Joe-Bob isn't thinking about a 30 percent increase in sales volume. (Remember, with a 15 percent price reduction, you need a 30 percent increase just to break even!) And Joe-Bob almost certainly isn't thinking about a 50 percent or 75 percent increase in sales volume — which is what you need to make money on the whole deal, as shown in Table 17-4.

Table 17-4	How Profits Look at Various Sales Levels		
Description	*1,300 Units Sold*	*1,500 Units Sold*	*1,750 Units Sold*
Revenue	$110,500	$127,500	$148,750
Variable costs	($45,500)	($52,500)	($61,250)
Fixed costs	($45,000)	($45,000)	($45,000)
Profits	$20,000	$30,000	$42,500

In summary, you can't reduce prices by, say, 15 percent, and then go for some penny-ante increase. You need huge increases in the sales volume to get big increases in profits. If you look at Table 17-4, you can see that if you can increase the sales from 1,000 doohickeys to 1,750 doohickeys — a 75 percent increase — you can more than double the profits. This increase assumes that the fixed costs stay level, as the table shows.

I want to describe quickly where you get the inputs you need for the formula:

- ✔ The profit figure can come right off the QuickBooks Profit & Loss Statement.
- ✔ The fixed costs figure just tallies all your fixed costs. (I talked about this in the paragraphs that describe how to estimate your break-even point.)
- ✔ The revenue per item is just the new price that you're considering.
- ✔ Finally, the variable cost per item is the cost of the thing you're selling. (I discussed this earlier in the chapter, too.)

Please don't construe the preceding discussion as proof that you should never listen to the Joe-Bobs of the world. The "cut prices to increase volume" strategy can work wonderfully well. The trick, however, is to increase the sales volume massively. Sam Walton, the late founder of Wal-Mart, used the strategy and became, at one point, the richest man in the world.

The Economic Order Quantity (aka Isaac Newton) Formula

Isaac Newton invented differential calculus. This is truly amazing to me. I can't imagine how someone could just figure out calculus. I could never, in a hundred years, figure it out. But I'm getting off the track.

The neat thing about calculus — and no, I'm not going to do any calculus here — is that it enables you to create optimal values equations. One of the coolest such equations is called the economic order quantity, or EOQ, model. I know this all sounds terribly confusing and totally boring, but stay with me for just another paragraph. (If you're not satisfied in another paragraph or so, skip ahead to the next secret formula.)

Perhaps you buy and then resell — oh, I don't know — 2,000 cases of vintage French wine every year. The EOQ model enables you to decide whether you should order all 2,000 cases at one time, order 1 case at a time, or order some number of cases in between 1 case and 2,000 cases.

Another way to say the same thing is that the EOQ model enables you to choose the best, or optimal, reorder quantity for items that you buy and then resell.

If you're still with me at this point, I figure that you want to know how all this works. You need to know just three pieces of data to calculate the optimal order quantity: the annual sales volume, the cost of placing an order, and the annual cost of holding one unit in inventory. You plug this information into the following formula:

$$\sqrt{(2 * \text{Sales Volume} * \text{Order Cost})} / \text{Annual Holding Cost per Item}$$

You buy and resell 2,000 cases a year, so that amount is the sales volume. Every time you place an order for the wine, you need to buy an $800 round-trip ticket to Paris (just to sample the inventory) and pay $200 for a couple of nights at a hotel. So your cost per order is $1,000. Finally, with insurance, interest on a bank loan, and the cost of maintaining your hermetically sealed, temperature-controlled wine cellar, the cost of storing a case of wine is about $100 a year. In this example, then, you can calculate the optimal order quantity as follows:

$$\sqrt{(2 * 2000 * \$1000)} / \$100$$

Work through the numbers and you get 200. Therefore, the order quantity that minimizes the total cost of your trips to Paris *and* of holding your expensive wine inventory is 200 cases. You could, of course, make only one trip to Paris a year and buy 2,000 cases of wine at once, thereby saving travel money; but you would spend more money on holding your expensive wine inventory than you would save on travel costs. And, although you could reduce your wine inventory carrying costs by going to Paris every week and picking up a few cases, your travel costs would go way, way up. (Of course, you would get about a billion frequent flyer miles a year.)

You can use the Standard view of the calculator to compute economic order quantities. The trick is to click the $\sqrt{}$ (Square Root) key last. For example, to calculate the economic order quantity in the preceding example, you enter the following numbers and operators:

2 * 2000 * 1000 / 100 $\sqrt{}$

The Rule of 72

The Rule of 72 isn't exactly a secret formula. It's more like a rule of thumb. Usually, people use it to figure out how long it will take for some investment or savings account to double in value. It's a cool little trick, however. And it has several useful applications for business people.

What the rule says is that, if you divide the value 72 by an interest rate percentage, your result is approximately the number of years it will take to double your money. For example, if you can stick money into some investment that pays 12 percent interest, it will take roughly six years to double your money because 72 / 12 = 6.

The Rule of 72 isn't exact, but it's usually close enough for government work. For example, if you invest $1,000 for six years at 12 percent interest, what you really get after six years isn't $2,000 but $1,973.92.

If you're in business, you can use the Rule of 72 in a couple other ways, too. If you want to forecast how long it will take inflation to double the price of an item, you can just divide 72 by the inflation rate. For example, if you own a building that you figure will at least keep up with inflation and wonder how long it will take to double in value if inflation runs at 4 percent, you just divide 72 by 4. The result is 18, meaning that it will take roughly 18 years for the building to double in value. Again, the Rule of 72 isn't exactly on the money, but it's dang close. A $100,000 building increases in value to $202,581.65 over 18 years if the annual inflation rate is 4 percent.

Another way business owners can use the Rule of 72 is by forecasting how long it will take to double your sales volume, given some annual growth rate. For example, if you can grow your business by, say, 9 percent a year, you will roughly double the size of the business in eight years because 72 / 9 = 8. (I'm becoming kind of compulsive about this, I know, but let me say again that the rule isn't exact, but it's very close. If a $1,000,000-a-year business grows 9 percent annually, its sales equal $1,992,562.64 after eight years of 9 percent growth. This really means that the business will generate roughly $2,000,000 of sales in the ninth year.)

Chapter 18
Ten Tips for Business Owners

. . . .

. . . .

*I*f you run a business and you use QuickBooks, you need to know the information in this chapter. You can learn these things by sitting down with your certified public accountant over a cup of coffee at $100 an hour. Or you can read this chapter.

Sign All Your Own Checks

I have nothing against your bookkeeper. In a small business, however, it's just too darn easy for people — especially full-charge bookkeepers — to bamboozle you. By signing all the checks yourself, you keep your fingers on the pulse of your cash outflow.

Yeah, I know this can be a hassle. I know this means you can't easily spend three months in Hawaii. I know this means you have to wade through paperwork every time you sign a stack of checks.

By the way, if you're in a partnership, I think you should have at least a couple of the partners co-sign checks.

Don't Sign a Check the Wrong Way

If you sign many checks, you may be tempted to use a John Hancock-like signature. Although this makes great sense if you're autographing baseballs, don't do it when you're signing checks. A clear signature, even with a sense of personal style, is distinctive. A wavy line with a cross and a couple of dots is really easy to forge.

Which leads me to my next tip . . . .

Review Canceled Checks Before Your Bookkeeper Does

Be sure that you review your canceled checks before anybody else sees the monthly bank statement.

This chapter isn't about browbeating bookkeepers. But a business owner can discover whether someone is forging signatures on checks only by being the first to open the bank statement and by reviewing each of the canceled check signatures.

If you don't examine the checks, unscrupulous employees — especially bookkeepers who can update the bank account records — can forge your signature with impunity. And they won't get caught if they never overdraw the account.

Another thing: If you don't follow these procedures, *you* will probably eat the losses, not the bank.

How to Choose a Bookkeeper If You Use QuickBooks

Don't worry. You don't need to request an FBI background check.

In fact, if you use QuickBooks, you don't need to hire people who are familiar with small-business accounting systems. Just find people who know how to keep a checkbook and work with a computer. They shouldn't have a problem understanding QuickBooks.

Of course, you don't want someone who just fell off the turnip truck. But even if you do hire someone who rode into town on one, you're not going to have much trouble getting that person up to speed with QuickBooks.

If the bookkeeper knows double-entry bookkeeping, that would be super-helpful. But, to be fair, it's probably not essential. I will say this, however. When you hire someone, find someone who knows how to do payroll — not just the federal payroll tax stuff (see Chapter 12) but also the state payroll tax monkey business.

Cash-Basis Accounting Doesn't Work for All Businesses

When you use QuickBooks, you employ either cash-basis accounting or accrual-basis accounting. (I describe the difference between these two methods in Appendix B.)

Cash-basis accounting is fine when a business's cash inflow mirrors its sales and its cash outflow mirrors its expenses. This isn't the case, however, in many businesses. A contractor of single-family homes, for example, may have cash coming in (by borrowing from banks) but may not make any money. A pawn-shop owner who loans money at 22 percent may make scads of money even if cash pours out of the business daily. As a rule of thumb, when you're buying and selling inventory, accrual-basis accounting works better than cash-basis accounting.

So this isn't earthshaking. It's still something you should think about. Note that you can easily switch to accrual-basis accounting by telling QuickBooks that you want reports prepared on an accrual basis and by promptly recording customer invoices and vendor bills.

If QuickBooks Doesn't Work for Your Business

QuickBooks is a great small-business accounting program. In fact, I guess I'd even go so far as to say that QuickBooks is probably the best small-business accounting program.

However, if QuickBooks doesn't seem to fit your needs — if, for example, you need a package that works for a manufacturer or that includes some special industry-specific feature — you may want one of the more complicated but also more powerful small-business accounting packages.

One possibility might be another popular (and more powerful) full-featured Windows accounting program: Peachtree Accounting for Windows from Peachtree. If that program doesn't work, you might talk to your accountant about industry-specific packages. (For example, if you're a commercial printer, some vendor may have developed a special accounting package just for commercial printers.)

I am amazed that PC accounting software remains so affordable. You can buy a great accounting package — one you can use to manage a $5 million or a $25 million business — for a few hundred bucks. It is truly one of the great bargains in life.

Keep Things Simple

Let me share one last comment about managing small-business financial affairs. *Keep things as simple as possible.* In fact, keep your business affairs simple enough that you can easily tell whether you're making money and whether the business is healthy.

This advice may sound strange, but as a CPA, I've worked for some very bright people who have built monstrously complex financial structures for their businesses, including complicated leasing arrangements, labyrinth like partnership and corporate structures, and sophisticated profit-sharing and cost-sharing arrangements with other businesses.

I can only offer anecdotal evidence, of course, but I strongly believe that these super-sophisticated financial arrangements don't produce a profit when you consider all the costs. What's more, these super-sophisticated arrangements almost always turn into management and record-keeping headaches.

Chapter 19

Ten Tips for Bookkeepers Who Use QuickBooks (and Anyone Else, Too)

* *

In This Chapter

▶ Tricks for learning QuickBooks

▶ Cross-referencing

▶ Reconciling accounts promptly

▶ Things to do at the end of every month

▶ Things to do at the end of every year

▶ Handling debits and credits

▶ Converting to QuickBooks from another system

▶ A word of advice on income tax evasion

▶ Being careful with payroll taxes

* *

An amazing number of people use QuickBooks for small-business accounting: dentists, contractors, lawyers, and so on. And, not surprisingly, a great number of small business bookkeepers use QuickBooks.

If you're jumping up and down, waving your hands, saying, "I do, I do, I do," this chapter is for you. I tell you here what you need to know to make your use of QuickBooks smooth and sure.

Tricks for Learning QuickBooks If You're New on the Job

First of all, let me congratulate you on your new job. Let me also remind you of how thankful you should be that you'll be using QuickBooks and not one of the super-powerful-but-frightening, complex accounting packages.

If you're new to computers, you need to know a thing or two about them. Don't worry. Using a computer isn't as difficult as you may think. (Remember that a bunch of anxious folks have gone before you.)

Turning On the Computer

Before you use the computer, you need to do the following:

1. **Find and flip on the computer's power switch (usually a big red switch).**
2. **Push a switch to turn on the monitor (the televisionlike screen).**
3. **Flip a switch to turn on the printer.**

Even if you're a little timid, go ahead and ask your boss how to turn on the computer and its peripherals. This question won't be considered stupid. You turn on different computers in different ways. For example, the switches on the computer and its peripherals may already be turned on, and the equipment may be plugged into a *fancy-schmancy* extension cord called a *power strip* — but this power strip thing may be turned off. (By the way, the word *peripherals* refers to things that work with the computer, such as the printer.)

Starting QuickBooks

Here are two different approaches for starting QuickBooks: Use one approach if you're using a previous incarnation of Windows, and use a different approach if you're using Windows 95. Windows 95 takes the place of DOS, and you won't see the characters on the screen that I mention in the section on Windows 3.1. Either way, you use Windows to start QuickBooks. If you don't "do" Windows, refer to your *Windows User's Guide* or to the *Windows For Dummies* book for your flavor of Windows, by Andy Rathbone (IDG Books Worldwide).

For Windows 3.1

After you turn on the computer, two things may happen. Windows may automatically appear, if someone has figured out how to configure the computer. Or you may see something on the screen that looks like this:

```
C:\>
```

This "something" is called the *DOS prompt,* but you don't have to remember this bit of trivia. To start Windows, type **win** and then press Enter. Windows starts. Look for a program group called, in a marketing coup, QuickBooks. When you find it, just double-click the QuickBooks icon, and the program starts.

For Windows 95

Windows 95 starts on its own when you turn on the computer. After it is finished booting up, click the Start button, and then choose Programs⇨QuickBooks⇨QuickBooks, and the program starts.

For Macintosh

When your Macintosh starts, look for an icon or folder (probably on your hard disk) called QuickBooks or something like that. If you find the folder, double-click the folder to open it and then double-click the QuickBooks icon to start the program.

Learning QuickBooks

When you know how to turn on the computer and how to start QuickBooks, you're ready to rock. Give Part II of this book a quick read. Then carefully read those chapters in Part III that apply to your work, too.

One last thing: Using QuickBooks is much easier than you think. Remember when you learned how to drive a car? Sure it was confusing at first: all those gauges and meters . . . the tremendous power at your fingertips . . . traffic. After you gained some experience, though, you loosened your death grip on the wheel. Heck, you even started driving in the left lane.

Give yourself a little time. Before long, you'll be zipping around QuickBooks, changing lanes three at a time.

Cross-Referencing Source Documents and Filing Them

Be sure to cross-reference and file (neatly!) the source documents (checks, deposit slips, and so on) that you use when you enter transactions. I won't tell you how to set up a document filing system. Chances are pretty good that you can do this better than I can — in fact, I usually use a crude, alphabetical scheme.

Invoice forms, sales receipts, and checks are all numbered, so you can cross-reference these items simply by entering form numbers when recording a check transaction.

Cross-referencing enables you to answer any questions about a transaction that appears in your QuickBooks system. All you have to do is find the source document that you used to enter the transaction.

Reconciling Bank Accounts Promptly

This is a pet peeve, so bear with me if I get a little huffy.

I think you should always reconcile, or balance, a business's bank accounts within a day or two after you get the bank statement. You'll catch any errors that you or the bank has made.

You also minimize the chance that you'll suffer financial losses from check forgery. If a business or individual promptly alerts a bank about a check forgery, the bank, rather than the business, suffers the loss in most cases.

Reconciling in QuickBooks is fast and easy, so there's no good excuse not to reconcile promptly. Chapter 11 describes how to reconcile accounts in QuickBooks.

Things You Should Do Every Month

In a business, everyone has some routine tasks: Go through the In basket. Return phone messages. Clean the coffee machine. Make macaroni and cheese for the potluck. You know.

Here are six bookkeeping chores that you should probably do at the end of every month:

1. **If the business uses a petty cash system, replenish the petty cash fund. Make sure that you have receipts for all withdrawals.**

2. **Reconcile the bank and credit card accounts.**

3. **If you're preparing payroll, be sure to remit any payroll tax deposit money owed.**

    The Internal Revenue Service can give you information about how this works for businesses in the United States.

    You may need to remit payroll tax money more frequently than monthly.

4. **Print one copy of the trial balance.**

Set this copy aside with permanent financial records. Chapter 13 describes how to print reports.

5. **Print two copies of the monthly cash flow statement, the profit and loss statement, and the balance sheet.**

Give one copy to the business's owner or manager. Put the other copy with the permanent financial records.

6. **If you haven't done so already during the month, back up the file containing the QuickBooks accounts to a floppy disk.**

You can reuse the floppy disk every other month. Chapter 14 describes how to back up files.

Don't view the preceding list as all-inclusive. You may need to do other things, too. I'd hate for people to say, "Well, it doesn't appear on Nelson's list, so I don't have to do it." Yikes!

Things You Should Do Every Year

Here are the things that I think you should do at the end of every year:

1. **Do all the usual end-of-month chores for the last month in the year.**

See the list in the preceding section.

2. **Prepare and file any state and federal end-of-year payroll tax returns.**

Businesses in the United States, for example, need to prepare the annual federal unemployment tax return (Form 940).

3. **Print two copies of the annual cash flow statement, the annual profit and loss statement, and the year-end balance sheet.**

Give one copy to the business's owner or manager. Put the other copy with the permanent financial records.

4. **Print a copy of the year-end trial balance.**

This report helps whoever prepares the corporate tax return.

5. **Back up the file containing the QuickBooks accounts to a floppy disk.**

Store the floppy disk as a permanent archive copy.

6. **Be sure to prepare and distribute any of the informational returns that the tax man wants: W-2s, 1099s, and so on.**

If you need help or have questions about these tax forms, call the local Internal Revenue Service office. If you're nervous and don't want them tracing the call, telephone them from a phone booth.

Again, don't view the preceding list as all-inclusive. If you think of other things to do, do them.

Using Debits and Credits

If you have worked with a regular small-business accounting system, you may have missed your old friends, debit and credit. (Is it just me, or do *debit* and *credit* sound like the neighbor kid's pet frogs to you, too?)

QuickBooks is a double-entry accounting system, but it doesn't require you to work with debits and credits. If you want to work with debits and credits — maybe you enjoy creating journal entries — you can use the Activities⇨Enter Special Transactions command. After you choose this command, QuickBooks displays the General Journal Entry dialog box where you can make journal entries till the cows come home.

Converting to QuickBooks

If you're converting to QuickBooks from a manual system or from another more complicated small-business accounting system, here are two important tips:

1. **Start using QuickBooks at the beginning of a year.**

   The year's financial records are then in one place — in the QuickBooks system.

2. **If it's not the beginning of the year, go back and enter the year's transactions.**

Again, the year's financial records are then in one place — in the QuickBooks system. (Entering the transactions takes quite a bit of time if you have many transactions to enter. In fact, you may want to postpone your conversion to QuickBooks to the beginning of the following year.)

Income Tax Evasion

A nice fellow wandered into my office the other day and told me that he had inadvertently gotten entangled in his employer's income tax evasion. He didn't know what to do.

He had (unwittingly, he said) helped his employer file fraudulent income tax returns. Then, already sucked into the tar pit, he had lied to the IRS during an audit.

I didn't have anything good to tell him.

I never did get the fellow's name, so I'll just call him Chump.

Helping his employer steal really didn't make any financial sense for Chump. Chump didn't get a share of the loot; he just helped his employer commit a felony. For free.

Although Chump didn't receive (supposedly) any of the booty, he is probably still in serious trouble with the IRS. The criminal penalties can be enormous, and prison, I understand, is not fun.

I'm not going to spend any more time talking about this. But I do have a piece of advice for you. Don't be a Chump.

Segregating Payroll Tax Money

While I'm on the subject of terrible things that the IRS can do to you, let me touch on the problem of payroll tax deposits — the money you withhold from employee checks for federal income taxes, social security, and medicare.

If you have the authority to spend the money you withhold, don't — even if the company will go out of business. If you can't repay the payroll tax money, the IRS will go after the business owners and also after *you*.

It doesn't matter that you're just the bookkeeper, it doesn't matter whether you regularly attend church, and it doesn't matter if you remember your wife's birthday (which, if you don't, is a whole different kind of trouble). The IRS doesn't take kindly to people who take what belongs to the federal government.

By the way, I should mention that the IRS is more lenient in cases in which you don't have any authority to dip into the payroll tax money and the business owner or your boss uses it. If you see that someone else is using the tax money, however, be darn careful not to get involved. And start looking for a new job.

Chapter 20

Tips for Handling Ten Tricky Situations

· ·

In This Chapter

▶ Selling an asset

▶ Tracking owners equity

▶ Doing multiple-state accounting

▶ Loans

· ·

*A*s your business grows and becomes more complex, your accounting does, too. I can't describe and discuss all the complexities you'll encounter, but I can give you some tips on handling nearly ten tricky situations.

In QuickBooks, you enter journal entries by using the Activities⇨Enter Special Transactions command. If you don't understand double-entry bookkeeping but you'd like to or you want help with using the Enter Special Transactions command, take a gander at Appendix B.

To track the depreciation on an asset that you have already purchased (and added to the chart of accounts), you need two new accounts: an asset account called something such as Accumulated Depreciation and an expense account called something such as Depreciation Expense.

After you set up these two accounts, you can record the asset depreciation with a journal entry such as the following one that records $500 of depreciation expense:

	Debit	Credit
Depreciation expense	$500	
Accumulated depreciation		$500

The federal tax laws provide a special form of depreciation called *Section 179 depreciation*. Section 179 depreciation enables you to depreciate the entire cost of some assets, which is a big break for small businesses. You can't, however, use more than $17,500 of Section 179 depreciation in a year. You also need to know about some other nitty-gritty details, so confer with your tax adviser if you have questions.

Selling an Asset

When you sell an asset, you need to back out, or get rid of, the asset's account balance, record the payment of the cash (or whatever) that somebody pays you for the asset, and record any difference between what you sell the asset for and its value as a gain or loss.

If you purchase a piece of land for $5,000 but later resell it for $4,000, for example, you use the following journal entry to record the sale of this asset:

	Debit	**Credit**
Cash	$4,000	
Loss	$1,000	
Asset		$5,000

Note: You may need to set up another income account for the gain or another expense account for the loss. Refer to Chapter 1 for information on setting up new accounts.

Depreciable Asset

Selling a depreciable asset works almost identically to selling an asset that you haven't been depreciating. When you sell the asset, you need to back out, or get rid of, the asset's account balance. You need to back out, or get rid of, the asset's accumulated depreciation. (This part of selling a depreciable asset is the only thing that's different from selling an asset that you haven't been depreciating.) You need to record the payment of the cash (or whatever) that somebody pays you for the asset. Finally, any difference between what you sell the asset for and what its net-of-accumulated-depreciation value is gets counted as a gain or loss.

This all sounds terribly complicated. But an example will help. Suppose that you purchased a $5,000 piece of machinery and have accumulated $500 of depreciation thus far. This means that the asset account shows a $5,000 debit balance and that the asset's accumulated depreciation account shows a $500 credit balance. Suppose also that you sell the asset for $4,750 in cash.

To record this transaction, you would use the following journal entry to record the sale of this depreciable asset:

	Debit	Credit
Cash	$4,750	
Accumulated depreciation	$500	
Asset		$5,000
Gain		$250

Note: You may need to set up another income account for the gain or another expense account for the loss. Refer to Chapter 1 for information on setting up new accounts.

Owners Equity in a Sole Proprietorship

Actually, tracking owners equity in a sole proprietorship is easy. You can use the single account that QuickBooks sets up for you, which it calls Opening Bal Equity, to track what you've invested in the business. (You may want to rename this account something like Contributed Capital.)

To track the money you withdraw from the business, you can set up and use a new owners equity account called something such as Owners Draws. Table 20-1 gives an example of owners equity accounts in a sole proprietorship.

Table 20-1	An Example of Owners Equity Accounts in a Sole Proprietorship
Account	*Amount*
Contributed capital	$5,000
Retained earnings	$8,000
Owner draws	($2,000)
Owners equity (total)	$11,000

Owners Equity in a Partnership

To track the equity for each partner in a partnership, you need to create three accounts for each partner: one for the partner's contributed capital, one for the partner's draws, and one for the partner's share of the distributed income.

Amounts that a partner withdraws, of course, get tracked with the partner's draws account.

The partner's share of the partnership's profits gets allocated to the partner's profit share account. (Your partnership agreement, by the way, should say how the partnership income is distributed among the partners.) Table 20-2 gives an example of owners equity accounts in a partnership.

Table 20-2	An Example of Owners Equity Accounts in a Partnership	
Account	*Partner A's Amount*	*Partner B's Amount*
Contributed capital	$5,000	$7,000
Profit share	$6,000	$6,000
Draws	($3,000)	($4,000)
Equity (total)	$8,000	$9,000

Owners Equity in a Corporation

Yikes! Accounting for the owners equity in a corporation can get mighty tricky, mighty fast. In fact, I don't mind telling you that college accounting textbooks often use several chapters to describe all the ins and outs of corporation owners equity accounting.

As long as you keep things simple, however, you can probably use three or four accounts for your owners equity:

- *A par value* account. You get the par value amount by multiplying the par value per share by the number of shares issued.

- A *paid-in capital in excess of part value* account for the amount investors paid for shares of stock in excess of par value. You get this amount by multiplying the price paid per share less the par value per share by the number of shares issued.

- A *retained earnings* account to track the business profits left invested in the business.

- A *dividends paid* account to track the amounts distributed to shareholders.

Table 20-3 is an example of owners equity accounts in a corporation.

Table 20-3	An Example of Owners Equity in a Corporation
Account	*Amount*
Par value	$500
Paid-in capital in excess of par value	$4,500
Retained earnings	$8,000
Dividends paid	($3,000)
Shareholders equity	$10,000

Multiple-State Accounting

For multiple-state accounting, the best approach is to set up a chart of accounts that includes a complete set of income and expense accounts (and if necessary, a complete set of asset and liability accounts) for each state. After you set up this chart of accounts, all you have to do is use the correct state's income and expense accounts to record transactions.

If you do business in both Washington and Oregon, for example, sales in Oregon would be recorded as Oregon sales and sales in Washington would be recorded as Washington sales. You would treat other income accounts and all your expense accounts in the same way.

Getting a Loan

Getting a loan is the hard part. After you get the money, recording it in QuickBooks is easy. All you do is record a journal entry that increases cash and that recognizes the new loan liability. For example, if you get a $5,000 loan, you record the following journal entry:

	Debit	**Credit**
Cash	$5,000	
Loan payable		$5,000

Note: You'll already have a cash account set up, but you may need to set up a new liability account to track the loan.

Repaying a Loan

To record loan payments, you need to split each payment between two accounts: the interest expense account and the loan payable account. For example, suppose that you're making $75-a-month payments on a $5,000 loan. Also, suppose that the lender charges 1 percent interest a month. The following journal entry records the first month's loan payment:

	Debit	Credit	Explanation
Interest expense	$50		Calculated as 1 percent of $5,000
Loan payable	$25		The amount left over and applied to principal
Cash		$75	The total payment amount

The next month, of course, the loan balance is slightly less (because you've made a $25 dent in the loan payment, as shown in the preceding loan payment journal entry). The following journal entry records the second month's loan payment:

	Debit	Credit	Explanation
Interest expense	$49.75		Calculated as 1 percent of $4,975, the new loan balance
Loan payable	$25.25		The amount left over and applied to principal
Cash		$75.00	The total payment amount

Get the lender to provide you with an amortization schedule that shows the breakdown of each payment into interest expense and loan principal reduction.

Note: You can record loan payments by using either the Write Checks – Checking window or the Enter Bills window. Just use the Expenses tab to specify the interest expense account and the loan liability account.

Part V
Appendixes

In this part . . .

Appendixes are like basements. Why? You use them to store stuff that you want to keep but don't know where else to put. The *QuickBooks 4 For Dummies* appendixes provide instructions for installing QuickBooks, an overview of accounting, and help with project estimating.

Appendix A

How to Install QuickBooks in Ten Easy Steps If You're Really Busy or Lazy

● ●

*I*f you haven't already installed QuickBooks, get it over with right now.

Macintosh

Installing QuickBooks on the Macintosh is as easy as breathing. Before you begin, close any programs you have running in the background, and turn off any antivirus programs that hide in the background of your computer (installation programs sometimes make antivirus programs think that your computer is under viral attack). Next, insert the QuickBooks installation disk, double-click on the disk's icon to open the disk's window if you need to, and then double-click the QuickBooks program to begin installation. The program will suggest a folder for the QuickBooks files; you can change the folder if you don't like its suggestion. For the speediest version of QuickBooks, Power Mac users should make sure that they install the PowerPC (or "native") version of QuickBooks.

Windows

If you're installing QuickBooks from a CD-ROM, Windows 95 may not notice the CD when you first click the Next button. That's because CD-ROM drives are like your car when it's freezing outside — slow, slow, slow; the disk drive may not be ready when you clicked the Next button. If Windows 95 tells you that it can't find the installation program, click the Back button to return to the first Add/Remove Programs window, and then click the Next button again. By this time, Windows 95 has probably noticed that you really do have a CD-ROM in your computer's drive.

1. Turn on the PC.

Find and flip on the computer's power switch. (I'm assuming here that you're using Windows 95, so don't be alarmed if your screen looks different than the figures here. Maybe you're still using Windows 3.1 or something.) Figure A-1 shows an example of the starting screen after Windows 95 has finished booting.

Figure A-1: The opening Windows 95 window.

2. Get the QuickBooks disks or CD-ROM.

Rip open the QuickBooks package and get out the disks (those plastic $5^1/_4$-inch or $3^1/_2$-inch squares) or the CD-ROM (which looks exactly like the ones that play music).

3. Open the Control Panel window.

Click the Start button, and then choose Settings⇨Control Panel from the Start menu. Figure A-2 shows the Control Panel window that appears.

Figure A-2:
The Control
Panel. Sort
of like the
bridge on
Star Trek.

4. Start the Windows 95 Install program.

Double-click the Add/Remove Programs icon. When the dialog box in
Figure A-3 appears, click Install.

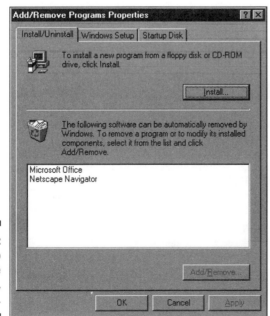

Figure A-3:
Ready to
install the
program,
Captain.

5. Insert the first disk or the CD-ROM, and then click Next.

Windows now shows a dialog box that looks like Figure A-4. Stick the disk that's labeled Install Disk 1 or the CD-ROM into the correct drive. (If you're not sure which one is the correct drive, don't worry. It'll usually fit into only one of the drives.) Then click Next.

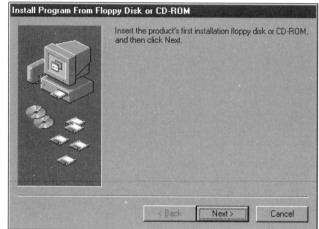

Figure A-4:
This one is pretty self-explanatory (I hope.)

The program searches through your drives, looking for Intuit's Install program. When it finds it, it stops and asks you if it has found the right one (see Figure A-5).QuickBooks is usually right, so go ahead and click Finish.

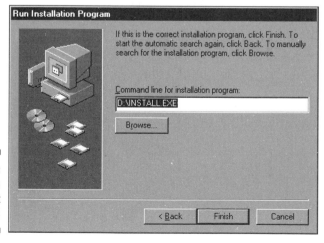

Figure A-5:
You're almost done!

6. (Optional) Keep your options open.

QuickBooks suggests a directory and program group using the QuickBooks Install window. (In Figure A-6, the suggestions are that you install QuickBooks in the C:\QBOOKSW directory and stick a program icon for the new QuickBooks program into the QuickBooks program group.)

If you want to change the directory, click the To button and then, when QuickBooks prompts you with a dialog box, select the directory. If you want to change the program group, click the Program Group button. When QuickBooks prompts you with a dialog box, select your preferred program group. The QuickBooks Install dialog box also provides an Install Quick Tour check box that you can use to tell QuickBooks whether it should install approximately 1MB of QuickBooks and Windows tutorials that come with QuickBooks. If you're low on disk space and you don't mind reading books like this one, not installing the tutorials is a pretty good idea.

Figure A-6:
The
QuickBooks
Pro Install
Options
dialog box.

7. Click the Install button with the left mouse button.

When you click the Install button, you tell the installation program that you want to install QuickBooks the easy way. As the installation program runs, you should see messages such as `decompressing`. Don't worry.

If you're installing QuickBooks from disks, QuickBooks asks you to remove one disk, insert another disk, and then press Enter. You better do what it says, or it won't do what you want — that's Intuit's Golden Rule.

8. Take a minute to contemplate the meaning of life, or get a drink of water.

9. **After the Install program finishes, restart Windows.**

   While the computer's rebooting, get a pencil and paper. You'll see some windows that tell you that you're finished with the installation and also provide some important information — including the current payroll tax table version and the payroll forms version, along with information on updating them, when necessary.

   Congratulations. You're finished with the installation. After you click OK, you see a new menu item: QuickBooks.

10. **(Optional) Celebrate.**

    Stand up at your desk, click your heels together three times, and repeat the phrase, "There's no place like home, Toto; there's no place like home." And watch out for flying houses.

As soon as you've celebrated, you may want to flip to Chapter 1 and find out how to register the program. You'll probably want to register QuickBooks before you begin using it.

The 5th Wave

By Rich Tennant

©RICHTENNANT

NO TALKING!

MORE! MORE! MORE!

EYES FORWARD, !MISTER!

HEY! GET TO WORK!

FASTER FASTER FASTER

WORK! WORK! WORK!

RK! DY!

"I TOLD HIM WE WERE LOOKING FOR SOFTWARE THAT WOULD GIVE US GREATER PRODUCTIVITY, SO HE SOLD ME A DATABASE THAT CAME WITH THESE SIGNS."

Appendix B

If Numbers Are Your Friends

• •

*Y*ou don't need to know much about accounting or about double-entry bookkeeping to use QuickBooks, which, as you know, is most of its appeal. But, if you're serious about this accounting business or serious about *your* business, consider learning a bit more; setting up QuickBooks and understanding all the QuickBooks reports will be easier, and you'll be more sophisticated in your accounting, too.

The Key Thing Is Profit

Start with the big picture. The key thing that an accounting system is supposed to do is enable you to answer the burning question, "Am I making any money?"

It's that simple. Really. So the rest of this appendix just talks about how to calculate a business's profits in a reasonably accurate but still practical manner.

Let me introduce you to someone: the new you

To make this whole discussion more concrete, I'm going to use an example. You have just moved to Montana for the laid-back living and fresh air. You're living in a cute log cabin on Flathead Lake.

To support yourself, you plan to purchase several rowboats and rent them to visiting fly fishermen. Of course, you'll probably need to do quite a bit of fly fishing, too. But just consider that part of the price of being your own boss.

The first day in business

It's your first day in business. About 5 a.m., ol' Peter Gruntpaw shows up to deliver your three rowboats. He made them for you in his barn, but even so, they aren't cheap. He charges $1,500 apiece, so you write him a check for $4,500.

Peter's timing, as usual, is impeccable. About 5:15 a.m. your first customers arrive. Mr. and Mrs. Hamster (pronounced *ohm-stair*) are visiting from Phoenix. They want to catch the big fish. You're a bit unsure of your pricing, but you suggest $25 an hour for the boat. They agree and pay $200 in cash for eight hours.

A few minutes later, another couple arrives. The Gerbils (pronounced *go-bells*) are very agitated. They were supposed to meet the Hamsters and fish together, but the Hamsters are rowing farther and farther away from the dock. To speed the Gerbils' departure, you let them leave without paying.

But you're not worried. As the Gerbils leave the dock, Ms. Gerbil shouts, "We'll pay you the $200 when we get back!"

Although you don't rent the third boat, you do enjoy a sleepy summer morning.

About 2 p.m., the Hamsters and Gerbils come rowing back into view. Obviously, though, a problem has occurred. You learn what it is when the first boat arrives.

"Gerbil fell into the lake," laughs Mr. Hamster. "Lost his wallet, too."

Everybody else seems to think the lost wallet is funny. You secretly wonder how you're going to get paid. No wallet, no money.

You ask Mr. Gerbil whether he would like to come out to the lake tomorrow to pay you. He says he'll just write you a check when he gets home to Phoenix. Reluctantly, you agree.

Look at your cash flow first

I have just described a fairly simple situation. But even so, answering the question, "Did I make any money?" is not going to be easy.

You start by looking at your cash flow: You wrote out a check for $4,500, and you collected $200 in cash. Table B-1 shows your cash flow.

Table B-1	The First Day's Cash Flow
Cash In and Out	*Amount*
Add the cash in:	
Rent money from Hamsters (pronounced *ohm-stairs*)	$200
Rent money from Gerbils (pronounced *go-bells*)	000
Subtract the cash out:	
Money to purchase rowboats	(4,500)
Equals your cash flow:	($4,300)

To summarize, you had $200 come in but $4,500 go out. So your cash flow was $4,300. From a strictly cash-flow perspective, the first day doesn't look all that good, right?

But does the cash flow calculation show you whether you're making money? Can you look at it and gauge whether your little business is on the right track?

The answer to both questions is no. Your cash flow is important. You can't, for example, write out a $4,500 check unless you have at least $4,500 in your checking account. But your cash flow doesn't tell you whether you're making money.

In fact, you may see a couple of problems with looking just at the cash flow of the rowboat rental business.

Depreciation is an accounting gimmick

Here is the first problem. If you take good care of the rowboats, you can use them every summer for the next few years. In fact, say that the rowboat rental season, which runs from early spring to late autumn, is 150 days long and that your well-made rowboats will last ten years. In this case, you can rent the rowboats for 1,500 days (150 days a year times 10 years equals 1,500 days).

If your rowboats each cost $1,500 and you can rent them 1,500 times, it's more accurate to say that only $1 per day of a rowboat's cost should be counted in a profit calculation.

Do you see what I'm saying? If you have something that costs a great deal of money but lasts for a long time, spreading out the cost makes sense. This *spreading out* is usually called *depreciation*. The little $1 chunks that are allocated to a day are called the *depreciation expense*.

Note: Accountants use the terms *cost* and *expense* differently. A *cost* is the price you pay for something. If you pay Peter Gruntpaw $1,500 for a rowboat, the rowboat's cost is $1,500. An *expense,* on the other hand, is what you use in a profit calculation. The little $1 chunks of the rowboat's $1,500 cost (that are allocated to individual days) are expenses.

If this depreciation thing seems wacky, remember that what you're really trying to do is figure out whether you made any money your first day of business. And all I'm really saying is that you shouldn't include all the cost of the rowboats as expense in the first day's profit calculation. Some of it should be included as expense in calculating the profit in future days. That's fair, right?

Accrual-basis accounting is cool

You don't want to forget about the $200 that the Gerbils owe you either. Although Mr. Gerbil (remember that it's pronounced *go-bell*) may not send you the check for several days, or even for several weeks, he will pay you. You've earned the money.

This brings up another very important point. The principles of accounting say that you should include sales in your profit calculations when you earn the money and not when you actually collect it. The logic behind this "include sales when they're earned" rule is that it produces a better estimate of the business you're doing.

I want to show you how this rule works. Say that the day after the Gerbils and Hamsters rent the rowboats you have no customers, but Mr. Gerbil comes out and pays you $200.

Different names, same logic

There's no sense in hiding a nasty little accounting secret from you. Here it is: Accountants call this cost-allocation process by different names, depending on what sort of cost is being spread out.

Most of the time, the cost allocation is called *depreciation.* You depreciate buildings, machinery, furniture, and many other things as well. But allocating the cost of a natural resource — such as crude oil that you pump, coal that you dig up, or minerals that you extract — is called *depletion.* And allocating the cost of things that aren't tangible — copyrights and patents for example — is *amortization.*

If you use the "include sales when they're earned" rule — or what's called *accrual-basis accounting* — your daily sales look like this:

	Day 1	**Day 2**
Sales	$400	$000

If you instead use what's called *cash-basis accounting* (in which you count sales when you collect the cash) your daily sales look like this:

	Day 1	**Day 2**
Sales	$200	$200

Please, please, please notice that the traditional accounting method shows that you have a good day when you rent two boats and a terrible day when you don't rent any boats. In comparison, when you use cash-basis accounting, both days look the same. It looks as if you rented a boat each day.

Now you know why accrual-basis accounting is a better way to measure profit.

By the way, accrual-basis accounting also works for expenses. The idea is that you should count an expense when you make it, not when you pay it. For example, you call the local radio station and ask it to announce your new boat rental business a couple of times for its fee of $25. Although you do not have to pay the radio station the day you make the arrangements for your announcement, you should still count the $25 as an expense for that day.

Now you know how to measure profits

With what you now know, you're ready to measure the first day's profits. Table B-2 is a profit and loss statement for the first day.

Table B-2   A Profit and Loss Statement for the First Day

Description	*Amount*	*Explanation*
Sales	$400	Rental money from the Hamsters and the Gerbils
Expenses		
Depreciation	3	3 rowboats x $1/day depreciation
Advertising	25	Radio advertising
Total expenses	28	Depreciation expense plus the advertising
Profit	$372	Sales minus the total expenses

Please notice that, although the first day's cash flow was terrible, your little business is quite profitable. In fact, if you really do make about $370 a day, you'll recoup your entire $4,500 investment in less than three weeks. That's pretty darn good.

Some financial brain food

Now that you know how to measure profits, I can fill you in on some important conceptual stuff.

Here's the first concept (and it's so simple, too): You measure profits for a specific period of time. In the rowboat business example, you measured the profits for a day. Some people actually do measure profits (or they try to measure profits) on a daily basis. But most times, people use bigger chunks of time. Monthly chunks of time are common, for example. And so are three-month chunks of time. Everybody measures profits annually — if only because the government makes you do so for income tax accounting.

When people start talking about how often and for what chunks of time you measure profits, they use a couple of terms. The year you calculate profits for is called the *fiscal year*. The smaller chunks of time for which you measure profits over the year are called *accounting periods* or *interim accounting periods*. (You don't need to memorize the two new terms. But now that you've read them, you'll probably remember them.)

One other thing that I want to say may be obvious, but it's important nonetheless. There's an awkward trade-off here. Daily profit and loss calculations show you how well you did at the end of every day, but you have to collect the data and do the work every day. And preparing a profit and loss statement is a great deal of work. (I made things purposefully easy by including only a few transactions, but, in real life, you would have many more transactions to worry about and fiddle with.)

If you use a quarterly interim accounting period, you don't have to collect the raw data and do the arithmetic very often, but you know how you're doing only every once in a while. In my mind, checking your profits only four times a year isn't enough. A great deal can happen in three months.

In the Old Days, Things Were Different

If you're new to the arithmetic and logic of profit calculation — which is mostly what modern accounting is all about — you won't be surprised to hear that not all that long ago, most people couldn't and didn't do much of it — profit calculating, that is.

What they did instead was monitor a business's financial condition. They used — well, actually, they still use — a balance sheet to monitor the financial condition. *A balance sheet* just lists a business's assets and its liabilities at a particular point in time.

For example, say that at the start of your first day in the rowboat rental business — before you pay Peter Gruntpaw — you have $5,000 in your checking account. To make things interesting, $4,000 of this money is a loan from your mother-in-law, and $1,000 is cash that you have invested in your business. Your balance sheet at the beginning of the day looks like the one in Table B-3.

Table B-3	The Balance Sheet at the Beginning of the Day	
Description	**Amount**	**Explanation**
Assets		
Cash	$5,000	The checking account balance
Total assets	$5,000	Your only asset is cash, so it's your total, too
Liabilities and owners equity		
Loan payable	$4,000	The loan from your mother-in-law
Total liabilities	$4,000	Your only liability is that crazy loan
Owners equity	$1,000	The $1,000 you put in
Total liabilities and owners equity	$5,000	The total liabilities plus the owners equity

If you construct a balance sheet at the end of the first day, things are only slightly more complicated. Some of these explanations are too complicated to give in a sentence, so the paragraphs that follow describe how I got each number.

Note: Even if you don't pay all that much attention, I recommend that you quickly read through the explanations. Mostly, I want you to understand that if you try to monitor a business's financial condition by using a balance sheet, as I've done here, things are messy. Later in this appendix, I talk about how QuickBooks makes all this stuff easier.

Table B-4 shows the balance sheet at the end of the first day.

Table B-4	The Balance Sheet at the End of the Day
Description	*Amount*
Assets	
Cash	$700
Receivable	200
Rowboats	4,497
Total assets	5,397
Liabilities and owners equity	
Payable	25
Loan payable	4,000
Total liabilities	4,025
Owners equity	1,000
Retained earnings	372
Total liabilities and owners equity	$5,397

Cash is the most complicated thing to prove. If you were really in the rowboat rental business, of course, you could just look at your checkbook. But if you were writing an appendix about being in the rowboat rental business — as I am — you would have to be able to calculate the cash balance. Table B-5 shows the calculation of the cash balance for your rowboat rental business.

Table B-5	The First Day's Cash Flow		
Description	*Payment*	*Deposit*	*Balance*
Initial investment		$1,000	$1,000
Loan from mother-in-law		4,000	5,000
Rowboat purchase	$4,500		500
Cash from Hamsters		200	700

The $200 receivable is just the money the Gerbils owe you.

The Rowboats' balance sheet value is $4,497 — which is weird, I'll grant you. But here's how you figure it. You take the original cost of the asset and you deduct all the depreciation expense that you've charged to date. The original cost of the three rowboats was $4,500. You've charged only $3 of depreciation for the first day, so the balance sheet value, or net book value, is $4,497.

The only liabilities are the $25 you owe the radio station for those new business announcements and that $4,000 you borrowed from your mother-in-law. I won't even ask why you opened that can of worms.

Finally, the owners equity section of the balance sheet shows the $1,000 you originally contributed and also the $372 of money you earned.

It's not a coincidence that the total assets value equals the total liabilities and total owners equity value. If you correctly calculate each of the numbers that go on the balance sheet, the two totals are always equal.

Here's another thing to remember: A balance sheet lists asset, liability, and owner's equity balances on a specific date. It gives you a financial snapshot at a point in time. By convention, you prepare a balance sheet whenever you prepare a profit and loss statement. The balance sheet shows account balances for the last day of the fiscal year and interim accounting period. (I think it's kind of neat that after only a few pages of this appendix you're reading and understanding terms such as *fiscal year* and *interim accounting period.*)

What Does an Italian Monk Have to Do with It?

So far, I have provided narrative descriptions of all the financial events that affect the balance sheet and the income statement. For example, I described how you started the business with $5,000 of cash (a $4,000 loan from your mother-in-law and $1,000 of cash you yourself invested). At an even earlier point in this appendix, I noted how you rented a boat to the Hamsters for $200, and they paid you in cash.

Although the narrative descriptions of financial events — such as starting the business or renting to the Hamsters — make for just bearable reading, they would be unwieldy for accountants to use in practice. Partly, this is because accountants are usually (or maybe always?) terrible writers. But an even bigger problem is that using the lots-and-lots-of-words approach makes describing all the little bits and pieces of information that you need difficult and downright tedious.

Fortunately, about 500 years ago an Italian monk named Lucia Pacioli thought the same thing. No, I'm not making this up.

Five hundred years after the fact, what this monk did is a little unclear. But according to one group, Pacioli developed the double-entry bookkeeping system. (According to the other group, by the way, Pacioli just described the system the Venetian merchants were already using. But I'm not one to cast stones at a dead accounting hero.)

In either case, however, what Pacioli really said was, "Hey, guys. Hello? Is anybody in there? You have to get more efficient in the way that you describe your financial transactions. You have to create a financial shorthand system that works when you have a large number of transactions to record."

Pacioli then proceeded to describe a financial shorthand system that made it easy to collect all the little bits and pieces of information needed to prepare income statements and balance sheets. The shorthand system he described? Double-entry bookkeeping.

His system is simplicity itself. Really. All he said was that rather than using a wordy explanation for every financial transaction, people should name the income statement or balance sheet line items, or accounts affected and give the dollar amount of the effect.

The profit and loss statement and the balance sheet line items are called *accounts.* You need to remember this term. (Just for your information, a list of profit and loss statement and balance sheet line items is called a *chart of accounts.* You may already know this term from using QuickBooks.)

Pacioli also did one wacky thing. He used a couple of new terms — *debit* and *credit* — to describe the increases and decreases in accounts. Increases in asset accounts and in expense accounts are *debits,* and decreases in asset and expense accounts are *credits.* Increases in liability, owners equity, and income accounts are *credits,* and decreases in liability, owners equity, and income accounts are *debits.* Keeping these terms straight is a bit confusing, so Table B-6 may help you.

I'm sorry to have to tell you this, but, if you want to use double-entry bookkeeping, you need to memorize the information in Table B-6. If it's any consolation, this information is the only chunk of data in the entire book that I ask you to memorize. Or, failing that, mark this page — with a dog-ear, for example — so you can flip here quickly, or just refer to the Cheat Sheet.

Table B-6	The Only Stuff in This Book That I Ask You to Memorize	
Account Type	*Debits*	*Credits*
Assets	Increase asset accounts	Decrease asset accounts
Liabilities	Decrease liability accounts	Increase liability accounts
Owners equity	Decrease owners equity accounts	Increase owners equity accounts
Income	Decrease income accounts	Increase income accounts
Expenses	Increase expense accounts	Decrease expense accounts

And now for the blow-by-blow

The best way to learn this double-entry bookkeeping stuff is to show you how to use it to record all the financial events discussed thus far in this appendix.

Start with the money you have invested in the business and the money you foolishly borrowed from your mother-in-law. You invested $1,000 in cash, and you borrowed $4,000 in cash. Here are the double-entry bookkeeping transactions — called *journal entries,* in case you care — that describe these financial events.

Journal entry 1: To record your $1,000 investment

	Debit	Credit
Cash	$1,000	
Owner's equity		$1,000

Journal entry 2: To record the $4,000 loan from your mother-in-law

	Debit	Credit
Cash	$4,000	
Loan payable to Mother		$4,000

(I numbered these journal entries 1, 2, and so on so that I can easily point you to them later.)

Journal entries are very cool for a simple reason. If you add up all the debits and credits, you get something called a *trial balance.* A trial balance isn't all that special — it's just a list of accounts and their debit or credit balance. But with a trial balance, you can easily prepare profit and loss statements and balance sheets. For example, if you add up the debits and credits shown in journal entries 1 and 2, you get the trial balance shown in Table B-7.

Table B-7	Your First Trial Balance	
	Debit	*Credit*
Cash	$5,000	
Loan payable to Mother		$4,000
Owners equity		$1,000

This trial balance provides the raw data needed to construct the rowboat business balance sheet at the start of the first day. If you don't believe me, take a peek at Table B-3. Oh sure, the information shown in Table B-7 isn't as polished. Table B-7 doesn't provide labels, for example, that tell you that cash is an asset. And Table B-7 doesn't provide subtotals showing the total assets (equal to $5,000) and the total liabilities and owner's equity (also equal to $5,000). But it does provide the raw data.

Take a look at the journal entries you would make to record the rest of the first day's financial events.

Journal entry 3: To record the purchase of the three $1,500 rowboats

	Debit	Credit
Rowboats	$4,500	
Cash		$4,500

Journal entry 4: To record the rental to the Hamsters

	Debit	Credit
Cash	$200	
Sales		$200

Journal entry 5: To record the rental to the Gerbils

	Debit	Credit
Receivable	$200	
Sales		$200

Journal entry 6: To record the $25 radio advertisement

	Debit	Credit
Advertising expense	$25	
Payable		$25

Journal entry 7: To record the $3 of rowboat depreciation

	Debit	Credit
Depreciation expense	$3	
Accumulated depreciation		$3

To build a trial balance for the end of the first day, you add all the first day journal entries to the trial balance shown in Table B-7. The result is the trial balance shown in Table B-8.

Table B-8	The Trial Balance at the End of the First Day	
	Debit	**Credit**
Balance sheet accounts		
Cash	$700	
Receivable	200	
Rowboats — cost	4,500	
Accumulated depreciation		$3
Payable		25
Loan payable		4,000
Owners equity		1,000
Profit and loss statement accounts		
Sales		$400
Depreciation expense	3	
Advertising expense	$25	

The trial balance shown in Table B-8 provides the raw data used to prepare the balance sheet and profit and loss statement for the first day.

If you look at the accounts I labeled as the "Balance sheet accounts" in Table B-8 and compare these to the balance sheet shown in Table B-4, you see that this trial balance provides all the raw numbers needed for the balance sheet. The only numbers that aren't directly from Table B-8 are the subtotals you get by adding up other numbers.

If you look at the accounts I labeled as the "Profit and loss statement accounts" in Table B-8 and compare them to the profit and loss statement shown in Table B-2, you see that this trial balance also provides all the raw numbers needed for the profit and loss statement. Again, the only numbers in Table B-2 that aren't directly from Table B-8 are the subtotals you get by adding up other numbers.

Blow-by-blow, part II

Do you understand what I've discussed so far? If you do, you grasp how accounting and double-entry bookkeeping work. I want to show you about a half a dozen more example transactions, however, to plug a few minor holes in your knowledge.

When you collect money you've previously billed, you record the transaction by debiting cash and crediting receivables (or accounts receivable). In the rowboat business, for example, you make this basic entry when Mr. Gerbil later pays you the $200 he owes you for the first-day's rental.

Journal entry 8: To record a payment by a customer

	Debit	Credit
Cash	$200	
Receivable		$200

Notice that you don't record a sale when you collect the cash. The sale has already been recorded in journal entry 5.

When you pay the radio station for the advertising, you record the transaction by debiting accounts payable and crediting cash.

Journal entry 9: To record your payment of $25 to the radio station

	Debit	Credit
Payable	$25	
Cash		$25

The one other thing I want to cover — ever so briefly — is *inventory accounting*. Accounting for things you buy and resell or the things you make and resell is a bit more tricky. And I don't have room to go into a great deal of detail.

When you buy items to resell, you debit an asset account, often named Inventory. If you purchase 300, $10 thingamajigs you hope to resell for $25 each, you record the following journal entry:

Journal entry 10: To record the cash purchase of thingamajigs

	Debit	Credit
Inventory	$3,000	
Cash		$3,000

When you sell a thingamajig, you need to do two things: record the sale and record the cost of the sale. If you need to record the sale of 100 thingamajigs for $25, for example, you record the following journal entry:

Journal entry 11: To record the sale of 100 thingamajigs for $25 apiece

	Debit	Credit
Receivable	$2,500	
Sales		$2,500

You also need to record the cost of the thingamajigs that you've sold as an expense and record the reduction in the value of your thingamajig inventory. If you reduce your inventory count from 300 items to 200 items, for example, you need to adjust your inventory's dollar value. You record the following journal entry:

Journal entry 12: To record the cost of the 100 thingamajigs sold

	Debit	Credit
Cost of goods sold	$1,000	
Inventory		$1,000

The cost of goods sold account, by the way, is just another expense. It appears on your profit and loss statement.

How Does QuickBooks Help?

Most of the time, all this debiting and crediting business goes on behind the scenes. When you invoice a customer, QuickBooks debits accounts receivable and credits sales. When you write a check to pay some bill, QuickBooks debits the expense (or the accounts payable account) and credits cash.

In the case in which a financial transaction isn't recorded automatically when you fill in some on-screen form, you need to use the Activities⇨Enter Special Transactions command. When you choose this command, QuickBooks displays the General Journal Entry dialog box, shown in Figure B-1, in which you enter the journal entry.

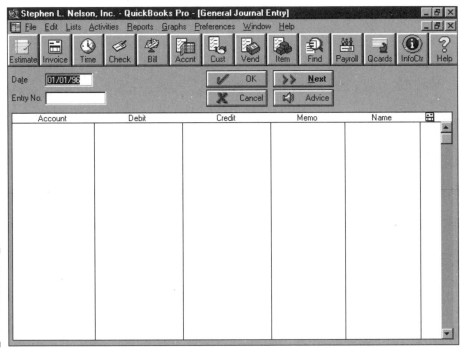

You use the General Journal Entry dialog box to record depreciation expense, for example.

QuickBooks automatically builds a trial balance, using journal entries it constructs automatically and any journal entries that you enter yourself using the General Journal Entry dialog box. If you want to see the trial balance, just choose Reports⇨Other Reports⇨Trial Balance.

QuickBooks prepares balance sheets, profit and loss statements, and several other reports as well, using the trial balance.

Two Dark Shadows in the World of Accounting

The real purpose of accounting systems such as QuickBooks is simple. Accounting systems are supposed to make succeeding in your business easier for you. You might think, therefore, that the world of accounting would be a friendly place. Unfortunately, this isn't quite true. I am sorry to report that two dark shadows hang over the world of accounting: financial accounting standards and income tax laws.

The first dark shadow

"Financial accounting standards," you say. "What the heck are those?"

Here's the quick-and-dirty explanation: Financial accounting standards are accounting rules created by certified public accountants. Ostensibly, these rules are supposed to make reading financial statements and understanding what's going on easier for people. (I happen to believe just the opposite is true, by the way.) But because of what financial accounting standards purport to do, some people — such as bank loan officers — want to see profit and loss statements and balance sheets that follow the rules. The exact catch-phrase is one you may have heard before, "prepared in accordance with generally accepted accounting principles."

Unfortunately, the rules are very complicated. The rules are inconsistently interpreted. And actually applying the rules would soon run most small businesses into the ground. (As you were running your business into the ground — you'll be happy to know — your certified public accountant would make a great deal of money helping you figure out what you were supposed to be doing.) So what should you do about this first dark shadow?

- ✔ Well, first of all, know that it exists. Know that people like your banker honestly think you should be following a super-complicated set of esoteric accounting rules.

- ✔ And here's my second tip: Don't get sucked into the financial accounting standards tar pit. Tell people — your banker included — that you do your accounting in the way that you think enables you to best manage your business. Tell people a small business such as yours can't afford to have an in-house staff of full-time CPAs. And, finally, tell people that you don't necessarily prepare your financial statements "in accordance with generally accepted accounting principles."

Do attempt to fully and fairly disclose your financial affairs to people who need to know about them. Lying to a creditor or an investor about your financial affairs or getting sneaky with one of these people is a good way to end up in jail.

The second dark shadow

And then there's the second dark shadow: income tax accounting laws. You know that Congress enacts tax legislation to raise revenue. And you know that it does so in a political environment strewn with all sorts of partisan, voodoo economic, and social overtones. It can't be any surprise to you then that what comes out of the nation's capital and your state capital are accounting rules that don't make much sense for running a business.

You need to apply the rules when you prepare your tax return, of course. But you don't have to use them the rest of the year. A far better approach is to do your accounting in a way that enables you to best run your business. That way, you won't use accounting tricks and gambits that make sense for income tax accounting but foul up your accounting system.

At the end of the year when you're preparing your tax return, have your tax preparer adjust your trial balance so it conforms to Mr. Taxman's rules.

The Danger of Shell Games

This appendix is longer than I initially intended. I'm sorry about that. I want to share one more thought with you, however. And I think it's an important thought, so please stay with me just a little longer.

You could use the accounting knowledge this appendix imparts to do the bookkeeping for a very large business. As crazy as it sounds, if you had 3,000 rowboats for rent — perhaps you would have rental outlets at dozens of lakes scattered all over the Rockies — you might actually be able to keep the books for a $200,000,000-a-year business. You would have to enter many more transactions, and the numbers would all be bigger; but you wouldn't necessarily be doing anything that was more complicated.

Unfortunately, the temptation is great — especially on the part of financial advisers — to let things get more complicated as a business grows. People start talking about sophisticated leasing arrangements that make sense because of the tax laws. Some customer or vendor suggests some complicated profit-sharing or cost-reimbursement agreement. Then your attorney talks you into setting up a couple of new subsidiaries for legal reasons.

All these things make accounting for your business terribly complicated. If you choose to ignore this complexity and go on your merry way, very quickly you won't know if you're making money. (I've seen plenty of people go this route — and it isn't pretty.) On the other hand, if you truly want to do accurate accounting in a complex environment, you need to spend a great deal of cash for really smart accountants. (This tactic, of course, supposes that you can find, hire, and afford these really smart accountants.)

If you're unsure about how to tell whether something is just too complicated, here's a general rule you can use: If you can't easily create the journal entries that quantify the financial essence of some event, you're in trouble.

So, what should you do? I suggest that you don't complicate your business's finances — not even if you think the new-fangled, tax-incentivized, sale-leaseback, profit plan is a sure winner. Keep things simple, my friend. To win the game, you have to keep score.

Appendix C

Project Estimating for Fun (But Mostly Profit)

● ●

*O*ne of the features found in QuickBooks Pro that isn't in the regular QuickBooks program is the capability to produce *project estimates.* This is particularly handy if you are in a business such as construction, where the customer must know potential costs. Not only that, but consider a construction project: You must estimate construction materials and employee hours. Some of the items that you need to consider will count as overhead and won't be billed back to the customer.

You want to add a markup to some of the materials that you use for the project. And, if you complete the project, you'll want to be able to turn the estimate into an actual invoice without jumping through a couple of million hoops or, worse yet, having to jump through hoops that you've already jumped through before. A lot to demand from a program, but what the heck — weren't computers supposed to make your life easier? This is one area where QuickBooks Pro really comes through and delivers on the promise.

The Birth of an Estimate

I have to make a few assumptions before I begin here.

- ✔ You should have a general knowledge of QuickBooks — an overall view of how the basic procedures work.

- ✔ Your lists should be up to date — your Item List, your Employee:Job List, and so on. If they're not, you should know how to update your lists as you go along. For example, if QuickBooks shows that an item you need to include on an estimate is not on the Item List, you should already have some idea of how to add the item.

A caveat before I begin: You can only produce one estimate per job. If you need more than one estimate for a job, list the estimates under different jobs. Maybe you can number them under the same customer, like Rec Room 1, Rec Room 2, and so on. You really should be creating a new job for any new work you do for a customer anyway, just to keep the records for each project straight.

Let's begin. On your mark, get set, go:

1. **Get the form.**

   Choose Activities⇨Create Estimates. QuickBooks opens a Create Estimates form, which bears an uncanny resemblance to Figure C-1.

2. **Start filling in the blanks.**

   Choose the appropriate Customer:Job from the drop-down list box at the top of the form. QuickBooks Pro automatically fills in as much information as it can — usually at least the Name/Address box — on the form. If the customer is on the Customer:Job list, but you're estimating a new job, choose the customer, click at the end of the customer's name in the Customer:Job drop-down list box, and then type a colon and the name of the new job. QuickBooks Pro gives you the opportunity to either Quick Add the job or set it up completely.

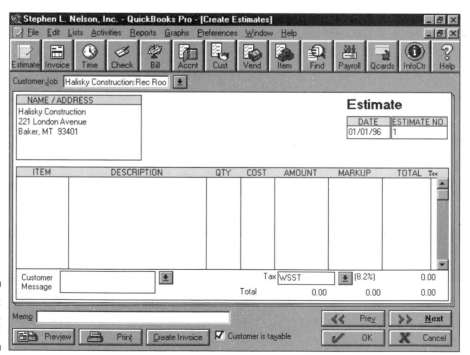

Figure C-1:
Estimates,
anyone?

If you have configured QuickBooks Pro to track classes, the appropriate drop-down list box will show up in the upper right-hand corner of the form. Go ahead and use it, if appropriate.

Feel free to change the default settings — the Date and Estimate No., for example. The Date Setting tricks on the Cheat Sheet in the front of this book may come in handy here.

3. **The Line Items — details, details, details.**

Ah, yes. This is where I separate the wheat from the chaff. Click the first line of the Item column and begin typing the name of the first item in your estimate. QuickBooks Pro tries to anticipate the item name, automatically filling in the rest of the name. If the name appears on your Item List after you're finished, QuickBooks Pro will fill in the description and cost for you. (If the name doesn't appear on your list, you'll have the opportunity to add it to your list or cancel out the line.)

Enter the quantity that you anticipate using in the Qty column. QuickBooks Pro automatically calculates the amount, markup, and total for you. QuickBooks Pro also places a T in the Tax column if the item is taxable and figures out the tax if you indicated that you were responsible to charge sales tax when you created the company file. If the customer is not charged tax, remove the check mark from the Customer Is Taxable check box at the bottom of the window by clicking the check box.

If you need to delete a line, no problem. Click the line that you need to delete, and then choose Edit⇨Delete Line. QuickBooks Pro takes the line out. No muss, no fuss, no dust.

At this point, you may be asking where QuickBooks Pro is getting all the information for its calculations. Well, if you choose Lists⇨Items, and double-click one of the items, you see an Edit Item window similar to Figure C-2. (I've chosen Chaff as an example.) This is the same window that you use to set up each item. Because the estimate is a document that you'll want to show the customer, QuickBooks Pro uses the Description on Sales Transactions in the Description column, the Cost in the Cost column, and so on. The Markup percentage (which, by the way, won't show up on the printed estimate) is calculated by comparing the Cost (in the Purchase Information box) to the Sales Price (in the Sales Information box).

Any part of the information on the estimate form can be changed. If you want to charge a higher markup for an item, for example, change the markup column on the form, and QuickBooks Pro will adjust the Total column accordingly. You won't affect the settings in the Item List by doing this.

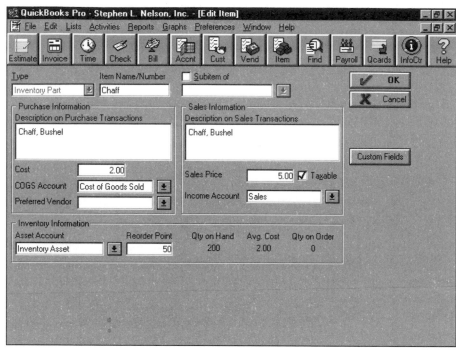

Figure C-2:
An Edit Item
window.

4. Optional information time!

If you want to, click the Customer Message drop-down list box, shown in Figure C-1, and write a friendly message or use one from the drop-down list. Try to avoid a tone like "Pleeeease! I neeeeed this job!" It's not becoming.

Then click the Memo line, and write a note to yourself regarding the project if you'd like. Or maybe some notes for the screenplay that you've been thinking about pitching to the studios. Whatever suits your fancy.

Figure C-3 shows an example of a Create Estimates window that has been completed. See the totals underneath the Tax list box, near the bottom of the window? The totals represent your cost ($896.00), the amount over your costs that you are charging ($919.00), and the final total ($1,963.83). I don't know about you, but I think this is pretty cool.

If you want to include other items on the Create Estimates window, you can customize that window. Choose Preferences⇨Estimates, and QuickBooks Pro brings up the Estimating Preferences dialog box, as shown in Figure C-4. Obviously, you create estimates for customers and jobs or you wouldn't be here, so leave the Yes option button marked for the first section. At the bottom of the window, if you're using duplicate estimate numbers on purpose — possibly one of those plots having to do with New Math — unmark the check box by clicking it.

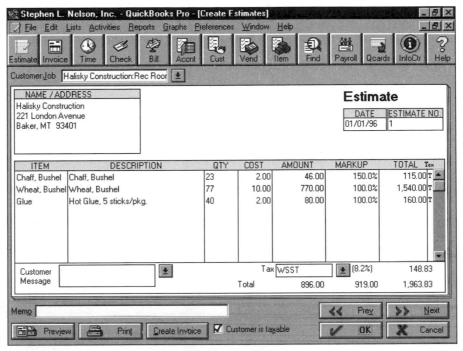

Figure C-3:
A completed
Create
Estimates
window.

Figure C-4:
Let's set up
some
Estimating
Preferences!
Yeah!

The Estimate Style box enables you to customize the on-screen and printed versions of the estimate form. If you click the Customize button, you get the Customize Estimate box, shown in Figure C-5. (I've clicked the Columns tab, which gives you an idea of the extent to which you can change the form.)

The first column lists the items you can include in the estimate. The Screen and Print check boxes determine whether the items appear. The grayed-out boxes can be changed only by the system, if at all. (For example, if you click the Markup Print check box, then the Amount Print check box is automatically checked, too.) When you change the columns, the Print Width and % of Page amounts adjust automatically. The Order column, of course, determines which items appear first on the page, going from left to right. The Title column changes the headings of each column.

On the Header tab, for example, you may want to call your estimates *Bids* or *Proposals.* Or John Jacob Jingleheimer Schmidt, for that matter. (Hey, that's my name, too!) Whatever your little heart desires. When you've made all your changes, click OK. If you experimented just a little too much and want to go back to the way the form was in the beginning, click the Default button. If you're giving up completely and you don't want to save your changes or see this window ever again, click the Cancel button.

The Create Estimate window returns. Before you print that estimate, remember that the Create Estimates window is *not* the same information that appears on the written estimate. To see how the printed version looks, click the Preview button at the bottom of the window. The result is a full-page image, shrunken down to fit on the screen (see Figure C-6).

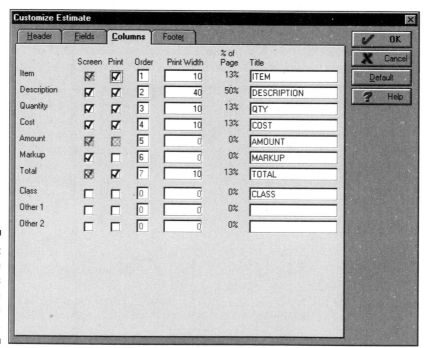

Figure C-5:
The
infamous
Customize
Estimate
dialog box.

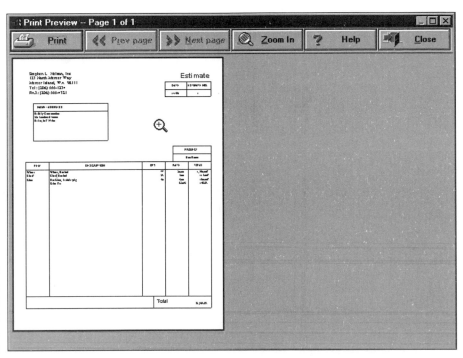

To examine the estimate more closely, either click the Zoom In button at the top of the screen, or move the mouse cursor over the image. When the cursor looks like a magnifying glass with a plus sign in it, click the left-hand button. Because you can only see part of the preview at a time this way, use the scrollbars at the bottom and right of the window to move around to the different areas. Note that the magnifying glass now has a minus sign in it, and the Zoom In button has changed to Zoom Out. If you've completed more than one estimate, you can use the Prev Page and Next Page buttons to look at other estimates. After you're finished, click the Close button.

We're now back to the Create Estimates window. You're the extremely confident type — I can just tell — and you can just feel in your bones that the estimate couldn't possibly be improved. Click the Print button, and QuickBooks Pro prints the estimate without any further ado.

Revising an Estimate

Let's say, however, that after consulting with your client, you decided that you don't really need that many bushels of wheat. Fifty-five bushels will do. Choose Lists⇨Customers:Jobs to open the Customers:Jobs list, and highlight the appropriate customer and job by clicking it. If you have previously created an estimate, the Estimate button at the bottom of the window will be activated.

Just click the button, and QuickBooks Pro brings the estimate right back up. Make your changes, and QuickBooks Pro recalculates all the totals. Smile. Imagine doing this by hand — the recalculations, the looking up of the prices, the retyping, the inordinate amount of time. Doing this by hand doesn't quite beat a hot dog with sauerkraut in the park on a sunny day, but it's pretty close.

Remember, though: You can only keep one estimate per job. After you click OK, any changes you make automatically take the place of the old estimate.

Turning an Estimate into an Invoice

Okay, you've fine-tuned the estimate, and it reflects exactly what you think it should. If your customer is paying a fixed amount, based on the estimate, you can turn the estimate into an invoice easily.

1. **Display the estimate.**

   Choose Activities⇨Create Estimates to open the Create Estimates window, then use the Prev and Next buttons at the bottom of the window to move to the estimate that you want to use.

2. **Click the Create Invoice button at the bottom of the window.**

   Go ahead. Live on the edge. Click that puppy with everything you've got.

3. **(Optional) Make any necessary changes to the resulting invoice.**

   The invoice that you see is a regular QuickBooks Pro invoice, and you can edit it the same way that you edit any invoice. Until you click OK, the invoice is not recorded in your records.

4. **After you've made all your changes, click OK to record the invoice.**

   That's right. You show them what you're made of. Click that thing. Yeah!

   Whew! What a workout!

Charging for Actual Time and Costs

If you're going to charge the customer for actual costs, you need to track the costs and time as you incur the charges for them. For example, Figure C-7 shows the Enter Bills window. Under the Items tab, we've bought red thingamajigs and some gizmos for the project at Dolliver Steel. (See how the customer is indicated in the Customer:Job column?) Now, we're going to charge Dolliver Steel for those costs.

1. **Open the Create Invoices window.**

   Choose Activities⇨Create Invoice to open the window. (I can only hope that you don't get too drafty.)

2. **Change the name in the Customer:Job drop-down list box to the proper customer.**

   This step is easy. Activate the drop-down list, and choose Dolliver Steele. You've done this a million times by now.

3. **Click the Time/Costs button on the right-hand side of the window.**

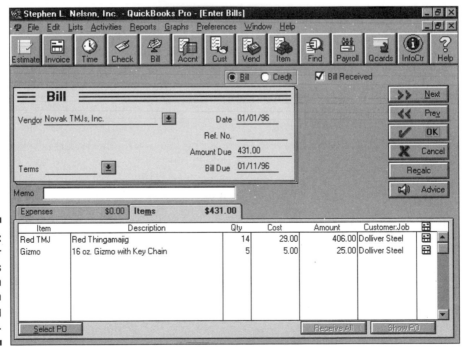

Figure C-7:
The Enter Bills window, in preparation for creating an invoice.

Figure C-8 shows the results of clicking the Time/Cos<u>ts</u> button — the Choose Billable Time and Costs dialog box. You probably haven't seen this dialog box before. (Didn't know there were any left, did you?) Note that the dialog box already shows the expenses from the bill that I entered at the beginning of this section.

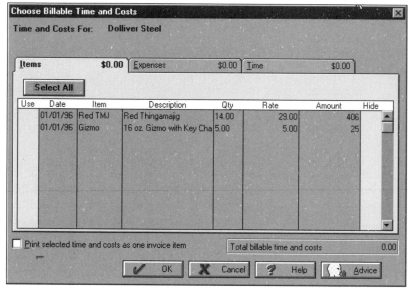

Figure C-8:
Hey, boys and girls! It's the Choose Billable Time and Costs dialog box!

4. **Choose the proper tab for the kind of expense that you're charging.**

   The <u>I</u>tems tab lists, well, items that you've bought specifically for the project. Parts, subcontracted services — that type of thing. The <u>E</u>xpenses tab is sort of a catch-all for anything that doesn't fit into the other two categories. The <u>T</u>ime tab lists billable time spent on the project.

5. **Choose the expenses that you want to charge the customer on this invoice.**

   If you want to charge the customer for everything that appears on this tab, just click the Select All button. Otherwise, click the Use column next to the charge that you would like to pass on. By the way, if you know for sure that you're going to accept a particular expense without charging the customer, just click the Hide column next to that expense so that doesn't show up on subsequent lists.

6. **(Optional, <u>E</u>xpenses only) Indicate the markup.**

   The <u>E</u>xpenses tab has a couple of extra fields at the top of the tab to indicate the Markup Amount or % and the Markup Account. If this is applicable, go ahead and fill in the fields with the appropriate information.

7. (Optional) Indicate whether you want the charges to appear as a single item on the invoice.

If you want to avoid detailing the gory details of the charges to your customer, click the Print Selected Time and Costs As One Invoice item check box to place a check mark in it.

At this point, the Choose Billable Time and Costs window looks something like Figure C-9.

8. (Optional) Repeat Steps 4-7 for the other tabs.

I am not even going to mention this. It's too obvious. Mmmmmmm, no, not me.

9. Click OK.

After you have everything the way you want, click OK. As if by magic (even if it was your hard work and the sweat of your own brow), the invoice appears (see Figure C-10).

10. (Optional) Add anything else you want to include on the invoice.

This invoice is a regular QuickBooks Pro invoice, remember? Bend the invoice or shake it — any way you want it. Intuit suggests that, at this point, you may want to click the Preview button to check to make sure that only the job costs that you want appear.

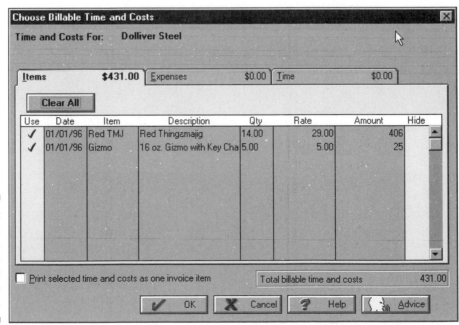

Figure C-9:
A completed Choose Billable Time and Costs dialog box.

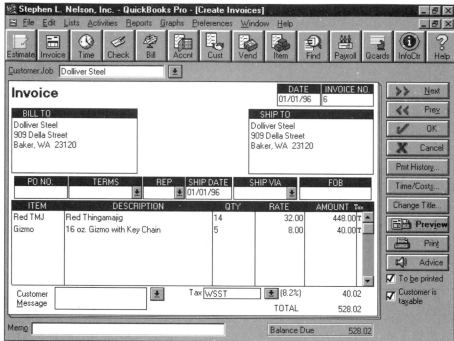

Figure C-10:
As if by
magic. Yeah.
Right.

11. Click OK.

Yes, again. That's how you record the invoice.

After the invoice is recorded, the job costs that have been billed are removed from the Choose Billable Time and Costs window. You're finished. Breathe easier.

You've got to admit, QuickBooks Pro makes this whole process a lot less time consuming. And, along the way, you have less chance for error — trying to juggle all those different files and items and bills and invoices could get slightly nerve wracking and drive anyone a little buggy.

But then, we don't have to worry about all that juggling anymore, do we?

Index

(continued)

Notes

IDG BOOKS WORLDWIDE REGISTRATION CARD

RETURN THIS REGISTRATION CARD FOR FREE CATALOG

Title of this book: QuickBooks 4 For Dummies, 2E

My overall rating of this book: ❏ Very good [1] ❏ Good [2] ❏ Satisfactory [3] ❏ Fair [4] ❏ Poor [5]

How I first heard about this book:

❏ Found in bookstore; name: [6]

❏ Advertisement: [8]

❏ Word of mouth; heard about book from friend, co-worker, etc.: [10]

❏ Book review: [7]

❏ Catalog: [9]

❏ Other: [11]

What I liked most about this book:

What I would change, add, delete, etc., in future editions of this book:

Other comments:

Number of computer books I purchase in a year: ❏ 1 [12] ❏ 2-5 [13] ❏ 6-10 [14] ❏ More than 10 [15]

I would characterize my computer skills as: ❏ Beginner [16] ❏ Intermediate [17] ❏ Advanced [18] ❏ Professional [19]

I use ❏ DOS [20] ❏ Windows [21] ❏ OS/2 [22] ❏ Unix [23] ❏ Macintosh [24] ❏ Other: [25]_____
(please specify)

I would be interested in new books on the following subjects:
(please check all that apply, and use the spaces provided to identify specific software)

❏ Word processing: [26]

❏ Data bases: [28]

❏ File Utilities: [30]

❏ Networking: [32]

❏ Other: [34]

❏ Spreadsheets: [27]

❏ Desktop publishing: [29]

❏ Money management: [31]

❏ Programming languages: [33]

I use a PC at (please check all that apply): ❏ home [35] ❏ work [36] ❏ school [37] ❏ other: [38] _____

The disks I prefer to use are ❏ 5.25 [39] ❏ 3.5 [40] ❏ other: [41]_____

I have a CD ROM: ❏ yes [42] ❏ no [43]

I plan to buy or upgrade computer hardware this year: ❏ yes [44] ❏ no [45]

I plan to buy or upgrade computer software this year: ❏ yes [46] ❏ no [47]

Name: _____ Business title: [48] _____ Type of Business: [49]

Address (❏ home [50] ❏ work [51] /Company name: _____)

Street/Suite#

City [52]/State [53]/Zipcode [54]: _____ Country [55]

❏ **I liked this book!** You may quote me by name in future
IDG Books Worldwide promotional materials.

My daytime phone number is _____

IDG BOOKS

THE WORLD OF
COMPUTER
KNOWLEDGE

☐ YES!

Please keep me informed about IDG's World of Computer Knowledge.
Send me the latest IDG Books catalog.